Images of Truth

Contemporary Studies in Philosophy and the Human Sciences

Series Editors:
Hugh J. Silverman and Graeme Nicholson

Published

* Also available in paperback

Images of Truth

From Sign to Symbol

◆

Carlo Sini

Translated by
Massimo Verdicchio

Humanities Press
New Jersey

Originally published as *Immagini di verità* © 1985 by Spirali/Vel srl

First published 1993 by Humanities Press International, Inc.,
Atlantic Highlands, New Jersey 07716

English Translation © 1993 by Humanities Press International, Inc.

Library of Congress Cataloging-in-Publication Data

Sini, Carlo, 1933–
   [Immagini di verita.   English]
   Images of truth : from sign to symbol / Carlo Sini ; translated by
Massimo Verdicchio.
     p.   cm. — (Contemporary studies in philosophy and the human
sciences)
   Translation of: Immagini di verita.
   Includes bibliographical references and index.
   ISBN 0-391-03763-3
   1. Signs and symbols.   2. Symbols.   3. Hermeneutics.
4. Nihilism (Philosophy)   5. Truth.   I. Title.   II. Series.
B3652.S533I513   1993
121—dc20   92-9063
          CIP

A catalog record for this book is available from the British Library.

Printed in the United States of America

Contents

Translator's Introduction

◆

In truth, it takes a strong stomach to do philosophy.
Carlo Sini, *Kinesis*

The task of a translator is always a rewarding one when it provides one with the opportunity of introducing to the English-speaking public the work of a philosopher who is already well known in other parts of the world. This is especially the case with Sini's *Images of Truth*, which, in many ways, is both a synthesis of the author's theoretical investigation of the last ten years and its culmination. In this work, the inquiry takes the form of a questioning of the notion of truth in Western metaphysics and of the impasse of nihilistic thinking to which it leads. *Images of Truth* is perhaps the best introduction to Sini's work as well as a good indicator of the present and ongoing development of his thinking.

Carlo Sini was born in Bologna, Italy, on December 6, 1933, and studied in Milan with the well-known phenomenologist Enzo Paci, under whom he graduated and worked as an assistant for many years. After teaching philosophy of history and history of philosophy at the University of Aquila, Sini was appointed to the Chair of Theoretical Philosophy at the University of Milan, where he still teaches.

His early studies were in Greek philosophy, an interest he still cultivates, and in the phenomenology of Hegel and Husserl, where his main concerns were the question of truth, the foundation of scientific knowledge, and the formation of self-consciousness. Afterward, he turned to British philosophy and concentrated particularly on Whitehead's metaphysics of process and his notion of subject. At that time he discovered Peirce's philosophy and semiotics, which proved to be a decisive influence in his later work. It should be mentioned at this point that Sini was one of the first, with Umberto Eco and Nynfa Bosco, to make the work of Peirce known in Italy.

Sini is the founder and present editor of *Man, a Sign* (*L'uomo, un segno*), a journal of philosophy and culture, and is responsible for the philosophical series of many publishing houses. He is a founding member of Perugia's *International Collegium Phaenomenologicum* and has taught and given papers in Europe and abroad. He is a contributor to many specialized journals as well as to dailies and magazines. He has appeared on both Italian and Swiss television. His books and essays have been translated into Spanish, French, German, and English. In 1980 he won the prestigious Palermo International Philosophy Award "F. Nietzsche," which has also been awarded to Popper and Derrida. *Images of Truth* is his first book to be translated into English.

Sini's major works, in their translated English titles, are: *Introduction to Phenomenology as Science* (1965), *Whitehead and the Function of Philosophy* (1966), *American Pragmatism* (1972), *Semiotics and Philosophy* (1978), *Beyond the Sign* (1981), *Kinesis. An Essay in Interpretation* (1982), *Images of Truth* (1985), *Silence and Word* (1989), *Signs of Soul* (1989), and *Symbol and Man* (1991).

Sini's greatest contribution has been to bring together Peirce's philosophy of the sign and notion of infinite semiosis, Heidegger's hermeneutic circle, and Nietzsche's notion of perspectivism and event of meaning. This unusual combination lies at the heart of his recent theories and constitutes the center around which many of his ideas revolve. The resulting hermeneutic of the sign, however, is not at all an ad hoc combination of fashionable theories but is made necessary by shortcomings in contemporary theories of the sign, not excluding Heidegger's. Theories of the sign seem to be concerned only with classification and description but avoid what naturally ought to be their primary concern, the essence of the sign. In Heidegger, too, the notion of sign is limited to its intermediary function and is denied any ontological status. What makes a sign possible is not a sign. The problem, for Sini, stems from a confusion between sign and sign relation, and between ontological sign and conventional linguistic sign. This is a confusion shared by modern semiotics, which also ignores the distinction between the ontological character of the sign relation (linking people, world, and things), language, and conventional signs.

The consequences of this misunderstanding have been dire for both Heidegger's philosophy and semiotics. In Heidegger's case, it has been largely responsible for reducing his philosophy to "silence" or to the mystic positing of the "mystery" of the event. In the case of semiotics, it has led to the total disregard of Peirce's contribution to the study of the sign, even on the part of those who have hailed him as their mentor.

Sini's insistence on combining Peirce and Heidegger no longer revolves around the "sign" but around the ontological sign relation. In a sign relation there is no subject which acknowledges an object as sign. Rather, there is an *Interpretant* that activates a relation between *Representamen* and *Object*, between sign and meaning. The resulting process is not an object in the world but a triadic relation between Interpretant, Representamen and Object. Thus, the "truth" of a sign relation is not meaning but yet another sign for other Interpretants. In this respect there is no difference between people and words, since both are the result of past interpretations and are destined for future interpretations. As Peirce observed, "Man is a sign."

On these bases, Sini elaborates his own theoretical program, which has its beginnings in a move away from the type of Husserlian phenomenology practiced by his mentor Enzo Paci. In his first work, *Introduction to Phenomenology as Science*, Sini is still working within the framework of Paci's brand of Husserlian philosophy, which attempted to bring together phenomenology, dialectics, and epistemology. Also in *Whitehead and the Function of Philosophy*, Sini deals with another of Paci's interests, Whitehead and his "phenomenological" approach to science. However, when he turns to American pragmatism, in the work by this title, as I indicated, his encounter with Peirce marks a major turning point in his career. The first stage of this new journey is *Semiotics and Philosophy*, which is Sini's first attempt at combining these two major trends by drawing on the similarities between Peirce, Nietzsche, and Heidegger and by contrasting them with alternative theories then popular such as Foucault's post-structuralist theory of discourse and those of Lévy-Strauss. But the key work of this period is *Beyond the Sign*, where, as a result of his continuing investigation of the ontological status of the sign and the issue of referentiality, Sini traces the genealogy of Western thinking from its origins in a cosmological view of the world to its displacement by a philosophy of the soul, which already foreshadows the boundaries and limitations of contemporary nihilism as well as of modern technology.

Sini's investigation takes up the question of cosmology and examines the conditions under which the cosmological view so predominant in the early development of Western thinking has gradually disappeared and been confined to the specialized study of astronomy. In ancient times cosmology was constitutive of being in the world. Humanity contemplated the cosmos and derived from it the measure and sense of its time and space, its certainty and bearing. With the advent of the birth of philosophy, there is no room for cosmological interpretation. Cosmology declines, only to resurface, now and then, at the margins of philosophy, as in the more "poetic" texts of Heidegger. Only the poets, for Sini, are allowed to speak of the universe.

The decline of cosmology follows an ambiguous path. While it appears that with Copernicus, Galileo, Newton, and Einstein cosmology becomes more and more scientific, at the same time it becomes marginal precisely because of the increasing predominance of scientific thought. We see this in Kant, for whom there is only one legitimate way of thinking the universe, which is the way of science. "Cosmology is either scientific or is nothing" (*Beyond the Sign*, Part II. 104). This philosophical stance, however, which privileges the scientific over everything else as the sole mode of thinking, has dire consequences since it leads eventually to the end of thinking. Science, says Sini, "does not *think*, does not think at all" (*Beyond the Sign*, II. 104). Science experiments, calculates, follows a theoretical praxis, uses the concept of infinity but does not "think" it. Science does not think because it is not its duty to think. Science is science, or proceeds as science, "*on condition*" that it does not think. That is to say, science does not "speculate." Any "speculating" for Kant is an "erring" (II. 104).

The inherent contradiction in scientific thinking is that while it posits a world in which science experiments and calculates, it also states that this world cannot be thought at all. Science, says Sini, quoting Heidegger, brings about the "annihilation" of the world while at the same time "annihilating" speculative thinking. Or, what is worse, since speculative thinking is part of the *ratio*, it is inevitably destined to nihilistic conclusions such as those that claim the experience of the world to be nothing or that the world is nothing (II. 104). Thus metaphysical speculation, science, has been engaged from the beginning in the destruction of cosmological experience. At the present time this destruction is being carried out in the name of technology, which is replacing theoretical and speculative thinking.

In the third part of *Beyond the Sign*, Sini takes up the issue of why technology puts thinking into question in much the same way that cosmology, the world, and the body had been displaced by science. Technology, he says, puts thinking into question because it asks the question at the limits of philosophy. Thus philosophy, understood as historical and scientific *ratio*, is displaced from its central role as interpretant of phenomena and reduced to the status of one of the many social sciences that vie for supremacy. In trying to determine the relation between technology and philosophy, Sini examines pronouncements from Plato to Husserl centered on, as in Plato's *Phaedrus*, the relation between the technology of writing and philosophy. First of all, there is no question that philosophy can dominate technology and bring it back to the living unity or totality of the soul, since philosophy is precisely that technology which institutes the soul. At issue, for Sini, is what he calls "the strategy of the soul," that strategy for power that from Plato on denotes the technology (*techne*) of discourse and which in the Platonic dialogues opposes the philosopher to the sophist. There are no significant differences between the philosopher's strategy and the sophist's, except the claim by the philosopher that he is giving the "scientific version." "Rhetorical discourse is transformed from Plato to Aristotle into logical-scientific discourse: *epistemology* of belief and perfect *organon* of persuasion" (III. 46). This is how *"soul," "psyche," "animal psychologicum"* are determined. "The art (*techne*) and science of discourse (*logos*) *constitute* the soul" (III. 46).

A similar relation exists between history and writing. There is no history first which writing then discovers and records. The technology of writing *constitutes* the historical view and historical reality. "This is how historical man is constituted. The *logoi*, the conflict of discourses, institute psychological man. Truth coincides with public persuasion" (III. 46). Similarly, modern technology moves from the philosophical fable and the syllogism to mathematical signs. The same strategy is at work.

The Socratic dialogue is a first instance of this "technology of consent" which eventually becomes the foundation of the present "technology of culture" and its "terrors" (III. 55). With the Socratic dialogue is born the correlation between individual and universal that goes under the name of "dialectic." In the play of the dialectic the particular must be suppressed, mediated, suppressed, negated. Vico in the *New Science* is the first to trace the genealogy of this new Western man "decentered by the strategy of the soul and thrown into the linear time of progressive history" (III. 55). Vico gives to modern man the awareness and the certainty of being worthy of entering into the totalizing journey of universal history. "To be on the way to the Promised Land." "And with it the certainty of being worthy of prevailing on any other humanity and to lead the earth to its ultimate destiny. With the help and guarantee of Divine Providence" (III. 55). Vico ushers in what Sini calls the *"psycho-historical strategy,"* the translation of Plato's strategy of the soul in a historical key and in the parameters of a "new science."

With the establishment of the "strategy of the soul," the place of truth is no longer limited to the cosmological relation man-god-nature-animal but is replaced by "souls" in dialogue and in conflict with one another. This is the place of "public opinion" which eventually becomes "public truth" or the "public place of reason." "This decentering transfers the 'monsters' of myth [those alluded to by Vico] in *interiore homine*, following a path that goes from Socrates (of the *Phaedrus*) to Vico to Freud without changing direction" (III. 66). Modern technology is precisely the outcome of this strategy of the soul and of the psycho-historical strategy proposed by Vico.

Modern technology is efficient, public, and objective. It is "efficient" by definition, but also because it is "neutral," it is its own end. "Neutral" means it is "self-sufficient," that "it removes anything that it is not itself" (III. 68). But this efficiency is not for the well-being of mankind, as one may believe. Although this is partly true, its main goal is "the production and reproduction of itself" (III. 68). Technology transforms everything as its own "appendix and extension," instrumentalizing everything, including body and soul (III. 68).

The second aspect of modern technology is its "public" character. This aspect depends on the neutrality and transparency of the linguistic sign as instrument of communication. What characterizes technological culture is its ability to communicate, to be measured and quantified. It makes possible a "public knowledge" available to everyone (II. 71). A central aspect is the *culture of information*, namely, the domination of the category of information, which includes everything from everyday news to computers but whose main aim is the "formation of public (political) opinion." Truth, as a result, is what everyone commonly believes. We do not ask, however, if the technology of information produces this "truth effect." The situation is always reversed to imply, rather, that "truth has always been based on the common agreement between peoples." This "public character" of truth, its becoming "public," is the last transformation of the metaphysical concept of truth (III. 71).

The third aspect of modern technology is its "objective" character. This is what we commonly believe, and rightly so, since technology is "neutral" and appears to take the world as it is, objectively. But for Sini this is not entirely so, since technology allows only for the existence of those neutral and "disenchanted" aspects of reality that it promotes, while removing or not recognizing others. "The practical reduction of nature to object becomes the objectivity of scientific knowledge" (III. 72). Science is objective in the sense that it reduces reality to object. Its interpretation of the world becomes the revelation of the universal and objective character of the universe. "Thus, what technology *makes* of the world becomes what the world is" (III. 72).

The dogmatic character of techno-scientific ideology, which Sini sums up in the imperative "Thou shalt have no other method outside of me," is not just fundamentally "irrational" but also "terroristic" since it labels those who speak against it, like Sini for instance, as "irrational" (II. 72). Anyone who does not fit within the parameters and criteria of truth set by technology are defined "terroristically" as irrational. The ultimate objectives of technology have changed little from those of the strategy of the soul. They are still, says Sini, "the complete taming of man and the world" (III. 72).

The natural outcome of technology's "terrorism" is the terrorism of institutions, the "pedagogical terror." The objective of modern institutions is not to educate or shape minds but "to promote themselves, by in-forming and taming minds to their own project" (III. 73). The same can be said of anti-institutional terrorism, similarly a product of technology, with which it shares the effectiveness and public character, and is equally based on the organization of "information." (The reference to "terrorism" must also be understood in the context of the 1970s in Italy, the time Sini was writing, when the terrorism of the Red Brigade was an everyday occurrence.)

The critique of the strategy of the soul, psycho-history, and technology in *Beyond the Sign* is fundamentally linked to the question of the sign. The effectiveness of modern technology, says Sini, depends on the neutrality of the linguistic sign, on its "*domestication*" (III. 70). The sign is deprived of all its "recalcitrant" and "wild" elements and made exact and quantifiable. As a result of its "domestication," language is regarded simply as a tool of communication between people, a mode of expressing our inner feelings. Language in and of itself is seen as neutral, that is, conventional and arbitrary.

Thus, in the next stage of his journey, Sini aims at recovering the lost cosmological interpretation of the sign, which entails combining Peirce with Heidegger, with all the necessary modifications this combination requires. In *Kinesis. An Essay in Interpretation*, Sini proceeds to an examination of the sign and its event in an attempt to think through some of the assumptions of modern hermeneutics that have been left unexplored. In these essays, Sini stresses first of all the importance of bringing together Peirce and Heidegger and justifying this choice. Peirce's notion of sign, compared to Husserl's ambiguous conception of sign as intermediary, middle, is more developed and profound. The sign for Peirce is "something which stands to somebody for something else in some respect or capacity." This "something" is also the Sign or Representamen; the "someone" is the Interpretant of the sign; the "something else" is the Object; and the ground is the point of view on whose basis something is taken as sign. But Peirce's most important advance in the theory of signs, according to Sini, concerns the question of "reference." The Representamen, the Object, and the Interpretant are not "things" among which a referential relation is established; they are the structural poles of the very same relation, "they are placed in existence [*in essere*] by the same referring function" (*Kinesis*, p. 23). For Peirce the sign is in actual fact a relation whose "reality" exists only within this relation. The sign, however, is also the outcome of an inferential-interpretive act unlike what is postulated by Husserl, for whom the sign is only the externalization of a supposedly intuitive act. "Things" says Sini, "the *real* things are for us within this sign relation and in the interpretive act that characterizes them" (p. 26). In the sign relation the interplay of reference between Representamen and Interpretant makes possible the emergence of the true nature of the sign. The Object brought nearer by the sign is at the same time distanced and deferred by it. This is Peirce's *infinite semiosis*, namely, that public process of signification and truth in progress, which Sini calls "the process of reality" (p. 27). We, the world, its meanings, its events are caught in this play of relations and are called on to play a definite role. Thus, the issue of the sign and its infinite referral coincides with the question of man and the world in which he lives as an Interpretant and in which he is always someone who has already lived and, thus, has interpreted.

For this reason Peirce's semiotics already announces itself as a hermeneutic, a philosophy of interpretation, as opposed to Husserl's philosophy of intuition. In Peirce's philosophy of infinite interpretation, truth and its meaning are not the privilege and possession of consciousness. "Rather, consciousness as Interpretant is always in truth and in meaning since it partakes of a sign process which involves it and assigns to it a similar destiny of truth. Thus, Peirce's semiotics becomes a hermeneutics" (p. 28). On this level, Peirce and Heidegger not only can be brought together but can also be said to be similar.

Similar echoes can be found in Heidegger, whose thinking is always hermeneutic, since what is at issue is always language and the sign. Likewise, at issue is always man (the Interpretant) and the world. Heidegger, says Sini, is always on the way toward a conclusion that goes:

Original saying (*Sagen*) means pointing (*Weisen*), and pointing out means showing (*Zeigen*), that is, pointing. Thus man, the one who points (*Zeigender*), the man who *is* a sign is the one who, because of this essence, finds himself "thrown" in the "destined destiny" (*Geschick*) of the sign. (p. 42)

At this level Peirce and Heidegger share the same view that man is in language rather than language in man and that the enigma of man and the world is inscribed in language rather than the other way around. Heidegger was always "on the way toward the sign," says Sini, but he can only be said to have begun to "formulate the question," since he never went much further than that (p. 46).

Heidegger's ambiguity toward the sign reflects the opposition at the core of contemporary philosophy, namely, the opposition between Heidegger the philosopher of the world of science and technology with its nihilistic ideology and the poetic Heidegger, the thinker of the "original saying," of *Sage* and *mythos*. For Sini, the opposition characterizes the difference between *signa* and signs. *Signa* are the original cosmological experience which ancient man interpreted to determine the dimension of his being and place in the world. Modern man, however, no longer interprets *signa* but signs, that is, a communicative and conventional language completely devoid of "cosmological dimension." This radical shift from *signa* to signs is made possible by a change in our ways of conceiving the truth. From the metaphysical definition of truth as *adequatio intellectus et rei* we have moved to the *adequatio notitiae et rei* of the present technological world where information ensures the supremacy of the sign by positing the "soul" and domesticating it. The shift is an "erring," says Sini, between an original cosmological meaning and a dissemination of information and "rumor." The history of Being is played out in this "double play" which needs to be thought, since it is really the history of the sign, of an erring between *signa* and signs. Thus, the task is to understand the connection that links semiotics to cosmology, language to *signa*.

The other aspect that Sini tackles in *Kinesis* is the question of the event of the sign, which he left suspended in *Beyond the Sign*. As Sini remarks in the introduction to the second part of *Kinesis*, his notion of event differs qualitatively from Heidegger's *Ereignis*, although he is very indebted to it. *Ereignis* in Heidegger is the letting-be of presence as the other of signification, which entails leaving metaphysical thinking behind and opening itself to a new thinking. But Heidegger shows he has not quite left metaphysics when he still thinks the event in terms of temporality and when he views *Ereignis* as the radical "'other" of presence, of the ontic world. Whether *Ereignis* is thought to be "close to" beings (and in this sense "different" from them) or "other" from them, it still has its norm (*misura*) in beings, of which it is "other." "The 'other' from beings is still 'something' even though in principle we cannot really say 'what' it is" (*Kinesis*, p. 187). In this case our attention is not at all removed from beings, as Heidegger would like. In fact, for Sini, our attention not only *cannot* be removed from beings but it *must not*. This alleged removal is at the root of Heidegger's "silence" and failure.

Sini's definition of "event" is radically different, since any event is at the same time the event of nothing. This is because any event, however important or insignificant, is always dual. The event is always both the event of an interpretation, a meaning, and the event of nothing. They are two ways of looking at and saying the event, which in itself is *indifferently* either one or the other. "The event," says Sini, "is precisely the in-difference of its recto and verso. This in-difference is the *kinesis* of the difference between meaning and nothing. This *kinesis* is the event itself" (p. 183). This "radical" nothing of the event, excluded and left unthought by metaphysics, allows us to go beyond metaphysics. Heidegger was unable to bring himself to equate Being with nothing and to think nihilism nihilistically to the end. Thus nihilism never fulfilled its destiny and the age of technology never achieved its truth (p. 193).

In *Images of Truth*, Sini brings together the many strands developed in his previous works, but especially in the last two, to attempt a radical rereading of the concept of truth in Western metaphysics entrenched in its original Parmenidean formulation of the identity of being and thinking. According to this view, truth is tautological. To think being, to say that it absolutely "is," is true. Thus, any other opinion and any other judgment is excluded except that of mere identity: A is A. With Plato the Parmenidean paradigm is altered slightly when it became obvious that the *logos* could not embody truth and that science could not exist if judgment could not justify being the unity of the many. Plato's solution, alluded to in the discussion of *Beyond the Sign*, is to say that Parmenides' mistake is to have confused non-being with nothing. Non-being does not only mean "nothing," just as non-white does not only mean black, but also what is *different* from white, i.e., red, green, yellow. Parmenides believed that since being can be thought, truth must consist in saying that being *is*. Plato and Aristotle added that it is not just a question of saying that being *is* but *how* it is, by means of a logic of judgment.

But for Sini, Parmenides' dictum also meant to say something radically different. We say and judge being not because being *is* but because we say and judge; truth consists in a being that can be thought and judged. In other words, the original place of truth is not being, which is revealed in judgment, but *logos*, judgment. Being is made to conform to the *logos* in its image and countenance and not *vice versa*. This was Parmenides' secret, says Sini, a secret that emerged more and more clearly in the unfolding of Western thinking and in particular in modern metaphysics from Descartes, to Kant, to Fichte, where the fundamental and foundational character of the *logos* becomes completely apparent.

Parmenides' knot between thinking and being begins to fall apart with Hegel and Heidegger, who put into question, respectively, the two places of truth as judgment and as correspondence between being and being true. These two steps taken into "the abyss of groundless ground," as Sini defines it, characterize the condition of contemporary man, who has totally "consumed" Being and can no longer "think" (p. 31).

But if Hegel brings about a reversal of Platonism by showing that judgment cannot be the place where truth can be expressed conceptually, since it can only speak in abstractions, for Hegel the place where truth takes place is in the disjunctive syllogism, which is "the adequate expression of rational mediation" (p. 27). In the *Science of Logic*, Hegel confirms the Parmenidean paradigm by demonstrating the total identification of being with rational thinking, at the same time that it brings Plato's "strategy of the soul" to its climax with the total spiritualization of reality, namely, its total historization and socialization. In Hegel, the very manifestation of phenomena, of experience, is logical, is science. Object and understanding come together and conform to one another, since the determinations of the Object, as understanding expresses them, are actual moments of the object although not in the way understanding believes. Thus Hegel, says Sini, fulfills the Parmenidean identity of being and thinking but at a price that

Parmenides would not have paid, namely, that all appearance or phenomenon is being and that being is appearance. This total dissolution of thinking in being and of being in thinking hurls the *ratio* into the abyss of "indistinction."

But in this reciprocal immanence, being is no longer "what it is" but rather the contrary, "what becomes"; and thinking is no longer "judgment," conceptual discrimination. Thus, the *ratio* enters into a vortex without exit, off a precipice with no way out. (p. 45)

In the last instance, Hegel's "concrete" thinking cannot say anything about the world and its truth because it coincides with them. About the world, says Sini, Hegel's thinking "has *really* nothing to *say*" (p. 46).

The second step in the abyss is taken by Heidegger with the destruction of the other place of truth which identifies Being with being true. In *On the Essence of Truth*, Heidegger says that being true and truth entail the accordance of a thing with what one assumes it to be and between what is thought in judgment and the thing. But judgment that describes beings as they are is for Heidegger not the origin of truth, since judgment is only a relation (*Verhältnis*) to the unconcealedness of beings, to the becoming manifest of beings. More basic than judgment is the becoming manifest of this place of truth, and since the unconcealedness requires the freedom of openness, this freedom is the origin of truth. For Heidegger, Being still remains to be thought by metaphysics; this thinking of Being is the unresolved question that metaphysics has always managed to avoid.

Although Hegel and Heidegger call thinking and Being respectively into question, they do not question the basic Parmenidean assumption of the identity of thinking and Being. They still believe that it constitutes the original and fundamental question to which one must return in order to be able to think. Thus both Hegel and Heidegger, says Sini, "complement each other in the inevitable nihilistic collapse of Western *ratio*" (p. 51).

For Sini, two hypotheses present themselves at this point. Either the truth of the world can be expressed by the *logos* or it cannot. In the first instance, judgment can be seen as a structure of signs that refer to things or events, which in turn are but signs that must be interpreted through other judgments and so on ad infinitum. Or truth cannot be expressed through the *logos*, which is Gorgias' anti-Parmenidean hypothesis also present in Hegel and in Nietzsche. In this case, as Wittgenstein says, there is nothing to be said about the world. But for Sini the conclusions of nihilism do not really make sense. He questions its assumptions and suggests that nihilism is merely one interpretation among many and not simply the only one. Similarly, he rejects the nihilistic claim that the world has no sense as a statement that belongs very much to the logic of sense. The basic assumptions of nihilism, says Sini, are fundamentally Parmenidean. Whereas thinking, traditionally, has always upheld the identity of thinking and being, nihilism denies it. In nihilism, as in other cases, the *logos*, judgment, produces being and the question of truth as correspondence to being. In the same way, from a public *logos*, are produced a public being and a public truth.

The issue of the "public" leads Sini to an examination of Heraclitus to determine "the constitutive movement of the *ratio* in its earliest stages" (p. 81). Heraclitus is the first to develop the notion of world both common and public, a world, that is, in that "thinking common to everyone," i.e., the *logos* (p. 84). Heraclitus suggests that one should rise to a particular type of vision since everything that happens happens *in the presence of the logos*, in the place of truth. Thus, to assume the point of view of the *logos* is to take on the universal point of view that oversees everything. The universal conscience or interpretant, says Sini, which is always taken for granted whenever one speaks of the truth of the world, originates in a similar fashion.

This panoramic view, or "public eye" (pp. 86ff.), is equivalent to the constitution of a pure mind for which the whole world is an object. In *Beyond the Sign* Sini called it the Platonic strategy of the soul where it was a question of the *dia-logos*, which constitutes the soul and its vision. The soul can gain access to the vision, since it possesses a fragment or a spark of the universal or divine soul. Or, in more modern terms, it is able to gain access to the vision because "the *logos* of every single man is *in* public thinking, as intersubjective-social activity" (p. 90).

But the incongruence or paradox of this universal pan-oramic or objective truth is that it is made possible *through* a vision that in itself is not objective. Rather, says Sini, it is the very principle of subjectivity, of consciousness. "The scientific ideal is objectivism, but the truth and *meaning* of that ideal cannot be objective since every 'objectivity' presupposes a constitutive subjectivity (or 'transcendental,' as Husserl calls it)" (p. 90). The crisis of European sciences, of which Husserl speaks, consists precisely in the fact that as objective sciences (sciences of the pure "how") they lose all *meaning* (all reference to the "what"), namely, all final purpose. At best, says Sini, meaning becomes private, the prerogative of the private, provided that it stays private, that is, without any consequence to public life and its institutions.

The private is a form of the public because it is only from the point of view of the public that a private truth can begin to exist. But since at the beginning the private does not yet exist, says Sini, something else is removed from experience and is displaced in the private by the institution of the *logos* and its public truth. For Sini the question becomes: "Of what is the private deprived" since its constitution as the other of the public? (p. 95). By working out this question and the answers it suggests, Sini elaborates a notion of "truth" unhindered by the limitations of metaphysical thinking. This is gradually accomplished through (*a*) the "destruction" of the panoramic view or public description of what actually occurs when one thinks; (*b*) the "destruction" of public objects that we are accustomed to conceive as real; and (*c*) the "destruction" of our common sense, on whose basis we live and perform. This entails thinking of our emotional relation to objects not as the result of objective knowledge but as the original and fundamental approach to objects *on* which the objective world of knowledge is founded and built.

This emotional relation is not constituted by feelings or moods that are added psychologically to real objects. Rather, it is a relation which "opens the world," opens up "being-in-the-world." Once again, for Sini, there is no world and no man already constituted; there are *determined* relations that are constitutive of being-in-the-world, which place man in relation with the world and open him to the *how* of the world, which make him "world." What the private is deprived of, then, are these constitutive relations which, for Sini, are best summed up as sign-symbol relations.

As an example of this relation, Sini quotes from Piaget an interview with a child who claimed that "Whenever I walk the moon follows me; I am the one who moves it" (p. 101). First of all, the relation child-moon, says Sini, is not to be taken in the public sense of a relation between moon and child. Rather, moon and child are constituted together and in correlation to one another. The moon is first of all an *event* in the constitution of being-in-the-world of man and it occurs as sign, as sign relation. "Everything which occurs, is a sign, a being-for or a standing-for, a referring. For us, there is no relation with events, with 'things' if not as sign relations" (p. 101). Furthermore, as I indicated earlier, a sign for Sini is not something that stands between two realities; rather, it is to be thought of as a sign relation which, in this case, situates the looking of the child and his looked-at as moon. Properly speaking there is neither moon nor child; there is rather a "cosmic" relation of (moon)light, of seeing or having-to-see. In Peircean terms, we can say that there is a triangular relation between Representamen, Object, and Interpretant, respectively, where the sign is the radiance of the moon, and the response of the Interpretant is the looking toward the light to what is revealed or made to appear by it, namely, the Object, and what public language calls "moon."

Stated as sign relation, the relation moon-child entails a further important feature: reciprocity. The essential nature of the sign relation child-moon, which can be simply stated as a "being-illuminated-having-to-see," is at the same time reciprocal. The child is not only "looking" but he is also being "looked-at" by the moon. The statement may seem "absurd," says Sini, but only because we persist in thinking "child" and "moon" as already constituted realities and in viewing "moon" as an object. The relation moon-child is not qualitatively different from the relation child-mother, where reciprocity is more comprehensible and sensible. The difficulty can be overcome when the primordial and constitutive character of the relation child-moon is grasped and we have succeeded in freeing ourselves of the dictates of common sense, for which such a statement is nonsensical. Then we will also be able to understand better the general character of the sign relation for which any such relation is necessarily always reciprocal.

Sini explains this general character of the sign relation as "distance." The sign relation created by setting up the two poles, child and moon, also puts them at a distance. Setting up the poles means placing them at a distance. "The relation, in essence, makes the *distance* happen" (p. 103). Or, "*The experience of the distance is the essential trait of the originary sign relation*" (p. 103). This being at a distance of the child also marks his *where*, which is such in terms of the *elsewhere* of the moon. Generally speaking, there is a distance which resides (*di stanza*) here, namely, the presence of an absence. (Sini plays on the words *distanza*, "distance," and *di stanza*, meaning "to reside.") In other words, the child measures the distance of the moon together with his relation to it as presence. On the basis of this distance two processes are at work that are as distinct as they are contemporaneous. Sini calls the "in-different difference" of these two processes the sign relation and the symbol relation. The unity or combination of the two he calls "experience," which he does not mean in the narrow sense of empirical experience but simply as the unity of sign and symbol relations.

The sign relation is defined as a having-to-respond. As such it determines the responding pole, namely, the *who* and *how* of responding, interpreting. The Interpretant, by activating the Signified of the sign, makes possible the appearance of the Object pole, *i.e.*, what the sign refers to. The light of the moon is the sign that sets up the corresponding pole, that is, determines the *here* as the *where* of the response by looking. Thus, the sign establishes a distance, since it directs the having-to-respond toward the *elsewhere*, *i.e.*, the Object, the moon.

Child and moon are placed in their difference because together they constitute a symbolic whole, a *symbolon*. Sini does not mean "symbol" in the ordinary sense of the term, as when we call scales a symbol of justice or the lion a symbol of strength. Sini employs the term in the original Greek meaning of *sym-ballein*, meaning "putting together," "uniting," "bringing together." The *symbolon* originally was the broken piece of an object that when brought together with the other half served as sign of recognition. The *symbolon* is the fragment of a whole that is not there or is no longer there. Although the symbol is a sign since it refers, it differs from a sign in that it does not refer to an "other" but always to itself (*"the other to which the symbol refers is still itself"* (p. 105). The broken half of the symbol refers back to the whole not yet broken.

Similarly, child and moon can be said to be the same, and this sameness is symbolic. On the basis of this very sameness, moon and child are determined as polarities of the sign relation, as poles of their distance and sign difference. The moment in which moon designates child as child-that-looks-at-moon and child designates moon as unreachable object of his looking, the distance bursts in and breaks up the whole of the "sameness" moon-child. The sign of moon places the child in the presence of his Other and conceals that this Other is still the Same. The Other, however, is really the *nothing* of what he is since this Other is his distance, his absence. "The symbolic relation is the relation to one's own sameness as to one's own nothing" (p. 106). But this "nothing" is not a negation, is not equal to "nothing." "Nothing" is what determines the child as what he is, as child-looking-at-the-moon. Nothing is the originary symbolic unity that makes the looking of the child possible. Thus, in the last instance, every sign can be said to be a sign of nothing. The child has his Sameness in nothing. In his looking at the moon, he is a sign of nothing. This conclusion marks also the end of the Parmenidean strategy. As Sini anticipates in his critique of Heidegger's *Ereignis*, since Being and nothing can be said to be the same, being is really equal to nothing.

The knot that unites sign and symbol relations, as I indicated above, constitutes the place of experience. This knot is a relation between two nothings, since for the sign the Object is in nothing, while for the symbol the Response in its decentering is in nothing. Similarly, for the sign, Meaning (*i.e.*, the public meaning of "moon") is the nothing of the event, namely, what erases the event by translating it into an Object that is always aimed for and deferred. For the symbol, instead, the event is the nothing of meaning, what by occurring annuls and keeps every meaning in nothing.

The crucial truth that moves us beyond metaphysics is based on this sign-symbol relation, which defines the place of experience. (Sini qualifies the statement by saying that the move beyond metaphysics is possible only because his thinking contains metaphysical thinking within itself.) By crucial truth Sini defines the experience of truth situated at the crossroads between event and meaning, sign and symbol. Every crucial truth is both event and meaning of interpretation. It moves from nothing to nothing and places two nothings in relation: nothing of the Response and nothing of the Object. The event of the Response occurs from a nothing of moon; the Response looks for the moon behind its countenance in an Object that in its turn is nothing. And since every interpretation goes after the truth, experiences its truth, every interpretation also *"goes after the truth of its own untruth,"* also experiences its not being "true" (p. 129). This inevitable and far-reaching conclusion marks for Sini not only the extreme radicalization of nihilism but also the turning point away from metaphysical assumptions.

Taking it one step further, it can be said that the experience of truth is the experience of the non-identity of one's identity or the catastrophe of one's identity, as well as of the identity of every truth. And since, says Sini, man is nothing more than his interpretation, we must conclude that "the catastrophe of our interpretations (of our being-in-the-world and of our having-the-world) is our very own catastrophe" (pp. 129–130). Differing from Heidegger, who claimed that we are in error because we err, Sini wants to say that we err because we are in error which, then, gives way to erring and to infinite interpretation. The symbolic relation is in error because it looks beyond the sign for what it is or has already, namely, the Same in countenance of Other.

This should not be taken to imply that for Sini interpretation is negligible or irrelevant. On the contrary, for him every interpretation is true since it occurs, but what occurs is not absolute truth but the becoming untrue of interpretation. Every interpretation is always on the way to the untruth of its truth, and this being on the way is the experience of truth. But this "crucial truth," which when it occurs is said to be a mystery (*i.e.*, in Heidegger), is still for Sini a public interpretation which leaves in the dark the non-public sense of experience: "enchantment."

The reason enchantment is always left in the dark, says Sini, is because it "*knows* nothing of truth and error" (p. 148). It is the experience of the Sameness of the Other and is characterized by the "equilibrium" between distance and presence, between sameness and difference. Enchantment is the experience of "part-icipation," which entails assuming the "part" in every sense of the word (*i.e.*, taking part, becoming part, *etc.*) and above all in the sense of being a "finite and perfect part," a *symbolon*. The relation between two nothings, mentioned earlier à propos of the correspondence between sign and symbol relations, has its correspondence in this equilibrium on the edge (*orlo*) of the Same, on the point of becoming sign and word. In this enchantment the finiteness of experience is finally complete and "perfect," since enchantment is really beings, what metaphysics calls "pure and simple *transcendens.*" In enchantment, the *transcendens* is the moon confronted and experienced in the tension of equilibrium "*as the nearest presence of occurring distance*" (p. 150). This is "*the enchantment of equilibrium.*" "Generally speaking, the entire human praxis is this equilibrium between participation and interpretive technique" (p. 151). Every technique requires a familiarity, a natural bent, which every rule presupposes but does not teach. Enchantment, in other words, is the root of every meaning since non-meaning, or unreason, gives meaning, or reason, and "says" the participation of man in the world. In this place of enchantment events and the meaning of these events take place. It is the place from where we speak, from where the public takes place with its public discourse and public *logos*.

The place of enchantment is also the place of the philosophical word. In the sign and symbol relations and in the experience of enchantment, says Sini, philosophy can find its own origin, its own justification and destiny. This new task consists in translating the mystery of enchantment into public words, as well as in interpreting the public, instead of abdicating this role to science, as is currently done. This new philosophical mandate also helps us to understand the direction taken by Sini's own philosophy after *Images of Truth*. The event of the sign, as event of the distance that makes interpretation and the infinite circle of reference possible, implies the overcoming of the metaphysical notion of truth and of philosophy understood as the science of truth. It implies, at the same time, that the way is open for a philosophical praxis that takes the form of an "ethics of thinking" or, more specifically, an "ethics of writing." This is the theme of Sini's next work, *Silence and Word* (1989), which is a study of corporeal and vocal gestures as events that open up the horizon of the world as a place of signification.

In *Signs of Soul* (1989), published just after *Silence and Word*, Sini reexamines the notion of image in Western metaphysics from Plato to Peirce to Sartre and attempts to reconstruct the genealogy responsible for its progressive Western psychicalization as well as for its constitutive paradoxes. Moving beyond the psychological subject, Sini opens the way for the constitution of an ethical subject that, despite the name, is completely unrelated to morality since *ethos*, as defined by Sini, means "residing," "having a place," "habit," or "praxis." Thus, Sini makes way for the constitution of a practice of subjectivity that proposes to inhabit the practices of the technological world by making it the object of a self-formative practice of knowledge. As a result, the metaphysical foundation is replaced with an ethics of distance as the formation of a subject open to the event of experience and to the always finite plurality of its enchantments. In Sini's last work, *Man and Symbol*, in press at the time of the writing of this Introduction, these issues are further examined with the more specific objective of providing an alternative to Heidegger's philosophy of destruction and Derrida's philosophy of deconstruction.

This is Sini's philosophical journey to date from the origins of philosophy to modern theories and back in an attempt to understand the movement of Western thought and the reasons why it has run aground in a nihilistic thinking that has led philosophy to its debacle in the acceptance of its impossibility. In questioning the dubious path taken by thinking, Sini attempts to restore philosophy to its original enchantment, to enable it once again to fulfill its task of *speaking* the mystery of the world, the ecstatic enchantment of the mystery that Kant, in a closing quote of *Images of Truth*, attempts to put into words:

> . . . and when I lift up my eyes to see the immense space teeming with worlds, atoms; no human word can express the feeling which this idea stirs up. And no subtle metaphysical analysis can even come close to expressing the sublimity and dignity of this intuition. (p. 154)

Sini's own journey is a "perfect" example of this task, of this philosophical "will to truth" founded on the relentless questioning of language. The non-philosopher, says Sini, has always viewed this questioning as "useless" and "futile," while at the same time he has feared it as dangerous and threatening. "How can this be so?" he asks. Sini's answer, in *Kinesis*, is to compare the work of the philosopher to that of the anatomist who removes the skin of the human body to dissect it and study it. The philosopher likewise removes the "skin" of everyday public language to analyze and investigate what lies beneath. To some this task may appear distasteful and even sadistic because of the pleasure the philosopher seems to take in it. As Nietzsche remarked, not all is well with the "will to truth." For Sini, too, to do philosophy is never a pleasant task. "In truth," he says, "it takes a strong stomach to do philosophy" (p. 158).

In conclusion, a word about this translation. In the Preface to *Images of Truth*, Sini tells the reader that he has tried to preserve the straightforward and colloquial tone of the original lecture format, in which his ideas were first expressed, by not overburdening the text with too many footnotes, which would have hindered the flow of his discourse. I have adhered to Sini's wish as much as possible by keeping references and notes to a minimum and inserting them only where I thought them necessary to make the book, the first by Sini to be published in English, more accessible to the English-speaking reader. At the same time, I hope to have succeeded in keeping unaffected, at least in part, the discursive tone of the original.

In doing so I have had a lot of help from friends who have guided me through some of the thorny stages of my own journey as a translator. My gratitude goes first to Alessandro Carrera, a student of Sini, for reading the manuscript and for his always pertinent and learned advice, especially on the subtleties of Sini's terminology and thinking, and for allowing me to read his own work on Sini, which I have found very helpful in putting together this Introduction. I would also like to thank the anonymous reader of Humanities Press who supported my translation and made very valuable suggestions on how to improve it. I would like to thank Robert Burch, my Hegelian and Heideggerean mentor, who took time to read the manuscript and helped me with some of the more obscure references. I also thank

Richard Bosley, who advised me on Aristotle and Greek philosophy. Bill Rankin helped edit and proofread the manuscript. Terry Butler assisted me with his computer expertise. I would also like to thank Hugh Silverman for suggesting that I do the translation and for his general support. My thanks also go to Keith Ashfield, the president of Humanities Press, for his patience in waiting for the manuscript and especially this Introduction. And last but not least I would like to thank the author, Carlo Sini, not only for always being very helpful in replying to my questions during our long-distance telephone conversations, and for providing me with material on his background and recent work, but above all for the learning and "enchanting" experience that translating his book, and becoming acquainted with his philosophy, has been for me. To all of them my sincere thanks. Of course, I alone am responsible for my "erring" and my "catastrophe."

MASSIMO VERDICCHIO

Preface

◆

The question of truth could not have remained silent in a journey that for years has involved questioning interpretation and the sign. The stages of this journey, if we can speak of it in these terms, are exemplified mainly by my *Semiotics and Philosophy*, *Beyond the Sign*, and *Kinesis. An Essay in Interpretation*.[1] Like these three works, *Images of Truth* was born out of the living experience of courses taught at the University of Milan. In the two years that have elapsed since then, I have had no reason to change any of the ideas expressed then, whether this is for the better or for the worse, or of no consequence at all. That is why I have tried to preserve in this book the simple and direct presentational style of the original lectures rather than burden the text with scholarly quotations and with those bibliographical "supports" which, with a bit of experience and effort, would suffice to confer on this book an external academic dignity and provide it with a formal "scientific" apparatus. I have preferred a text bare of references and notes, as well as an almost colloquial tone so that it may be easier for the reader to understand and evaluate the basic narrative, as well as the importance and the soundness of the theoretical thesis expressed in it.[2]

However, since there are two sides to every coin, by proceeding in this fashion, the theoretical pretensions of the book (as well as its grandiose theme, not to mention the great authors who are too quickly dismissed) are thus entirely "exposed," especially since the book cannot avail itself of the backing of any "authority," unless indirectly and, for that matter, very freely interpreted. On the other hand, the aim of the book is such, as the reader will find out if he is patient enough to read it, that any device aimed at securing in whatever way the *truth* or truthfulness of what it says, would seem, first of all, contradictory and, then, what is worse, nonsensical and against the "spirit" of the book. This does not mean, however, that the author is masochistically looking for detractors; on the contrary, as anyone who writes, he is looking for consonances and elective affinities. Thus, to achieve this frank purpose, it is better to risk being refuted because of a flaw in the text than to be praised for an excess of the same. In presenting itself with disarming simplicity, the text wants to say to the potential friend: "Beware in whom you trust," all the more when the common cause which unites us is the question of truth.

What the role of truth in interpretation is, especially when interpretation takes on the form, as in this case, of "infinite semiosis," is an issue which is as inescapable as it is disquieting. How can anyone speak of truth, authentically, if its form and image are constantly deferred in a movement which, from the point of view of truth, is literally without either head or tail? On the other hand, whoever possesses truths which in one way or another, knowingly or not, are not interpretations, *i.e.*, signs and relations of signs which infinitely refer, let him come forward to cast the first stone. Otherwise, we have to agree that where the question of truth is concerned we are all debtors, whether we care to admit to it or not.

What I have been saying for the past few years, namely, that there is theoretical congruence and complementarity between interpretation and infinite semiosis (Peirce) and hermeneutics (Heidegger, but also Nietzsche, who insists that we cannot avoid the possibility that the world "contains infinite interpretations"), is finding today ample acceptance as well as the support of influential authors and works both here in Europe and in North America. This in itself should leave one satisfied and even gratified for having pursued a lucky as well as a timely intuition, except that the conclusions which have been reached land us in the arms of the purest nihilistic disenchantment and relativism which, all things considered, is neither the easiest nor the most pleasant place to find oneself. But this is the least of it, since it depends on personal as well as on inessential psychological tendencies. So if Euthyphro does not know what he is doing (to himself) or why he does it, whether we like it or not, it behooves the philosopher to make the fact known because the philosopher is first of all the friend of truth.[3]

But what truth value can the nihilistic declaration of truth have, whether it is Euthyphro's or it comes from those who, like him, wish to avoid infinite discussion and interpretation? With what right does nihilism speak in the name of truth, or at least intimate that its critique is truthful or "more" truthful? Isn't nihilism, in the history of truth (already an ambiguous phrase), the most dogmatic and inconsistent of forms? It is impossible to remain in nihilism for long, without having to pay the price of refusing to think through what in nihilism, as Heidegger would say, "makes one think." In fact, for one thing, it is intuitively plausible that truth may lie precisely in this thorough thinking of nihilism; and this, moreover, is the thesis on which our present investigation rests. Equally self-evident and necessary, it seems to me, is an assessment of the images of truth that have accompanied or, better, characterized and founded our overall history, whether thinking still has a sense for us or whether we think that this and any other sense have now declined. For even so it will be necessary to show the *reasons* behind this history and to explain eventually what new image of truth supports it.

Another important aspect of the problem that nihilism and the resulting disenchantment of the world pose today is, precisely, the question of the image. The questioning of the images of truth turns into the questioning of the truth of the image. At the heart of this question is what I defined earlier in *Beyond the Sign* as the "strategy of the soul," the keystone of the whole metaphysical strategy whose coherent conclusion is precisely the "weak nihilism" (as Nietzsche says) of the "psychological" men of our time afflicted by the "social sciences" and by the spirit of resentment (in turn playful and serious) toward the world or universe.

In this book, the strategy of the soul exhibits its deepest ground of origin in that knot between thinking and being whence the image and the problem of truth arise. The complementary side or other face is the question of the metaphysical creation of the image as place and law of the soul; a problematic and elusive place, to this day inexplicable and unexplained, but nonetheless essential if truth is to be thought and stated. This is what Plato says literally in the *Sophist* and Aristotle takes up again at the beginning of *De interpretatione*. I have not been able to discuss this complementary aspect in the present investigation, but I hope to set down in another book analyses pertaining to the problem of the image: a phantasm of public reason on which the human sciences are founded metaphysically, mostly unconsciously, and unproblematically.[4]

With the discussion of the question of truth, as approached and clarified here, seems to be brought to a conclusion the theoretical aim which has inspired and has ideally given unity to my work of the past ten years. This does not mean, naturally, that all the problems have been solved. As this book will show, every work of interpretation pays the penalty of a radical being-in-error, quite apart from the personal limitations of the writer—hence the constitutive "erring" of any discourse and the *experience of truth* that emerges from it. The "conclusion" I meant above pertains rather to the entirely subjective feeling of a "complete(d)" experience and thus is not relevant for "public" ends. This experience can be said to be provisionally "perfect" precisely because, in essence, it is insurmountably and irremediably "concluded."

CARLO SINI

PART I

◆

Images of Truth

1

◆

The Eyes of the Bat

In Book II, chapter 1 (993bff.) of Aristotle's *Metaphysics* we read:[5]

The investigation of the truth is in one way hard, in another easy. An indication of this is found in the fact that no one is able to attain the truth adequately, while, on the other hand, no one fails entirely, but everyone says something true about the nature of things, and while individually they contribute little or nothing to the truth, by the union of all a considerable amount is amassed. Therefore, since the truth seems to be like the proverbial door, which no one can fail to hit, in this way it is easy, but the fact that we can have a whole truth and not the particular part we aim at shows the difficulty of it. Perhaps, as difficulties are of two kinds, the causes of the present difficulty are not in the things but in us. For as the eyes of bats are to the blaze of day, so is the reason in our soul to the things which are by nature most evident of all. It is just that we should be grateful, not only to those whose opinions we may share, but also to those who have expressed more superficial views; for these also have contributed something, by developing before us the habit of thinking [*exin*].[6] It is true that if there had been no Timotheus we should have been without much of our lyric poetry; but if there had been no Phrynis there would have been no Timotheus. The same holds good of those who have expressed views about the truth; for from the better thinkers we have inherited certain opinions, while the others have been responsible for the appearance of the better thinkers. It is right also that philosophy should be called the science of truth. For the end of theoretical knowledge is truth, while that of practical knowledge is action (for even if they consider how things are, practical men do not study what is eternal but what stands in some relation at some time). Now we do not know a truth without its cause; and a thing has a quality in a higher degree than other things if in virtue of it the similar quality belongs to the other things (*i.e.*, fire is the hottest of things; for it is the cause of the heat of all other things); so that that which causes derivative truths to be true is most true. Therefore the principles of eternal things must be always most true; for they are not

2

merely sometimes true, nor is there any cause of their being, but they themselves are the cause of the being of other things, so that as each thing is with respect to being, so is it with respect to truth.

No commentary can ever exhaust the richness and complexity of this Aristotelian passage. For our purposes, let us keep in mind first of all the following six points:

1. *Anyone can say something about the truth (reality or the nature of things).* Man and his "speech," therefore, are always already placed in the truth. We partake of the truth; thus the truth concerns us; it is our business. Man is not on one side and truth on the other, and they meet occasionally. Man and truth have a *being in common.* Keeping in mind the conclusion of the Aristotelian passage, it could also be said that man has as much truth as he has being. But how much being? What is the deep sense of this "situation" or "place" of man in the truth? In what sense are man and his *legein* (his speech, his "combining" or gathering) already situated in the truth?

In order to provide an answer, one would need to know first of all what the meaning of "truth" is. This is the purpose of our questioning of Aristotle, and, to be sure, we will be discovering a lot more. Meanwhile, we can observe that the question of truth also involves being and man. What does "being" mean? What does "man" mean? Can we explain either one of these terms without making reference to the other? We are faced thus with basic questions. Precisely the forgetting of the fundamental importance of these questions is what constitutes the meaninglessness of modern "scientific" knowledge, which believes that it can ignore metaphysical questions including its own unquestioned foundations in metaphysics. Typical, in this regard, are the methodologies of the contemporary "Human Sciences." As a rule, they have no answer to the fundamental questions since somehow they have already *decided*: "Being is equivalent to Nature (the sum total of "physical" events); Man is equivalent to social animal (equipped with *logos*); truth is equivalent to accord of judgment (*logos*) with the things of Nature (with physical events). On what authority do these assumptions rest, these opinions that for the most part are left implied and shape the common outlook of our time?

2. *Truth requires investigation, a theory.* Man, in fact, attains easily the whole, the general truth (just as anyone knows how to hit a door with an arrow) but has difficulty hitting the truth in its particulars. Therefore, we should say that man is and is not in the truth. Or maybe he is in it and does not know it?

3. *The cause of the difficulty in the investigation of the truth is not in the things but in us.* Therefore, is there a "we" in man that is not in the truth or that does not know itself to be in it? Aristotle employs the image of the bat.

But why, we should ask ourselves, is reason blind to the things most evident of all? Why does the most evident (*aletheia, alethestaton*) elude us?

4. *Aristotle clearly conceives the investigation of truth not just as a fact but as a "social" process.* His observations in this regard still concern us. Everyone contributes to the search for truth (which thus is a process, a way of attaining an end by amassing knowledge). From everyone's collaboration one obtains the most considerable results, even if each single contribution is in itself insignificant. Aristotle is saying literally what Peirce has stated in our time, namely, that truth is a public process, a social convention (a social "custom") always in motion (Nietzsche said something similar in *On Truth and Lie in an Extra-Moral Sense*). In this regard we could use a typical Peircean image: truth is like a strong rope made up of many intertwining strands. Each strand is by itself frail, but the rope that binds them is, in contrast, very strong.

5. *Philosophy is the science of truth.* In this sense it is theoretical and not practical. It aims at truths that are eternal and not contingent. Furthermore, it aims at the first cause that is the origin of truth in the highest degree. Naturally, these are statements that are decisive for the entire meaning and destiny of our culture. Aristotle (as elsewhere in the *Metaphysics*) distinguishes here between a theoretical and a practical humanity. There is a philosophical and a non-philosophical humanity, *i.e.*, one that does not pose the "theoretical" problem of truth. This is its "historical" character, as Heidegger says in his own way, as we shall see. Other peoples and cultures addressed what we could call particular truths and stopped at them, limiting themselves to the contingency of the "when" (neglecting the true and the eternal). For example, the hunter is concerned that the footprint is a true sign of the animal; the sailor that the North Star points truly to the north, so he can return home. Further, every man desires that the loving words of the woman he loves are the expression of her sincere feelings, without lies, design, or reserve. And every woman wishes the same from the man she loves. Finally, every man takes for granted that there is a real connection between his feelings, his desires, and the ability to move his body in accordance with his will; that his perception of the tree and its fruit is true and that his desire to climb the tree and eat the fruit translates into a command that the body is capable of following.

We have, thus, four types or images of particular truths, characterized by natural and celestial signs and signs from interpersonal and internal communication. These particular truths are not "disinterested," as are those of philosophy, which are pursued, as Aristotle says, for the sheer pleasure of knowledge. Differently from the philosopher, the hunter, the sailor, the lover, and the man who desires the fruit are "interested," to be sure. The sailor turns to the North Star to find the way home and not out of sheer astronomical interest. Here truth is not a general problem as it is for the science we call philosophy. There can be conflict among particular truths: "Is it true that the plague comes from the stars?" Or, "Is the plague the result of a crime committed by a member of the community?" The solution does not lead to a theory of the plague but to the ability to confront the situation. Nevertheless, philosophy too aims at the causes that produce phenomena and, more than that, at first causes. Philosophy is not limited to the *what* but also looks for the *why*. Aristotle (as Plato before him) calls this investigation "science," "philosophy," and confines to the merely practical all prescientific and prephilosophical knowledge. What is the meaning and true basis of this decision? On what authority does it rest? Because of this decision, philosophy relies on that instrument (*organon*) for investigating the truth and first causes which takes the name of "logic," a *synonymic* investigation, as it is called, on which judgment is founded, on its two values: truth and falsity.[7] But what is logic's sense of truth? Is it because philosophy is based on logic that it is a "science of truth"? And can one conceive of a science that is not "logical," that is, not based on the philosophical gesture of distinguishing between theory and practice and thereby establishing the "logical" image of truth?

6. *Everything has as much being as it has truth.* Aristotle sets up here a correlation between being and being true (which brings to mind the Hegelian identity of real and rational, but whether this connection has any sense and what this may be will be discussed later). For the moment it is more urgent to ask: "What is the meaning of being?" Furthermore, it seems that one can speak of truth in two ways: (*a*) as a problem that concerns the soul's reason, whereby the problem of truth does not depend on the things but on "us," is a problem which is "in us"; (*b*) as the essential, "causal" characteristic of what "is" or, we could say, of what "truly is." What is the connection between these two meanings of the word *truth*? How do they define, together and separately, truth and its (logical) image? We must turn once again to Aristotle to help us clarify these difficult meanings.

2

◆

The Two Places
of Truth

In Book VI, chapter 4 of the *Metaphysics* (1027b–1028a), Aristotle confronts the problem of "that which *is* in the sense of being true, or *is not* in the sense of "being false." He remarks that they depend "on combination and separation" and that "together they are concerned with the apportionment of a contradiction." And he adds, "for truth has the affirmation in the case of what is compounded and the negation in the case of what is divided, while falsity has the contradiction of this apportionment." For "falsity and truth are not in things but in thinking." And he further explains, "while with regard to simple things and essences falsity and truth do not exist even in thinking." Aristotle, clearly, follows the Platonic doctrine of judgment developed in the *Sophist*. Discursive thinking (*dianoia*) proceeds by affirmation and negation ("*a* is *b*," "*a* is not *b*"). These affirmations and negations combine and distinguish between them notions or concepts or, more simply, words. The question of truth and falsity pertains precisely to these relations insofar as they reflect or do not reflect reality. Beings, too, in fact (the "ideas," for Plato) are combined or separated. This does not mean that beings are true or false; all beings *are*, while non-being applies more properly to our judgments insofar as they say what is not, that is, the false; truth and falsity thus are more properly in us, in our thinking. For instance, if we said that fishing is an acquisitive art we would be stating the truth. If, on the contrary, we said that it is a productive art we would be stating a falsehood. Both acquisition and production *are*, but only the former applies to fishing, not the latter. In the same way, we could say, truthfully, that fishing is an acquisitive art by coercion, while it would be a falsehood to say that it is an acquisitive art by hunting. In so doing judgment combines beings according to the sense of truth or falsity.[8]

6

Aristotle goes on:

> But since the combination and the separation are in thinking and not in the things, that which *is* in this sense is a different sort of being from the things that *are* in the full sense. For thinking attaches or removes either the "what" or quality or quantity or one of the other categories.

That which *is* in the sense of being true is not therefore that which *is* accidentally (*on e on*). That which *is* in the sense of being true consists "in some affection of thinking" (*tes dianoias ti pathos*). Aristotle alludes here to his famous and fundamental thesis that "being has several meanings." These meanings or modes of being he expresses in the categories of essence or *ousia*, quality, quantity, relation, and so on. For judgment consists precisely in attributing categories or more general predicates to things. For example, we can say that snow is a substance (an essence or *ousia*), or that it is white (quality), and so on. This is how snow is "thought"; its being is said in many ways. This pertains to the faculty of speech which is proper to reason and to the *logos*. But snow, whiteness, *etc.* are themselves indifferent to this process. The snow is not any less white if we say that it is black, nor does it disappear from the world if we negate its *ousia*. In this important chapter Aristotle has thus cleared up the first part of point 3 of the six points listed above. But a question arises: What happens to the identity of being and being true asserted in point 6?

In the *Metaphysics* (Book IX, chapter 10, 1051b) Aristotle reiterates first of all:

> The condition of this [of truth and falsity] in the objects is their being combined or separated, so that he who thinks the separated to be separated and the combined to be combined has the truth, while he whose thinking is in a state contrary to that of the objects is in error.

And goes on, "This being so, when is what is called truth or falsity present, and when is it not? . . . It is not because we think that you are white, that you *are* white, but because you are white we who say this have the truth." In other words, we speak the truth. Having established these premises, we can deduce three consequences:

1. some things are always combined;
2. some things are always separated;
3. some things can sometimes be combined and separated.

It follows that opinion (*doxa*) and discourse (*logos*) will be, respectively:

1. always true, if they combine; always false, if they separate.
2. always true, if they separate; always false, if they combine;
3. sometimes true and sometimes false.

At this point Aristotle introduces a further problem: "With regard to incomposites [*asuntheta*], what is being or not being, and truth or falsity?" (1051). The issue had already come up for simple beings and essences. In this regard, in the *Metaphysics*, Book VI, Aristotle had stated that truth and falsity cannot even be in thought, besides not being in things. This statement was not discussed then, and it is now time to take it up.

It is generally accepted that the above-mentioned incomposites are the essences. For example, Ross remarks that incomposite beings or terms are obviously the essences or the pure forms, God or the prime mover,[9] and adds that so are the simple terms that judgment combines such as "man," "plant," "wood," "white," *etc*. With regard to these beings and terms, truth and falsity cannot take place in the same manner as in composite ones. Aristotle says: "In fact, as truth is not the same in these cases, so also being is not the same; but truth or falsity is as follows—contact and assertion are truth (assertion not being the same as affirmation), and ignorance is non-contact" (*Metaphysics* IX, chapter 10, 1051).

What Aristotle is pointing out here is that where incomposites and simple beings are concerned the pair truth-error does not apply; rather the pair should be truth-ignorance. In fact he writes:

> About the things, then, which are essences and exist in actuality, it is not possible to be in error, but only to think them or not to think them. Inquiry about their "what" takes the form of asking whether they are of such and such a nature or not. (1051)

The fact *that* they are, therefore, is not subject to error. That is, intuition (and assertion) relative to these beings is always true; at worst it can fail out of ignorance. For example, I may not know that there is an animal like the ornithorhyncus or that there is a quality like ultrasounds.

Once this is established, we can say that Aristotle has cleared up the relationship between being and being true in its difference with respect to truth and falsity that are in us, that is, in the judgment that combines and separates, stating the many meanings of being (apophantic judgment). The solution in fact is just before our eyes. In simple beings, truth corresponds to being, that is, to their being directly intuited, asserted, or thought. Thinking, having grasped them, can define them, say what they are, *to ti esti*. The opposite of this operation is not falsity (one cannot *intuit* what is false, what is not) but simply ignorance. One can ignore that Socrates existed. With regard to simple beings one can either think or not think them, but one cannot think what is false. In composite beings, instead, what is true concerns reason's judgment, the affirmation that states what is combined and what is separated (always or necessarily, or sometimes yes and sometimes no, or by accident). Here its opposite is precisely what is false, that falsity which is in us and consists of saying that what is combined is separated (*i.e.*, that Socrates is bad, when he is good, *etc*.).

We can sum up as follows: being is above all by itself, in itself, and for itself the true from the moment that it "is." Since being is revealed to the intuition of the senses and of thinking it is *alethes*: manifest, not latent, *i.e.*, true. But in the *logos* which speaks being, in the affirmation and negation of judgment, we encounter another type of truth (and its opposite which is falsehood); it is thus that truth and falsehood take place in the soul's reason, since judgment says *how* the being which is is, says being in all its manifold meanings. Naturally the issue requires further elaboration, and this constitutes the heart of Aristotle's *Metaphysics*, especially Books IV and VII. The question pertains to the unity of being with respect to the multiplicity of its categories or predicates (the question from which Heidegger began his inquiry into the meaning of being) and more generally to the question of the relationship between the one and the many, which Aristotle thought crucial. We cannot ourselves conduct a similar analysis here, but it is sufficient to be reminded that the question does not start or end with Aristotle.

3

◆

Parmenides' Knot

In Parmenides' poem, the *Way of Truth*, we read:

> That which can be spoken and thought needs must be; for it is possible for
> it, but not for nothing, to be; . . . [It] is uncreated and imperishable, for it
> is entire, immovable and without end. It *was* not in the past, nor *shall* it
> be, since it *is* now, all at once, one, continuous. . . . This is the real and
> true way. . . . Wherefore all these are mere names which mortals laid
> down believing them to be true—coming into being and perishing, being
> and not being, change of place and variation of bright colour.[10]

In the *Sophist*, Plato takes up the famous Parmenidean assertion that "Never
shall this be proved, that things that are not are, but do thou, in thy inquiry,
hold back thy thought from this way" (237a and 258d).[11] We are here in the
presence of what we could call the Parmenidean knot which ties together
being, thinking, and truth and which lies at the origin of our entire culture.
The question of truth is at the center of this knot. For Parmenides truth is
characterized by the fact that to think being, to say that it absolutely "is," is
true. The force of this statement lies precisely in the absolute character of its
truth, namely, that the non-being of being cannot even be thought. But here
is also the weakness of this proposition which excludes from speech every
other judgment and from thinking every other opinion which is not that of
mere identity: being *is* being (*A* is *A*). In the *Sophist*, Plato exposes this
difficulty. "The isolation, he says, of everything from everything else means
a complete abolition of all discourse" (259e). In other words, it is impossible
to establish and justify the unity of judgment, which is unity of the many (*A*
is *B*). Therefore the door is open to sophistry and heuristic, which manipu-
late Parmenides' assertion any way they like. If one can only think and state
being, what *is*, and not not-being, then every statement is true. There is
practically no more distinction between truth and falsity. If everything is
true and nothing is false, truth no longer has any connotation of its own, no
longer has any difference. Therefore there cannot be a science of discourse

founded on the science of being. There is only the *practice* of discourse, with its greater or lesser rhetorical effectiveness, with its power of persuasion. Combating all this, Plato aims at salvaging the Parmenidean identity between being, thinking, and truth (*i.e.*, science), but in order to do this he has to defy Parmenides' ban that forbids us to think non-being. One must somehow be able to think and express non-being if one wants to be able to distinguish truth from falsity, true discourse from false. Plato's solution is well known. Parmenides' error consists in identifying non-being with nothing; but non-being does not mean nothing just as non-white does not mean only black. Non-white means also that which is *different* from white, *i.e.*, red, green, yellow and the entire gamut of colors, except white. Therefore non-being also means that which is *different* from being, that is, motion, becoming, rest, birth, death, and all those things that Parmenides had banished to the deceptiveness of opinion, to the path of the night (error) as opposed to the path of the day (truth).

In the *Sophist*, Plato expounds on the question of the logical relation between the one and the many as follows: "any discourse, he says, owes its existence to the weaving together of forms" (260). Thus, being is not unique, compact, motionless and so on. Rather it is a universe of relations between essences or ideas. The form of judgment reflects these relations. When I say that fishing is an acquisitive art, I am expressing in discourse the relational mode proper to things: how things are in their relation. The idea of art is like a great genus that comprises a large number of heterogeneous things. The being of all these things is expressed in terms of multiple identities and differences. Every thing is itself, has its own being, because it is not the others. It is *different* from the others that together with it make up the same genus. Thus hunting and fishing are both identical, since both are arts and not natural products such as trees and mountains, and different, since one is an art of capture by enclosure and the other by angling (220c). This is how judgment is able to express the relation among the various types of being, and how it can be either true or false. It is true, as Aristotle says, if it expresses exactly the relations among beings, that is, if it declares identical what is identical, *i.e.*, Socrates and goodness, and different what is different. It is false if it says the opposite.

With Plato we have the birth of what we could call onto-logy: the science of discourse, of truth and falsity, since it is founded on beings or, better, on the being of beings, that is, on the relations among beings that constitute their being, their way of being, and, finally, the reason that makes them be what they are. Behind this conception, however, even if modified or developed in its implications, lies Parmenides' knot: the powerful and equally enigmatic statement of the identity of being, thinking, and truth. Without this identity and its characteristic knot (with the related question of the one and the many, that is, of the unity of meaning of the meanings of being, of what is) there is no truth, no *logical* thinking, and not even that science of truth that Aristotle calls philosophy.

The situation, therefore, looks like this. There is a true being that is the unity and the cause of its appearances, of its becoming *alethes*, manifest. We see the appearances but we do not see equally well what holds them together, being. On the one hand, it is *alethestaton*, the maximum manifestation or truth, since it is what is manifested in all appearances; but for us, as for the bat mentioned by Aristotle, the most manifest is precisely what is difficult to grasp. Dispersed and blinded by the manifold, we are blinded by too much light; we cannot grasp the unity that surrounds us everywhere. This explains the typical way in which man, as we have seen with Aristotle, dwells in the truth. He is in it:

a) since he knows (intuits) appearances;
b) since he places them in relation by means of the *logos* (judgment).

But also he is not in it:

a) since he does not know all the appearances. He *ignores* them. Spinoza would say that it is because man ignores the infinite attributes of being except for two: thought and extension.
b) since he posits false (*erroneous*) relations, for the side of the truth which is "in us," as *pathos tes psyches*. For this reason man needs the science of truth, philosophy.

Furthermore, we understand even better now what Aristotle means when he says that every thing has as much being as it has truth. It is man's finitude of being that partially makes possible being in the truth, even though man is in it more than any other animal and, generally, more than any other natural being, because he possesses the *logos*, that is, the capacity to speak or to combine appearances, phenomena. Hobbes too, for instance, situates in the *logos* this prominent capacity to combine and calculate, and it is certainly not unrelated to these basic premises that modern and contemporary thinking develops the science of logic.

But what can be said of man applies also to every other thing: every thing embodies a fragment of its relation with the whole. Every plant embodies in its own way the essence of being vegetable and every animal the essence of being animal. Every thing has the being of its "form," of its specific essence; in fact, it *is* this form in actuality. But no being (not even man) has the form of all the forms, the uniting essence of all the manifold essences. This pertains to God alone, the ultimate form, the final and conclusive act of everything which is. This form can only be, as Aristotle says clearly, the thinking of all the forms, their first and ultimate "cause": a complete thinking which has nothing outside itself (which is totally act and in actuality); which has no further potentiality to fulfill and no further matter to translate into form; which is the thinking of thinking. Thus, at the height of Aristotelian metaphysics, we have once again the Parmenidean knot, the identity of being and thinking. Man's specificity, one could say, is to be in the truth, since he is a fragment of divine thinking. (This is what medieval philosophy will say more explicitly, as Heidegger, we shall see, points out.) Human science, too, is thus essentially "theological"—"onto-theo-logical," as Heidegger says.[12]

Let us briefly summarize what we have said so far. The question of truth concerns being and thinking and is connected with them in two ways: (*a*) every thing has as much being as it has truth and vice versa (correspondence between being and being true); (*b*) truth is an affection of the mind, since it unites and separates in judgment the modes of being (categories, predicates). The place of truth thus appears to be twofold: being (*to on*, what is); judgment (the *logos tes psyches*). Man partakes of it in two ways: as the being that he is (*animal rationale*); and because he is rational, that is, endowed with *logos*, capable of logical judgment. The dominion of truth, therefore, has its foundation in being, in the truth of being, *i.e.*, in its becoming manifest (*alethes*) in all its manifold ways that judgment tries to gather (to "speak"). The *logos* depends on being, so that thinking and being, as Parmenides says, belong to one another. Thinking speaks being, but being is "rational," ordered according to the "logical" correlation of genus and species. The dominion of truth, as well as its image, is onto-logy, which does not so much adhere to Parmenidean logic (which, in fact, from Plato to Aristotle inevitably has to be modified in order to lay the foundations for logic) as it is based on the Parmenidean principle *einai kai noein tauton*, being and thinking are one and the same. The foundation of onto-logy and thus of science, both ancient and modern, is the Parmenidean knot of being, thinking and truth.

4

◆

Parmenides' Secret
or the
Truth of His Truth

But what is the truth of the Parmenidean knot? The truth of its truth is exactly the opposite of what it says. This is the radical turning point that must now be understood. It will shed light on the rest of our journey. The truth of the Parmenidean statement is the following. Since being *is* absolutely and can be thought, truth consists precisely in speaking it, in speaking that being *is*. Plato and Aristotle, on the strength of this argument, add the truth of judgment. It is not just a question of stating *that* being *is* but also of *how* it is, through the logical relation of judgment. The truth of the Parmenidean assertion, however, is the opposite of what it says. Because we speak and judge, truth consists in a being that can be thought and judged, that is, in conformity with the structures and demands of the *logos* and judgment. In other words, the original place of truth is not the being that is and which then is revealed in judgment. The original place is precisely the *logos*, judgment. It is being that is assimilated to judgment, not judgment, thinking, to being. Being con-forms to the *logos*, *i.e.*, is formed in its image and likeness. In Parmenides' phrase, one can only speak or think being. The original revelation is not "being" but precisely that which concerns "speaking" and "thinking." We could call this "Parmenides' secret," which Parmenides himself must have ignored. The truth of this secret, in fact, does not pertain to his assertion but rather to the destiny of his assertion, that is, to what it was destined for and the use to which it was put.

The truth of this secret is already apparent in that exceptional passage in Plato's *Sophist*, which we have already quoted. "The isolation of everything from everything else means a complete abolition of all discourse" (259e).

Therefore, being *must* be and must then be manifested in a multiplicity of essences, categories, or "logical" relations; otherwise there can be no truth, no science of truth, *i.e.*, philosophy. Thus, when we read in the *Sophist* that "any discourse we can have owes its existence to the weaving together of forms" (260) we should in fact read, "the forms and their relations owe their existence to our discourse and to *its* weaving them together." The "logical" image of truth depends on it.

In bringing about this reversal of meaning by reading in the truth of the Parmenidean knot the opposite of what it says and has kept on saying throughout our entire tradition, we are only placing in evidence the coming of the Western *ratio*, of its onto-logical reason, namely, the coming of that "discursive" *logos* which investigates, debates, defines, contradicts, *etc.* and in so doing, and as we shall see later, founds "*public truth*." The founding of "public truth" is at the same time bestowing "being to the world," in every sense of the expression. This event entails the reduction of the word to a mere conventional sign of thinking, to an external apparel of the internal intentions of the soul, which in turn is edified in terms of the Platonic "strategy of the soul" which is at the very heart of philosophical reason. However, this is an issue that cannot be taken up here. For a discussion of this point, the reader is referred to the third part of my *Beyond the Sign*.[13]

After Aristotle and the theological-Christian assumptions of the Middle Ages, the question of truth shows the increasing predominance of thinking over being. That is, the fundamental and foundational character of the *logos* gradually emerges to slowly unveil Parmenides' secret. This is made completely clear by modern metaphysics from Descartes to Kant and to Fichte. The certainty of thinking and, later, the transcendental character of the synthetic á priori, determine the structure of being, of what is, even though this happens and continues to happen on the basis of the never clearly resolved Parmenidean knot of the identity of being and thinking. The knot is resolved only at the moment when the two places of truth established by tradition, and which not even Kant's Copernican revolution was able to affect, undergo an irreversible crisis. The first commonplace to be put into question and then totally demolished was that of truth understood as judgment and affection of the soul. The second commonplace was that of the correspondence between being and being true. It was literally a question of two fatal steps taken toward the abyss, toward the groundlessness (*Abgrund*) of ground. These two steps usher in the contemporary era and exemplify the present condition of man, who has completely "consumed" being and can no longer "think." The first step toward the abyss is taken by Hegel, as he is the first to declare and to show that judgment *is not* the place of truth. In so doing, Hegel reverses an ancient tradition, opening the way for a decisive turning point in the destiny of our civilization, a shift whose importance on the ideal and conceptual scale is not inferior to that of the French Revolution for history. After all, we must not forget the importance that Hegelian logic had for Marx's thinking and the ideological revolution that resulted. For all these reasons it is only fair to speak of Hegel's modernity, not only because he marks a turning point in philosophical thinking, which is still relevant for us today, but also because the underlying importance of that shift, in some cases even in its simple literal sense, is still largely ignored or misunderstood, as is the case with the entire tradition of contemporary logic. Thus, it will probably be a long time before Hegel's real contribution will be universally recognized.

5

◆

The Destruction
of Judgment

How and why does Hegel arrive at the conclusion that judgment is not the place of truth? The answer can be found in the "Preliminary Notion" of the *Science of Logic* in *The Encyclopedia of the Philosophical Sciences* (§19–83).[14] Hegel confronts here the question of the first, second, and third "positions" of thinking with respect to objectivity, namely, metaphysics, empiricism, and critical philosophy (Kant's), and immediate knowledge. For our purposes, we shall be concerned only with the first "position" of thinking with respect to objectivity which characterizes traditional and pre-Kantian metaphysics, namely, the way of representing reality and thinking the object in general.

In general, one could define this first position as "naive." "It involves the *belief*," says Hegel,

> that the truth is *known* by meta-thinking, and objects brought before consciousness as they really are. In this belief, thinking heads straight for objects, transforms the content of sensations and intuitions into a content of thinking, and is satisfied with this as the truth. (§26)

This is how "the old pre-Kantian metaphysics" is "the *view that mere understanding* takes of the objects of reason" (§27). This view can be said to be "old" only for the history of philosophy, since it is rather "eternal," for it exemplifies the intellectual method of inquiry to which the so-called common sense also subscribes.

What is the modus operandi of traditional metaphysics? We perceive many horses and we ask ourselves: what is the truth of these perceptions? By reflection we discover that all these individual perceptions generate in us a common and complex image; we then assume this image, idea, or general concept and call it "essence," "truth," and maybe even "cause" of these

17

individual perceptions. Basically, truth is said to reside in the concept thus deduced.

However, in the next paragraph (§28), Hegel makes a very important observation.

This science (traditional metaphysics) took the determinations of thinking to be the *fundamental determinations of things*. It assumed that to think what is, is to know in itself; to that extent it occupied higher ground than the critical philosophy that succeeded it. [Sini's emphasis]

Hegel is lashing out here at Kant's phenomenalism whereby "all that is left to men is the dross." In fact, Kant attributes to thinking the faculty of determining à priori the structure of phenomena, of the phenomenal world, but phenomena, as is well known, are not the things as they are in themselves. They are the reality *for us* that know them but not the reality *in itself*. Therefore, thinking cannot grasp reality but only "its dross." In making this claim, Hegel reiterates the fundamental Parmenidean correlation between being and thinking, and in fact he brings this relation to fruition. Traditional metaphysics, however, insofar as it does not disown the unity of being and thinking, is, in this respect at least, more philosophically advanced than Kant's critique.

Nonetheless, Hegel quickly distances himself from traditional metaphysics since (*a*) It assumed that the determinations of things in their abstraction are valid in themselves and capable of being *predicates of the truth*. (It is true that the thing is white, salty, smooth, etc.) (*b*) It generally assumed that "a knowledge of the absolute was gained by assigning predicates to it" (§28). (*c*) "It investigated neither the peculiar content and value of the determinations of the understanding, nor even this way of determining the absolute by assigning predicates to it" (§28). In fact, "Nobody asked whether such predicates had any intrinsic and independent truth, or if the judgmental form could be a form of truth" (§28). With this observation and with this question, a first step is taken toward the abyss.

But let us consider the Addition to the text: "The Metaphysics of the past assumed, as unsophisticated belief always does, that thinking apprehends the very self of things, and that things, to become what they truly are, require to be thought" (Addition to §28). In this "naive belief" Hegel recognizes a grain of truth. It is true that things are what they are insofar as they are "thought," but "that metaphysics . . . never went beyond the province of the *analytic* understanding." That is, it never went beyond a thinking that transforms its abstract determinations into truth predicates, *i.e.*, a thinking that predicates "existence" with regard to God, "finiteness" or "infiniteness" with regard to the world, "simple" or "complex" with regard to the nature of the soul, and "unity" or "whole" with regard to things. In other words, it was a form of thinking that transformed its abstractions, its abstract concepts derived through simple reflection from empirical experience, into truth. Traditional metaphysics, moreover, does not differentiate between two quite different modes of thinking. "But in using the term thinking," says Hegel,

> we must not forget the difference between *finite* or discursive thinking and the thinking which is only *infinite* and *rational*. The categories, as they meet us *prima facie* and in isolation, are finite forms. But truth is always infinite, and cannot be expressed or presented to consciousness in finite terms. . . . The understanding, itself finite, knows only the nature of the finite. (Addition to §28, emphasis Sini's)

Hegel here states his famous distinction between understanding (*Verstand*) and reason (*Vernunft*). Only the latter has to do with non-abstract, intellectual thinking and thus with the truth. Now the defect of traditional metaphysics was to try to determine the objects of reason (soul, world, God) through finite predicates. As we shall see, judgment, its abstract and analytical form, is precisely the expression of this defect.

Paragraph 31. Any proposition or judgment indicates through the predicate ("or in philosophy, the category") "*what* the subject, or the conception we start with, is." For instance, "In such a sentence as 'God is eternal,' we begin with the conception 'God,' not *knowing* as yet what he *is*; to tell us that is the business of the predicate" (emphasis Sini's). In so doing we commit a double error: (*a*) we pretend to define the absolute (reality in itself, the objects of reason) with finite predicates, whose truth is to be predetermined and, anyway, could only be *within* the absolute and not outside as its predicate; (*b*) in order to define the absolute, reality in itself, we appeal to something other than thinking, that is, to a simple conception, denying thus that truth has its foundation in thinking. In conclusion: "The form of the proposition or, more precisely, judgment, is not suited to express the concrete—and the true is concrete—or the speculative. The judgment is by its form one-sided and, to that extent, false." The destruction of judgment as the place of truth is already announced here.

Paragraph 32. Traditional metaphysics falls into dogmatism since it believes that judgment constitutes the place of truth. For instance, it assumes "that of two opposite assertions . . . one must be true and the other false" (§32) which, as is well known, is still the cornerstone of contemporary logic. By proceeding in this manner, the one-sided determinations of understanding are kept fixed. They exclude, in fact, the opposites in accordance with the "cybernetic" rigidity of the *aut aut*: either the world is finite or infinite. On the other hand, truth as a totality "holds in union as a totality [those determinations that] for dogmatism are something fixed and true in their isolation" (Addition to §32).[15] The determinations, instead, "are of value only when overcome. The battle of reason is the struggle to break up the rigidity to which the understanding has reduced everything" (Addition to §32). The meaning of this "overcoming" (dialectic overcoming, *Aufhebung*) alluded to here by Hegel is on the one hand well known; later on we will discuss its wider implications. Meanwhile we should note that from the above quotations emerge three fundamental characterizations of truth. Truth, says Hegel, is the *infinite*, the *concrete*, the *totality*. None of these three aspects, however, can be grasped by judgment, which is the finite, abstract, and one-sided form of understanding.

Paragraph 33. The truth of a proposition consists in this: "Whether a concept is or is not with truth to be attributed to a subject." It follows that "untruth lies in the contradiction between the subject of the idea, and the concept to be predicated of it." Truth, then, is nothing more than the absence of contradiction. However, every concept "and every determinacy in general is essentially a self-contained unity of distinct determinations." Concepts such as being, existence, finiteness, simplicity, *etc.* are not intrinsically true concepts in their abstract isolation but in their manifold relations. A simple contradiction or non-contradiction expressed in the form of judgment cannot express the truth.

Paragraph 36. The understanding makes use of judgment to "demonstrate" its own truths. For instance, it wants to define and demonstrate God, the reality in itself and for itself or absolute reality. This entails an "absurd inversion." Instead of passing from the finite to the infinite (which is the true problem of thinking which aims at the truth), one wants to ground the absolute (the infinite) in a finite concept. For instance, one attributes to God finite properties, such as goodness, intellect, *etc.*; thus "God's being . . . acquires the appearance of being derived from something else" (Wallace, §36). Nor does it help to specify that here it is a question of *infinite* goodness, *infinite* intelligence, and so on. This quantitative exaltation of the determination only destroys the property, and the mere name is all that is left.

And further in the Addition to §36, we read that if from God, the most real of beings and the most true, we exclude negation as understanding would have us do, we get a result opposite of what understanding supposes it to be. Instead of the richest being, we get the poorest and emptiest since it is conceived solely through the abstraction of all the concrete characteristics of reality. "It is with reason," Hegel writes,

> that the heart craves a concrete body of truth; but without definite feature, that is, without negation, contained in the concept, there can only be an abstraction. When the concept of God is apprehended only as that of the abstract or most real being, God is, as it were, relegated to another world beyond: and to speak of a knowledge of him would be meaningless.

Where there is no definite quality, knowledge is impossible. Mere light is mere darkness. (Wallace, Addition §36)[16]

This last remark shows how Hegel is working a kind of reversal of Platonism, but we should also note that if God, the absolutely real, is reduced by understanding to a simple noumenal beyond, Hegel reduces God to a simple here and now. What is more important, however, is that Hegel shows the incongruence between the two modes of truth as they are found in Aristotle and transmitted by tradition. If truth is the *ens verum*, the *ens realissimum*, then judgment is not at all the proper place to exemplify this truth in conceptual form. Judgment, by rejecting negation and contradiction and by proceeding by abstract, fixed, and finite determinations can only state the abstraction of reality, its reflexive ghost. To conclude:

Instead of arriving at a concrete identity (concrete identity of God, concrete unity of being and thinking), this metaphysics insisted on an abstract one. Its good point was the perception that thinking constitutes the essence of all that is. (Wallace, Addition to §36)[17]

But if judgment is not the place of truth, what then is its proper place? As Hegel says, where does "the journey of rational demonstration" take place? This journey takes place in the syllogism and, more precisely, in the disjunctive syllogism. This is, for Hegel, the place of truth.

6

◆

Everything Is
a Syllogism

At first one is perplexed by the statement that the syllogism is the place of truth. Is not a syllogism, as everyone knows, the simple union or inferential relation of three judgments? Are we not falling back, once again, on that judgmental understanding that Hegel has shown to be inadequate to grasp and express the truth? Let us go to §181 of the *Encyclopedia*, which deals with the syllogism. For Hegel, the syllogism "is the unity of concept and judgment" (Wallace, §181).[18] The concept is the simple identity, *i.e.*, "animal"; judgment adds its formal distinctions or determinations, *i.e.*, "animal is horse"; the syllogism, instead, presents distinctions that are no longer formal but "set in reality." Thus, the syllogism, says Hegel, is also the concrete concept turned on itself and determined in reality. Therefore, "the syllogism is the *rational*, and *everything* rational." What does this mean?

First of all it is clear that Hegel distinguishes between the formal and concrete concept, one intellectual (*Verständlich*), the other rational. Similarly, he speaks of rational syllogism to distinguish it from traditional syllogism, which is purely formal. As is well known, traditional syllogism has two judgments as premises ("All men are mortals," "Socrates is a man") and a concluding judgment ("Socrates is mortal"). The inferential play consists in that the major and minor terms, or "extremes," of the conclusion ("Socrates is mortal") are shown to be congruent by virtue of a third, or "middle" term ("man") which, in fact, mediates between them and makes their relation possible. In other words, "mortal" can predicate "Socrates" because it predicates "man" and, at the same time, "man" can predicate "Socrates." That is to say, since the genus "mortal" comprises the species "man" and this has "Socrates" as one of its members, then "Socrates" too belongs to the genus "mortal." This procedure is defined by Hegel as formal and purely intellectual. The syllogism, he says, is not the "form" of the rational, as is believed. In fact, formal syllogism "really presents what is rational in such a non-rational way that it has nothing to do with any rational matter." Concrete syllogism, instead, is "but an explicit putting, *i.e.*, *realizing of the concept.*" "(Concrete) Syllogism, therefore, is *the essential ground of whatever is true*: and at the present stage the *definition of the Absolute* is that it is the syllogism or, stating the principle in a proposition: *Everything is a Syllogism.*"

He explains:

Everything is a *concept*, the existence of which is the differentiation of its members or functions, so that the *universal* nature of the concept gives itself external reality by means of the *particularity*, and thereby, and as a negative reflection-into-self, makes itself an *individual*. Or, conversely: the actual thing is an *individual*, which by means of particularity rises to *universality* and makes itself identical with itself.

To summarize, we could say that "the actual is one: but it is also the divergence from each other of the constituent elements of the concept, and the syllogism represents the orbit of intermediation of its elements, by which it realizes its unity." The sense of these Hegelian remarks, even if well formulated as such, are inevitably obscure at first. For the time being, however, let us draw attention to the similarities between Hegel's position and Peirce's.

The statement that everything is a syllogism is similar to Peirce's. Peirce identifies reality with the inferential sign; everything is a sign.[19] This is to say that the real is the infinite mediation of signs, where the concept, too, is a concrete sign. For Peirce, too, as for Hegel, the syllogisms of traditional logic are empty abstractions. And with Hegel, Peirce also believes that the syllogism, in its living concreteness, is at the heart of every experience and every reality. Everything that happens in fact is a syllogism, a mediated concept and not a "material" individual, as common sense or empiricism have supposed. Hegel illustrates all this with an example that Peirce would have approved of without hesitation.

If anyone, when awaking on a winter morning, hears the creaking of the carriages on the street, and is thus led to conclude that it has frozen hard in the night, he has gone through a syllogistic operation: —an operation which is every day repeated under the greatest variety of conditions. (Addition, §183)

Having said this, the question remains: What is meant by concrete syllogism? In what way is disjunctive syllogism concrete; is it the real concept and the real ground of every truth?

To give an answer to these questions we must pass to a closer examination of the problem and turn to the *Science of Logic* and, more specifically, to the

Subjective Logic or *The Doctrine of The Concept*, and to Section I, chapter 3; The Syllogism.[20] Hegel divides the argument into three parts: A. The Syllogism of Existence; B. The Syllogism of Reflection (Allness, Induction, Analogy); C. The Syllogism of Necessity (Categorical, Hypothetical, Disjunctive). We are concerned only with part C and its last subsection.[21]

In the Disjunctive Syllogism, says Hegel, the middle term "has determined itself as *totality*, as *developed* objective universality. Consequently the middle term is not only universality but also particularity and individuality" (§701). From this first remark we are warned of at least two things: (*a*) the middle term is the means to arrive at the truth as it has to do with totality, as we noted earlier; (*b*) Hegel's disjunctive syllogism is characterized by a middle term completely different from the traditional syllogism. In the latter, the middle term "mediates" between universality and individuality, between "mortal" and "Socrates," placing them in a relation. Here, however, and surprisingly, the middle term is said to be both universal and particular and individual. Let us see how this is analytically possible.

First of all, says Hegel, the middle term is "the substantial identity of the genus," its substantial universality. For instance, it is *A*, where *A* stands for Animal. In the second place, the middle term is the universal sphere, but "developed" in its internal particularizations. *A* is as much *B*, as *C*, as *D*; Animal is as much horse, as dog, as lion, *etc.*, for the sake of brevity, let us suppose that the sphere of animality comprises only these three species. In the third place, these particularizations are a reciprocal *aut aut*, *i.e.*, between *B*, *C*, and *D*. Here the middle term is a negative unity, born out of the reciprocal exclusion of the determinations since they are more properly distinctions. We could say that *A* is either *B* or *C* or *D* and at the same time and in the same sense that *A* is neither *B* nor *C* nor *D*. These two propositions, taken together as both *true*, express with one formula the movement of the reciprocal exclusion of the particularities within the universality of the genus. This movement, however, is not a mere "relative" determination, "relative" of the particular terms, as in the Saussurean concept of *langue*; it is not a question of a mere reciprocal exclusion, "but it is just as essentially a *self-related* determination, the particular as *individuality* to the exclusion of the *others*" (§701). For instance, *B* relates to itself, to its concrete individuality, since it excludes the other determinations *C* and *D*. Horse is a concrete individual as it excludes the determinations of the dog and the lion. This is how *B* fulfills its own concrete animality, that *B* is *A*. We could also say that at the level of concrete reality *A* does not exist. Animality is not encountered in the world, *sic et simpliciter*, even if *A* is understood as the place of a reciprocal relating, determining and excluding of its species. There is *B* instead (there are horses in the world) as concrete refusal and difference with respect to *C* and *D* (dogs and lions). It is by relating to itself, to its concrete individuality, that *B* embodies *A*, that horses are animals, *like*, but also different from, dogs and lions. This is how Hegel expresses in a formula the disjunctive syllogism:

> *A* is either *B* or *C* or *D*,
> But *A* is *B*,
> Therefore *A* is neither *C* nor *D*.

Or again:

> *A* is either *B* or *C* or *D*,
> But *A* is neither *C* nor *D*,
> Therefore *A* is *B*.

Hegel comments on these two formulas as follows:

> *A* is subject not only in the two premises but also in the conclusion. In the first premise it is a universal, and in its predicate, the *universal* sphere particularized into the totality of its species; in the second premise it appears as *determinate* or as a species; in the conclusion it is posited as the exclusive, *individual* determinateness. Or again, it already appears in the minor premise as exclusive individuality and is positively posited in the conclusion as the determinate which it is. (§702)

If we take into account the entire movement of the disjunctive syllogism, which obviously is to be taken as a single movement that the formula exemplifies graphically in three successive movements, we observe that what is *mediated* is the universality of *A* with its individuality (animal since it is horse), but the *mediating* factor, what mediates, is also *A*. We are faced, as Hegel had indicated, with the unity of the mediated and the mediating: "That which is mediated is itself an essential moment of what mediates it, and each moment appears as the totality of what is mediated" (§703). In *B* there is the totality of the moments in *A* by inclusion since it is *A*, and by exclusion since it is neither *C* nor *D*. In order to have horses one needs dogs and lions. This is how each one is the entire animality, *i.e.*, an animal, but as a concrete animality, individually determined by the exclusion of all other animalities.

However, at this point we cannot help but comment on the strangeness of this kind of syllogism. How can a syllogism be a succession of judgments in which the middle term is the subject of all three judgments, premises, and conclusions, and where the middle term and the extremes between which it mediates are the same term? Hegel recognizes this fact. The disjunctive syllogism, he says, "*is no longer a syllogism*" (§702). "For the middle term, which is posited in it as the totality of the concept, contains itself the two extremes in their complete determinateness." Thus, "The extremes . . . appear only as a positedness which no longer possesses any determinateness peculiar to itself as against the middle term" (§702). But this is how we obtain the concrete concept, and not merely the abstract or intellectual one, namely the concept "in its determined difference and at the same time in the simple identity of the concept" (§702).[22] This is how Hegel "overcomes," in the sense of *Aufheben*, which is a "sublating" and also a "preserving," the logic of understanding that proceeded by finite and abstract determinations. It assumed, for instance, that the concepts of horse, dog, and lion in their determination are simple truths in themselves. Against these abstract concepts is posited the concept of animality as the product of a further abstracting reflection. Naturally all these abstract operations remained enigmatic. The understanding has to know already that these are horses, those are dogs, and those others lions in order to be able to "abstract" the concept, *i.e.*, it must already possess the concept, hence the attempts by traditional metaphysics to resolve the problem by means of theories of memory or by distinguishing between active and passive understanding, *etc.* With these abstractly formulated concepts, traditional formal logic played its inferential game: animality comprises the fish, the cod is a fish, the cod is an animal. In so doing, formal logic was precluded from an understanding of the real movement of the concept, which is an interpenetration of being and thinking, of reality and concept. This is what Hegel wants to demonstrate, as he says, by entering into the logic of reason. He writes, for instance: "In this way (*i.e.*, with disjunctive syllogism) *the formalism of the syllogistic process*, and with it the subjectivity of the syllogism and of the concept in general, has sublated itself" (§702).

This last observation is particularly important. We will recall that Aristotle defines being in the sense of truth as "some affection of the understanding" [*tes dianoias ti pathos*].[23] In the old metaphysics the question of truth is based on three rational premises: there is a reality in itself already constituted (there are "horses"); opposite there is the soul, man's reason, also a reality in itself. Somehow these two realities in themselves come into contact and then the soul receives the impressions, the images, of things. The understanding abstracts the common traits of these images and forms the concept. The concept, thus, is a subjective production of human understanding, an abstracting reflection. But how do we know that in reality there are "horses," if not from the concept? To sublate the subjectivity of the concept implies, then, that reality in its movement is determined according to rational structures and that understanding is only an abstract determination of these forms in movement, taking them as complete in themselves and not in their concrete process of determination.

It is precisely this process that Hegel shows unfolding in the syllogism through those three moments (Syllogism of Existence, Syllogism of Reflection, Syllogism of Necessity) which we cannot examine here in detail. This process, says Hegel, exhibits "the stages of *impregnation* or concretion of the middle term" (§703). The pivot is the middle term understood first of all as the understanding presents it, in its pure formalism and in its determination and extraneousness with respect to the extremes. In the various syllogistic forms, the middle term acquires concreteness (*i.e.*, reality) to the point of absorbing entirely the extremes in itself, as we saw, presenting itself as concrete reality. At this point, "the form of the syllogism which consisted in the difference of the middle term from its extremes has thereby sublated itself" (§703). To sublate this difference means, at the same time, to arrive at the concrete concept. Of this concrete concept, as of disjunctive syllogism, one can say that everything pertains to it, that everything is a concept. Concrete concept and disjunctive syllogism are essentially the same. Everything is a concept, but every concept, in its unfolding movement, in its determined indifference, and in its simple identity, is a syllogism. Says Hegel, "Thus the concept as such has been realized; more exactly, it has obtained a reality that is *objectivity*" (§703).

The concept ("horse," "animal") is first of all the mere *internal* (the content of subjective understanding) of an *exteriority* (so-called external reality) whose externality is "its own" (the concept's), but the concept does not know it; the concept is concerned with it intellectually, and it appears as the concept's externality. Then the concept determines itself, still by abstraction, through judgment ("the horse is an animal"). Finally,

> . . . the course of the syllogisms is that this externality is equated with the inner unity. . . . The various determinations return into this unity through the mediation in which at first they are united only in a third term, and thus the externality exhibits in its own self the concept. (§703)

The real presents itself as rational, as equal—identical—to thinking. The real individuals themselves—the horses, the dogs, the lions—exhibit the rational and true totality of animality. The syllogism, therefore, is the adequate expression of rational mediation. "The syllogism," says Hegel,

> is *mediation*, the complete concept in its *positedness*. Its movement is the sublating of this mediation, in which nothing is in and for itself, but each term is only by means of an other. The result is therefore an *immediacy* which has issued from the *sublating of the mediation*, a *being* which is no less identical with the mediation, and which is the concept that has restored itself out of, and in, its otherness. This being is therefore *a thing* which is *in and for itself*, objectivity (§704).[24]

7

◆

Philosophical Truth

In the *Science of Logic*, Hegel reaches the culmination of what we could call the total logification of the world (in Peirce's terms, its total semiotization). Hegel shows the complete articulation of being (in genera and species, Plato would say) and thus its identification with rational thinking, without residue. The Parmenidean identity finds here its fulfillment, together with Plato's dialectic. Of course, the return of the term "dialectic" is not casual— obvious terminological and historical differences aside. Meanwhile, and it could not have been otherwise, Hegel brings the strategy of the soul to its culmination with the total spiritualization (historicization, socialization) of reality. But the *expression* of this culmination precipitates a crisis for the language of philosophy, still founded (again, it could not have been otherwise) on the subjective, conventional, and abstract Platonic-Aristotelian sign. The unified totality of being and thinking is not ultimately "speakable." Hegel himself demonstrates in the *Logic* why and how this occurs (as he does in the *Aesthetics*): judgment, understanding, cannot speak the whole, the concrete, the totality, *i.e.*, the concept. Furthermore, the concrete concept is no longer a concept but, properly speaking, is rather a "praxis" or the "work" of God in *Objectivity*, as Hegel himself says. In another respect (actually, in the same respect, but considered from another point of view), the concept is our "habit of thinking" (*exin*), as Aristotle defined it earlier, a living inference in action.[25] (One is reminded of the example of the noise of carriages on the icy streets.) Here Hegel is once again very close to Peirce's future conclusions.

How then is the "putting forth," the exhibition (the phenomeno-logy), of philosophical truth possible? How can philosophy "speak" its truth (*i.e.*, the truth *tout court*)? How can philosophy still be defined as "science," in fact, the only true, infinite, concrete, total science? In order to give an answer to these questions we must now turn to Hegel's *Phenomenology of Spirit*.[26] The Preface (*Vorrede*) to the *Phenomenology* begins significantly, with this ques-

28

tion: "*How* is philosophical truth to be expounded?" First of all, it does not consist in "the antithesis of truth and falsity."

> The more conventional opinion gets fixated on the antithesis of truth and falsity, the more it tends to expect a given philosophical system to be either accepted or contradicted; and hence it finds only acceptance and rejection. It does not comprehend the diversity of philosophical systems as the progressive unfolding of truth, but rather sees in it simple disagreements. The bud disappears in the bursting-forth of the blossom, and one might say that the former is refuted by the latter; similarly, when the fruit appears, the blossom is shown up in its turn as a false manifestation of the plant, and the fruit now emerges as the truth of it instead. These forms are not just distinguished from one another, they also supplant one another as mutually incompatible. Yet at the same time their fluid nature makes them moments of an organic unity in which they not only do not conflict, but in which each is as necessary as the other; and this mutual necessity alone constitutes the life of the whole. But he who rejects a philosophical system [*i.e.*, the new philosopher] does not usually comprehend what he is doing in this way; and he who grasps the contradiction between them [*i.e.*, the historian of philosophy] does not, as a general rule, know how to free it from its one-sidedness, or maintain it in its freedom by recognizing the reciprocally necessary moments that take shape as a conflict and seeming incompatibility. (p. 2)

The exposition of philosophical truth, therefore, consists in stating a "process" (the "progressive unfolding of the truth," for Aristotle). The famous example of the "life of the plant" in its vanishing manifestations (bud, flower, fruit) expresses admirably those three characteristics of truth that we already noted in our reading of the *Logic*: the concrete and infinite totality, an always open circular movement that has negation and contradiction as its internal moments. The whole history of philosophy, the whole history of truth, is to be understood, then, as just such a process in which understanding with its opinions wants to keep the moments determined (true versus false), while reason is aware of the dialectic process of the whole which is both overcoming of its distinct moments and their preservation in a higher—more "true"—viewpoint (the moments of the organic unity are all equally necessary).

Truth, therefore, is at one with "the real issue" (*die Sache selbst*), which is an organic unity (one is reminded of the question of the unity of the meanings of being in Aristotle): "For the real issue," says Hegel, "is not exhausted by stating it as an aim, but by carrying it out, nor is the result the actual whole, but rather the result together with the process through which it came about" (p. 2). The actual is not the fruit alone but the entire process that is concretized in the fruit. "The aim by itself," says Hegel, "is a lifeless universal, just as the guiding tendency is a mere drive (the Aristotelian "power") that as yet lacks an actual existence; and the bare result is the corpse which has left the guiding tendency behind it" (pp. 2–3). The "real issue" is actual and thus true since it is conceived as the totality of its process, as "life of the whole."

Let us apply this notion to the concept of truth in its pregnant sense, that is, to philosophical truth: "The true shape in which truth exists can only be the scientific system of such truth" (p. 3). The *shape*, the image of truth, of absolute truth, is neither Plato's idea, nor Aristotle's substance, nor Descartes' *cogito*, nor even Kant's transcendental ego. Each and every one of these shapes, insofar as each assumes intellectually a rigid point of view, pretends to embody by itself absolute truth by positioning itself in opposition to and in contradiction to others. But the *true* shape of truth is neither this nor that shape; rather, it is the whole process of shapes and images since they, in their becoming, are a "system." To understand this system is, for Hegel, the "scientific" character of truth and thus "philosophical" in the true sense. We shall see later how the "scientific" character of the "system" is to be understood. Meanwhile let us observe how truth, even though distinguishable from "intellectualism," does not exclude the contribution of the intellect. It is necessary, says Hegel, rather "to arrive at rational knowledge through understanding"; thus it is not a question of "gagging consciousness and doing away with understanding," as all philosophies do when they appeal to intuition or to faith against understanding and its insufficient and abstract truth. To renounce understanding is equivalent to renouncing science, just as to uphold the point of view of understanding is equivalent to being satisfied with the "dead corpse" of knowledge and truth. "In my view," says Hegel, "everything turns on grasping and expressing the true, not only as substance, but equally as subject" (pp. 9–10). As is well known, here Hegel is in polemics with Spinoza's view of substance, where "self-consciousness was submerged" (p. 10). The living shape of truth is also the shape of consciousness; its movements are also moments and images of consciousness, its "formations."

How consciousness relates to knowledge and truth is a question that we will address later. For the moment let us note how Hegel attempts the maximum possible identification between being and thinking (*logos*). Being is the very same self-consciousness; self-consciousness is the very same reality ("the living substance is being which is in truth *Subject*") (p. 10). Self-consciousness is not the simple empirical consciousness and Subject does not imply psychological and "private" subjectivity. Here is operative a type of difference completely similar to the one already established between formal and "subjective" concept and real Concept. But the point Hegel wants to make here is that one cannot arrive at self-consciousness as reality, at the subject as living subject without going through the "suffering of the negative" (p. 10). Substance is not a motionless substratum, mere intellectual concept of substance. Instead, it is a process, a movement. In particular, substance is a self-positing, a mediation that entails the becoming-other-from itself; from this being-other it returns with a movement of reflection, in itself. This is how the process of substance is the same as the process of truth: "The true is the process of its own becoming," it is a "circle" (p. 10). This self-positing, this becoming of itself, is precisely what Hegel calls Subject. A substance which is mere "objectivity," mere "thing," deprived of self-consciousness, can neither become nor be posited in a process; that is why substance is also subject.

As Subject, substance is above all *negation*, movement of negation, *negativity*. At first it is the separation of the simple in two parts, or the oppositional duplication. This is the function of understanding, of *Urteil*, of the original separation performed by understanding judgment, which then becomes "intellectual" as it keeps the opposing poles determined in their abstract truth—*i.e.*, I and the world, being and thinking—and takes them to be real and true in their abstraction. Then, substance is the negation of negation, that is, negation of that indifferent diversity and of its opposition (the reflection in itself begins from its being-other). Finally, and for this reason, substance is the reconstituting equality of itself with itself through the mediation of its movements and *in the* mediation of its moments. This is the veritable work of reason (p. 80). Thus, Hegel concludes:

> The true is the whole. But the whole is nothing other than the essence consummating itself through its development. *Of the absolute it must be said that it is essentially a result* (not a "bare" result, but a result in its process) that only in the *end* is it what it truly is; and that precisely in this consists its nature, *viz.* to be actual, subject, the spontaneous becoming of itself. (11) [Sini's emphasis]

As we saw, mediation and reflection are essential moments of the life of the whole and are, at the same time, *in the* whole, or the whole would not have development or actuality. In fact, this is the great function of understanding what Hegel describes and celebrates in an important as well as famous passage. (This celebration of understanding recalls the analogous celebration of the bourgeoisie which Marx sketches in the *Manifesto*.) Even though we cannot give here a close commentary on the words and images employed by Hegel, we can remark at least that in the union of the concepts of negation and death is the key to understanding the Hegelian notion of Spirit (*Geist*). It is in the Spirit that the dialectical unity of real and rational, being and thinking is summed up. Spirit is "life" since it is negation and at the same time the acceptance, transcendence of death:

> The activity of dissolution is the power and work of the understanding, the most astonishing and mightiest of powers, or rather the absolute

power. The circle that remains self-enclosed and, like substance, holds its moments together, is an immediate relationship, one therefore which has nothing astonishing about it. But that an accident as such, detached from what circumscribes it, what is bound and is actual only in its context with others, should attain an existence of its own and a separate freedom—this is the tremendous power of the negative; it is the energy of thinking, of the pure I. Death, if that is what we want to call this non-actuality, is of all things the most dreadful, and to hold fast what is dead requires the greatest strength. Lacking strength, beauty hates the understanding for asking of her what it cannot do. But the life of Spirit is not the life that shrinks from death and keeps itself untouched by devastation, but rather the life that endures it and maintains itself in it. It wins its truth only when, in utter dismemberment, it finds itself. It is this power, not as something positive, which cares nothing for the negative, as when we say of something that it is nothing or is false, and then, having done with it, turn away and pass on dismissively to something else; on the contrary, Spirit is this power only by looking the negative in the face, and tarrying with it. This tarrying with the negative is the magical power that converts it into being. This power is identical with what we earlier called the Subject, which by giving determinateness an existence in its own element supersedes abstract immediacy, *i.e.* the immediacy which barely is, and thus is authentic substance: that being or immediacy whose mediation is not outside of it but which is the mediation itself. (pp. 18–19)

Let us compare this conclusion with what was said earlier of the concrete concept as indifferent determination of its moments, immediacy *resulting* from its syllogistic mediation, that is, finally, "thing," "objectivity," living presence of the universal in the individual and of the individual in the universal. On the basis of this same conclusion, Hegel models philosophical truth as well as the task of philosophy. Truth is the "life of truth," a process that has in itself the mediation of its moments, "repose" of immediate being that contains in itself the "negative labor" of thinking (p. 10). It is the actual which is made transparent in the knowledge of itself, knowledge which is embodied in a real organism. This is truly the Dionysiac revelry of life that moves around and exists in the motionless "ether" of the concept, of its nullifying and realizing power. But beyond these images, what is to be emphasized above all in the passage that follows is the identity to which Hegel brings truth and falsity, their reciprocal belonging, the intrinsic, corresponding necessity of both. This is the decisive step that Hegel takes with respect to tradition. By this path, "traditional metaphysics" in reaching its fulfillment plunges decisively into the abyss of it own dissolution.

Philosophy, on the other hand, has to do, not with *unessential* determinations, but with a determination in so far as it is essential; its element and content is not the abstract or non-actual, but the actual, that which posits itself and is alive within itself—*existence within its own concept*. It is the process which begets and traverses its own moments, and this whole movement constitutes what is positive [in it] and its truth. This truth therefore includes the negative also, what would be called the *false*, if it could be regarded as something from which one might abstract. The evanescent itself must, on the contrary, be regarded as essential, not as something fixed, cut off from the true, and left lying who knows where outside it, any more than the true is to be regarded as something on the other side, positive and dead. Appearance is the arising and passing away that does not itself arise and pass away, but is "in itself" [*i.e.*, subsists intrinsically], and constitutes the actuality and the movement of the life of truth. The true is thus the bacchanalian revel in which no member is not drunk; yet because each member collapses as soon as he drops out, the revel is just as much transparent and simple repose. Judged in the court of this movement, the single shapes of Spirit do not persist any more than determinate thoughts do, but they are as much positive and necessary moments, as they are negative and evanescent. In the whole of the movement, seen as a state of repose, what distinguishes itself therein, and gives itself particular existence, is preserved as something that recollects itself, whose existence is self-knowledge, and whose self-knowledge is just as immediately existence. (pp. 27–28) [Sini's emphasis]

The *Phenomenology of Spirit* is the concrete exemplification of this vital and true process (of this movement of the "life of truth"); it is the exemplification applied, precisely, to the "spirit."

8

◆

The Science of Experience

The immediate existence of spirit is consciousness. As such, consciousness, which is always "consciousness of," contains two moments: (*a*) knowledge and (*b*) the negative objectivity opposed to knowledge. In other words, as *consciousness of*, consciousness *knows what* it knows, and these two moments are in antithesis. The process of consciousness, or more properly the process of spirit in the shape of consciousness, is as follows. The spirit brings out its moments, is the subject that posits itself, that "externalizes" itself, so that the opposition supervenes with respect to the knowledge of consciousness. These moments appear as *shapes of consciousness*. The science of this process expressed in concepts is the "science of the *experience* that consciousness goes through," (p. 21) namely "phenomeno-logy": the science of phenomena, that is, of the "shapes" of consciousness that all together constitute the movement of spirit. In order to understand the above, let us turn to the Introduction (*Einleitung*) of the *Phenomenology of Spirit*.

The *Phenomenology of Spirit*, says Hegel, takes its starting point from the "way it appears," namely, as it appears. In some ways, this exposition can be regarded as

> the path of the natural consciousness which presses forward to true knowledge; or as the way of the soul which journeys through the series of its own configurations as though they were the stages appointed for it by its own nature, so that it may purify itself for the life of the spirit, and achieve finally, through a completed experience of itself, the awareness of what it really is in itself. (p. 49)

Simplifying somewhat we could say that this is a journey that moves from common sense to the "scientific" truth of philosophy. A truth, moreover, that the sciences cannot reach, since they are founded—or better still, since they are "unfounded"—on the dogmas and paradoxes of common sense. On

34

the basis of these premises, Hegel observes that this journey has at first a "negative significance." Consciousness, in fact, loses its initial truth, its shape and initial image and then, one by one, all the others. It is a "pathway of doubt and despair" (p. 49). Since every truth that consciousness affirms fails, is revealed untrue; since every shape or image of consciousness' knowledge is revealed through experience to be untrue the entire experience of consciousness appears afflicted by a thoroughgoing skepticism, and the entire history of truth, of knowledge, of philosophy, seems to be the history of an error. Universal doubt reigns supreme (*dubitamus et dubitabimus*).

This point of view stems, however, from the inability to think of untruth and error as anything but the opposites of truth: *aut aut*, either this or that, as we saw earlier. However, this is not the case at all, since at issue is the "detailed history of the *education* of consciousness itself to the standpoint of Science" (p. 50). Through doubt and despair, namely negation, consciousness is raised to true knowledge, or absolute knowledge, to that level in which it is what it is "in truth," as a process that contains all its moments or passing "stages." Furthermore, what natural consciousness, common sense, common logic, looks upon as doubt and despair is really a process of "determinate negations." From the negation of a form of knowledge, common sense deduces the skeptical universal conclusion that "We do not know anything and we shall never know anything." This is a dogmatic conclusion, since it presupposes that knowledge is such only if it arrives at an immovable truth, absolute in the sense of separate from the life process and the experience of truth, and totally unjustified since it claims at the same time to affirm something universally eternal: "We shall *never* know anything." This failure of the Aristotelian truth, in which consciousness believed and with which it identified, seems to leave us no other choice but to commiserate or piously meditate over our human finitude. We would be forgetting, however, that what fails is only the truth *of* Aristotle, the knowledge *of* that knowledge, and not knowledge in general; and that negation is just a determined negation. Let us see how this actually works.

Hegel says that consciousness exhibits first of all its two abstract determinations, just as they are found in it: *knowledge* and *truth*. Or, "Consciousness simultaneously *distinguishes* itself from something, and at the same time *relates* itself to it, or, as it is said, this something exists *for* consciousness" (p. 52). Now, "the determinate aspect of this *relating*, or of the *being* of something for a consciousness, is *knowledge*" (p. 52). We know something determinate relative to a something that exists for consciousness, which is the object of its knowledge. But from this "being for an other," being for consciousness, we distinguish "being-in-itself," the object of knowledge as it is or as it will be found to be in itself: "whatever is related to knowledge or knowing is also distinguished from it, and posited as existing outside of this relationship" (pp. 51–52). The object is what it is independent of the knowledge that has consciousness of it. Now "this *being-in-itself* is called *truth*" (p. 53). This way Hegel has admirably described how *knowledge* and *truth* are found in consciousness as its determinations. Why these determinations are also "abstract" is what we shall see presently, although very few have truly understood this even today. A typical example is Karl Popper's ridiculous objections to Hegel's dialectic which only prove that he himself is one of those "thinkers" incapable of raising the level of their thinking to that of the *Einleitung* of the *Phenomenology of Spirit*. For, if Popper had succeeded, he certainly would not have proposed the notion of an "objective world" or "world 3" so incredibly imbued with metaphysical dogmatism, that is, naive common sense.[27]

Having defined knowledge and truth as moments of consciousness, Hegel applies the "phenomenological method" to these determinations. This method consists first of all in taking the knowledge of consciousness just as it appears, that is, with its determinations as they immediately offer themselves, without preconceived notions or norms of knowledge or truth. In other words, we do not measure the knowledge and truth that consciousness offers immediately to us with other notions of knowledge and truth gathered elsewhere. At this point, the investigation of the "truth of knowledge," which consciousness offers, can begin.

At first it may seem that we are investigating that which is in-itself, the object in-itself, in order to determine whether it corresponds to the knowledge that consciousness has. But since this object in-itself is in our investigation *our* object, it is really *for us*. Its supposed or possible in-itself is only its being for us. It follows that what we would be affirming as its essence, its truth in-itself, would not be its truth in-itself but only our *knowledge* of this truth. In so doing, consciousness has simply compared itself to itself. In fact, the posited distinctions (what is in-itself, what is for consciousness; truth, knowledge) are posited by *consciousness*: they all fall *in consciousness*, they occur in it. Hegel says:

> In consciousness one thing exists *for* another, *i.e.* consciousness regularly contains the determinateness of the moment of knowledge; at the same time, this other is to consciousness not merely *for it*, but is also outside of this relationship, or exists *in-itself*: the moment of truth. (p. 53)

But this only means that consciousnesss designates what for it is the *object* (the in-itself "external" to it) and what for it is the *concept* (its knowledge of the object). The investigation of the "truth of knowledge" consists, then, in seeing whether the concept corresponds to the object and vice versa. (Let us keep in mind this notion of correspondence when we read Heidegger, since he takes Hegel to task on this account, as we shall see.)[28] Both the concept and the object fall, clearly, within the knowledge which is being phenomenologically investigated by us, namely, they fall within the shape of consciousness under investigation. Thus the phenomenological method assumes the thing "as it is *in and for itself*" (p. 54). That is to say, assumes it as it appears and presents itself in a concrete shape of consciousness, in a determinate knowledge of consciousness and not on the basis of a preconceived notion of the "thing"; thus "all that is left for us to do is simply to look on" (p. 54), namely, all that is left is the pure description of what happens to consciousness. In fact consciousness itself makes the experience of *its* truth in the form, one could say, of its "erring." It is (*a*) consciousness of the object and (*b*) consciousness of itself, consciousness of what for it is true and consciousness of its knowledge of the truth. For consciousness itself, then, is opened the process of comparison: whether or not knowledge, or the concept, corresponds to the object. What happens then if (or *when*, "historically") there is no correspondence? Consciousness is forced to alter its own knowledge, to make it conform to the object. "But," Hegel says, "*in the alteration of the knowledge, the object itself alters* for it too, for the knowledge that was present was essentially a knowledge of the object; as the knowledge changes, so too does the object, for it essentially belonged to this knowledge" (p. 54) [Sini's emphasis]. Consciousness comes to find that "what it previously took to be the *in-itself* is not an *in-itself*, or that it was only an in-itself *for consciousness*. Since consciousness thus finds that its knowledge does not correspond to its object, the object itself does not stand the test" (p. 54). Now, "*Inasmuch as the new true object issues from it*, this *dialectical* movement which consciousness exercises on itself and which affects both its knowledge and its object, is precisely what is called *experience (Erfahrung)*" (p. 55). In this sense the *Phenomenology of Spirit* is a science—a mere looking on—of *experience* that consciousness has. The new object, Hegel concludes, "contains the nothingness of the first; it is what experience has made of it" (p. 55). This is how Hegel sums up the process:

> Consciousness knows *something*; this object is the essence or the *in-itself*; but it is also for consciousness the in-itself. This is where the ambiguity of this truth enters. We see that consciousness now has two objects: one is the first *in-itself*; the second is the *being-for-consciousness of this in-itself*. The latter appears at first sight to be merely the reflection of consciousness into itself, *i.e.* what consciousness has in mind is not an object, but only its knowledge of that first object. But, as was shown previously, the first object, in being known, is altered for consciousness; it ceases to be the in-itself, and becomes something which is the *in-itself* only *for consciousness*. And this then is the true: the being-for-consciousness of this in-itself. Or, in other words, this is the *essence*, or the *object* of consciousness. This new object contains the nothingness of the first. (p. 55)

Let us try to illustrate what Hegel has just stated with an example, keeping in mind the imperfection of every example. Consciousness knows something which is the object of its knowledge. For instance, it knows that there are gods. The gods, the object of this knowledge, are in themselves the truth of that consciousness. The knowledge of this consciousness is determinate: not only are there gods, but they are also jealous of men; they quarrel among themselves; they make love and they betray each other, and so on. Now, at a certain point, a poet-thinker like Xenophanes arrives on the scene and claims that our knowledge of the Gods does not say at all how the Gods are in themselves (*i.e.*, the *concept* of the divine does not correspond to how the divine is in itself), but says only how *we* think of them, how we attribute to them, anthropomorphically, our vices and virtues.[29] What we thought was in-itself turns out to be only for us. This negation, however, takes on the form of a new object that does not tolerate its former object. The divine being is now a being entirely spiritual, a God completely whole that sees and thinks, motionless and perfect like a sphere. This is now the new in-itself, the truth of the new knowledge, the new object, which originates out of the experience consciousness had of the first, the anthropomorphic gods.

If, however, we question natural or common consciousness, we realize, says Hegel, that consciousness does not understand *experience* as we have described it. Consciousness, in fact, believes that the falsity or falsification of the first concept (of its former knowledge) is determined by the encounter with the new object in-itself. It does not believe that the new object "shows itself to have come about through a *reversal of consciousness itself*" (p. 55). Hence the naiveté of natural consciousness that continues to believe in the existence of objects in themselves positioned in a world in-itself, "visible" from a consciousness conveniently placed. Such a consciousness does not understand that the objects encountered are correlatives of its "knowledge," of its "shape," so by altering it one also alters the objects, which is why consciousness "finds" them on its path.

At the same time natural consciousness draws from this experience the conviction that the result of an untrue knowledge is equal to nothing, to an empty nothing, to the empty nothing of pure skepticism with regard to the object of that abandoned knowledge, and not that it is the "determinate nothing" (p. 56), namely, that that experience is the condition of the opening of a new world, with its objects, its images and its determinate forms of knowledge—a new shape of the spirit. This is what common consciousness, overwhelmed by its own experience, cannot comprehend. But "for us," as Hegel says, the truth of experience is something altogether other. "For us" here stands for the phenomenological subject which, in its "merely looking on," turns to "a scientific consideration of the object" and so traverses the "scientific system of truth." The "for us," in short, is reason, the result of what it truly is, the knowledge which is known at the end of the whole process, the knowledge which "historically" is embodied or manifested by Hegel's utterance.

Therefore, for us, what has happened is the following. The lowering of the object to knowledge of consciousness gives life to a new object with which *a new shape of consciousness* appears, with a different essence from the former. In fact, "we see" from our phenomenological perspective the "reversal of consciousness" in its forms of knowledge and in its images, while natural consciousness knows nothing of this reversal: "the entire series of the patterns of consciousness . . . is just this necessity . . . which proceeds for us, as it were, behind the back of consciousness," since it "is not present to the consciousness comprehended in the experience itself" (p. 56). Now, "Because of this *necessity, the way to science is itself already science:* . . . science of the *experience of consciousness*" (p. 56). This experience embraces "the entire system of consciousness, or *the entire realm of the spirit*" (p. 56). In the light of this realm, of this result, the moments of truth appear (*a*) as abstract in themselves (none of them is true or *the* truth); (*b*) as moments of the whole, *i.e.*, as patterns of consciousness (moments in the life of truth). In moving ahead along this path, consciousness "will arrive at a point at which it gets rid of its semblance of being burdened with something alien, with what is only for it, and some sort of "other"; at a point where appearance becomes identical with essence" (pp. 56–57). At this point the presenting of the experience of consciousness coincides with the "authentic science of Spirit" (p. 57), that is, with the shape of "absolute knowledge," the shape of the "for us," since we are witnesses to the truth as "result." The entire experience of consciousness, of which every moment is together sublated and preserved, made true in the totality of the process, takes shape then as the science itself. Self-consciousness contains here all its moments just as the disjunctive syllogism contained in itself its species and particularizations— unmediated being and truth of infinite mediation.

9

◆

Phenomeno-Logical Truth

Now we must evaluate, in the light of what we have learned from Hegel, the progress made so far. Let us concentrate on the following points:

1. *Aristotle defines philosophy as the "science of truth."* We saw how Hegel understands this "science." Science is the same as experience, if understood phenomenologically and not in terms of naïve common sense or past and contemporary empiricism. In fact, Hegel has shown the immanence of science in experience, its being already on the way as science of the experience that consciousness has, and finally the resolution of experience in science. This is what Hegel defines as "raising the actual to the concept." To be more precise, the actual *raises itself* to the concept, namely, to explicit concept (knowledge of reason), having been formerly, in its abstract immediacy, implicit knowledge of the understanding.

2. *Now the question: "How can man and his speech be already in the truth?" becomes clear, since "anyone can say something about truth."* Now we can answer: "Any image or shape of consciousness is in the unfolding, in the pathway of truth; is there as necessary dialectical moment of that process." Thus error is assimilated to truth, becomes part of it. Since understanding makes absolute every shape of consciousness, it is incapable of "comprehending" literally this unity of truth and error, even though this is, so to speak, a necessary error, since the process could not exist without the distinctions and the negations of the understanding. Thus, what man speaks is already "comprehended" in truth, even though it is not *the* truth.

3. *The cause of the difficulty in investigating the truth, Aristotle says, is not in things but in us.* And he adds that like the bat, the understanding is blind to those things that by nature are the most self-evident.[30] Why this should be, we can now explain with Hegel's phrase that consciousness, steeped as it

is in the experience of truth, cannot see what is going on behind its back. But what goes on after all is itself, *i.e.*, for it, that which ought to be the most self-evident of all. Consciousness, however, can see itself only when its shape reaches the place of "absolute knowledge," that is, when it is separate from the arbitrariness of other shapes and reaches the self-conscious vision of the whole process of its shapes. That is why, says Hegel, philosophy is like the owl that flies at dusk, at the setting of a spiritual world already entirely *become*. Absolute knowledge, in fact, is the last shape of consciousness, when the concept becomes equal to being.

4. *The investigation of truth is a social process to which everyone contributes, even if in small amounts.* We could say that the process of truth is like a chain or a stage on which everyone plays his part, while the truth is the entire script. This chain constitutes the entire reality of spirit, *i.e.*, reality in the proper sense; it contains the series of self-interpretations of consciousness, that is, of its images and shapes. Truth, in other words, is infinite interpretation and this, too, is reality. In Hegelian terms, there is no reality that is not spirit, interpretation of truth.

5. *The relationship between being and being true and between being and judgment (the two traditional places of truth).* This is the most complex and delicate point. It is above all in the light of this question that we must gauge the progress we made with Hegel. The particular difficulty arises from the fact that we find ourselves once again confronting the foundations of the entire Western *ratio*: the Parmenidean correspondence of being and thinking. The *quaestio veri (et falsi)* has always depended on it. This question is made even more complex in the light of Hegel's pronouncements, making it necessary for us to weigh its proper significance for *our own* question, without letting the richness of Hegel's analysis lead us too far afield.

A) *To think is to correspond to what is.* This correspondence is truth. We have, thus, stated the foundation of the question of truth, as Parmenides posed it, and on which unfolds the entire tradition until Hegel. However, what is the sense of truth of this foundation? This question constitutes a turning point in our considerations, to which obviously Hegelian thought has largely contributed. Although Parmenides posited a correspondence between being and thinking, it was based on a distinction. Only in this way could he *posit* the correspondence. Only by keeping separate the terms of the correspondence could he state their identity. Being could be determined then as what "is," as what is "opposed to" thinking. To this opposition of *einai* corresponds the being true of *noein*. The identity of the two terms is made possible by their previous difference or distinction. This distinction was never restored. In fact, it is the condition of philosophical truth, of the scientific, epistemological *logos*. One can think what-is only within the space of this overlooked distinction, only on these terms. Thinking is the

movement that overcomes this space and erases the tracks. But every movement of thought reproduces at the same time the difference, reiterates it
while exhibiting its identity of being and thinking; thus the problem of truth
passes over into tradition, giving life to what we call the "history of philosophy," the "history of truth."

The moment in which thinking accomplishes its ultimate labor, *i.e.*,
realizes its destiny, that is, the moment in which the "Parmenidean difference" is restored without any residue, then, the *ratio* reaches its fulfillment.
From this moment on philosophical truth ceases to be. Being ceases to have
meaning, and thinking, as the "rational" thinking of truth, is no longer
possible. In fact, the premises have failed and so also has their condition,
namely, the difference between being and thinking as the place from which it
was possible to state their identity. This is what happens in Hegel, as we
shall see now. But let us keep in mind what we said earlier, that being is
posited by the *logos* as its premise (the truth of Parmenides' truth). If this
positing is also being (its self-positing, as Hegel says), the meaning of truth
fades away and truth itself "corresponds" to nothing. The revelation of
"Parmenides' secret," *i.e.*, the discovery of the *logos'* secret, erases the *ratio*,
revealing its non-sense. That is to say, it *pretends or imagines* to be looking
for something that actually it has already assumed beforehand. This assumption is called "being," but its truth is really nothing (*nulla*).[31] Hegel is the
first to have taken, although only partially, this fatal step.

B) *Being, what is, takes shape in the tradition as determined this way or
that (as idea, substance, transcendental ego, etc.), and is modeled from time
to time on thinking, on what is held to be thinking, the logos.* From Plato on,
especially, thinking has been for the most part defined in relation to two
aspects: as intuitive thinking, *nous*, the intuition of what is, which for
Aristotle, as we saw, corresponds to the two alternatives of knowledge and
ignorance: thinking or not thinking; and as discursive thinking, *dianoia*, it is
the judging *of* what is, which gives way to the two opposing alternatives of
truth and falsity: speaking the objects as they are and as they are not. The
demands of *dianoia*, of judgment, of the *logos* of logic, "complicate" being
by positing more than Parmenides had ever supposed, for instance, the soul
and its relations, as Plato suggests in the *Sophist*. In fact, without this
complication "science" would not be possible. The *logos*, assured of its truth
through the presupposition of being, could proceed no further, that is, could
not inscribe the articulation of its discourse within the realm of truth. From
these complex circumstances the two places of truth emerge to which we
have alluded many times and which we found exemplified in Aristotle. Now
we could say that truth, since it partakes of these two places, takes shape, at
least starting from Aristotle, as *phenomeno-logical truth*:

phenomeno: The manifestation of what is as being true, that is, as manifest and not as latent (*aletheia*). (This is how Heidegger, for instance, understands the phenomenon in *Being and Time*; furthermore, he is also aware that he has to go back to Aristotle, even more than to Husserl.)

logical: Judgment as adequate assertion, as *will* to adequation; as adequation of understanding (*dianoia*) to the self-manifesting object, as intuition (*nous*) attests.

Let us see now what happens in Hegel with this truth "situation." We could say that in Hegel there is a sublation of any difference between phenomenon and logic (the sublation of the phenomenological difference). The manifestation of the phenomenon (the *experience*) is logical (*science*). This is achieved by Hegel through the conscious elimination of two aspects of thinking passed on by tradition: intuition (*nous*) and judgment (*dianoia*). Hegelian anti-intuitionism is the first death sign of the Western *ratio*. (The same happens with Peirce's anti-intuitionism, even though Peirce is even less aware than Hegel of the "nihilistic" consequences of his thought.) Insofar as Hegel denies immediate intuition, he bans at the same time "pure being," being in itself. Being is never "pure." "Pure" being is equal to nothing (*nulla*). (In these very narrow terms Hegel proposes the question of the nothing (*nulla*).[32] There is no "pure" being in itself (the being of Parmenides) because being is always in one of its "forms," *i.e.*, in one of its interpretations, images or meanings, in one form of its "experience." Pure being is a mere abstraction of the understanding (like the "absolute" abstraction of an unaffected God sheltered from the contradictions of the world). This being is reality's residue once abstract thinking has sublated all the characteristics and all the determinations of reality.

On the other hand, Hegel sublates even the truth of judgment, the instrument that ancient metaphysics had posited as the foundation of the distinction between truth and falsity. Hegel, however, as we have seen, coherently sublates even *this* distinction. In so doing, Hegel accomplishes the complete *adaequatio intellectus et rei* (*non intellectus ad rem*). Understanding has no reason to want to "reach" the thing (*ad rem*). If the question were put in these terms, the understanding would need an intuition. This, as Kant observed, would be possible only for divine understanding, since human understanding is not capable of intuitions but only of judgments, that is, of arguments and inferences. But the question *cannot be put* in these terms. Intuition does not exist, and the Kantian "divine intuition" is only an intellectualistic fantasy. What we call intuition is only a "result," something "mediated." On the other hand, understanding does not need to reach the thing, since it is already there. Thing and understanding fuse and are confused in one another. The determinations of the thing expressed by understanding (that it is white, salty, smooth, *etc.*) are actual moments of the thing even though not in the rigid and abstract form that understanding believes. They are "vanishing" moments but not any the less real and necessary than the bud, the flower, and the fruit for that thing which is the life of the plant. Thus, with the total identity of thinking and being, we are witnessing Parmenides' fulfillment, although at a price that Parmenides himself had refused to pay, that is, that all "appearance" (phenomenon) is being and being is appearance—a circle which moves "in repose," as Hegel says. It is true that this price has been paid at every turn by the history of philosophy, the history of being and its truth, from Plato on, for whom becoming and the *doxa* of judgment, which Parmenides rigorously left out, come somehow into "being." Of this history, Hegel writes the final chapter.

Thus with Hegel we reach the conclusion that *being is the history of being*. All the "real," in fact, is process, a "historical" gallery of the shapes of truth; and all the process is "rational," *i.e.*, "true." With this conclusion, the project of the "ratio," as the edification of being on the basis of the *logos*, arrives at the total sublation of every thinkable limit, since there are no objects, events, or facts radically outside of reason, that are radically non-rational. The totality of what is is identified with the concrete concept, so that everything is a syllogism, without notable residue, as Hegel states. In order to arrive at this conclusion Hegel must overcome, however, the traditional formal logic of understanding and deny that the form of judgment is the place of truth. Judgment, with its (for all that) necessary distinctions, stops at abstract universality. The syllogism (the logic of reason), instead, represents the identity of abstract and concrete, of universal and individual. In this way, the process of thinking, as syllogistic process, is the same process productive of reality (*Wirklichkeit*), so that "science" is nothing more than the production and the becoming of the actual, its "experience" translated in concepts. The absolute knowledge of philosophy (absolute truth) is the entire conceptual system which is also the entire "logical" structure of reality. Science, therefore, is "history" (becoming and the coming-to-be of experience), and being is the "history of being," which becomes transparent to itself, *i.e.*, is "known" through concepts. This total resolution of thinking in being and of being in thinking, this absolute fulfillment of the Parmenidean "premise," or of "traditional metaphysics" as Hegel would say, throws the *ratio* headlong into the abyss. The outline of this abyss is precisely what must be described now.

First of all Hegelian thought is no longer a judging, a gathering and an unfastening, *i.e.*, the original utterance of the metaphysical *logos*, and not even an evaluation. The assimilation of truth and error entails the parallel assimilation of good and evil. The Hegelian resolution of Platonism is at the same time its undoing. One has often spoken of Hegelian "mysticism." In fact, Hegel's position is the opposite of mysticism and thus, in a certain sense, it is "the same," as is the case with any opposites. After all, mysticism, especially "Christian" mysticism, just like "skepticism," is the other side of the Western *ratio*. But to clarify this question would require a separate treatment, and we cannot go into it here.

For Hegel, to think is to carry out the total mediation of the existing, that is, to transform the existing into an interpreted (a *mediated*) and thinking into an interpretant (a *mediating*). This is exactly what we pointed out in the discussion on the disjunctive syllogism. Everything is, thus, always already an "interpreted being" of which one must exhibit the producing middle, the interpreting concept. The whole reality is contained in reason. The Hegelian expressions "rise to the concept," "give the concept," urge us to understand that everything is always already a concept and that the concept always already "is."

The Parmenidean tautology being-thinking no longer retains a possible difference, whether implicit or explicit. Being is con-fused in thinking and thinking in being. Thinking no longer is anything "in and for itself" but is "movement" of the real which is not separate from the real. The totality of the mediations is the immediate "resolved" in its mediations. Thus, Hegel arrives paradoxically at that abyss of indistinction which he wanted to avoid in his youthful and fundamental critique of Schelling. And, what is more, he arrives precisely by the main road of triumphant reason which has "subdued" understanding and has made it its slave, that is, by a "conceptual" road which believes itself to be immune from the "wonder" of reason, *i.e.*, from the acknowledgment of its own impotence, which instead we find in Schelling.[33]

By completely tying together truth as "quantum of being" and truth as judgment, "affection of the intellect", that is, by con-fusing indissolubly the two traditional places of truth, Hegel makes being and truth radically immanent to themselves, without further residue. But in this reciprocal immanence, being is no longer "what it is"; it is rather the contrary, "what becomes"; and thinking is no longer "judgment," conceptual discrimination. The *ratio* enters, thus, in a vortex without exit and onto a precipice without a way out. We can state this condition in the simplest way with reference to the Hegelian outcome by remarking that if everything is truth, nothing is truth. Thus, the distinctive character of the *ratio*, its being founded on the true *logos*, its being "logical," comes to nought. The *ratio* in its foundations is revealed to be "historical," meaning that it is "a story," a *mythos*, a peculiar form of myth with a particular kind of image.

Nietzsche remarked that with Hegel the existing "is made divine," as it is raised to reason and truth. We should add, then, that nothing is any longer divine. Total rationality is irrationality. That is why it is totally useless to confront Hegel with the irrationality of the world, since he claims it to be rational. This approach, employed by Kierkegaard, Schopenhauer, Nietzsche, and Heidegger and then repeated foolishly ad nauseam by so many others who were neither Kierkegaards nor Nietzsches, *i.e.*, who themselves did not possess an authentic pathos of truth to oppose to Hegel, is a sterile approach that leaves the *ratio* untouched, since Hegel, after all, has always more "reasons" than his detractors. What becomes evident with Hegel *is not* that, contrary to what he thought, the real is irrational. The real of the *ratio*, as we shall see better later, *is* really rational. Here Hegel is absolutely right. What becomes clear with Hegel is that Western *thought* and its project of being and world is irrational. This irrationality has two sides which embody the rational project in its alpha and omega. Either thinking is abstract, as for the Eleatics and the Platonists who are the eternal founders of Western thought, and then negates the world, its concrete determinateness and vitality. Truth, then, as Nietzsche would say, is posited in a world behind the world, that is, in a pure nihilistic fantasy and image. Or thinking is concrete (as Hegel would have it), in which case the world becomes the realm of meaningless arbitrariness (or "disenchanted arbitrariness," as Weber would say).[34] Truth is, then, posited in a meaningless "here and there," which again is a pure nihilistic fantasy and image, a nightmare of reason. In the final analysis, "concrete" Hegelian thinking says that the world is so because it *has become* so, as it is; and that finally, in the light of absolute knowledge, we discover that it could not have become other than exactly what it is. This thinking, in other words, says that about the world and its truth there *really* is nothing to *say*.

10

◆

Truth as Accordance

With Hegel we have taken what earlier was defined as the first step toward the abyss. This consisted in the destruction of the place of truth understood as affection of the understanding or judgment. We also saw that the price paid by Hegel is the abolition of being understood as the *transcendens* with respect to thinking or experience, understood in its Hegelian sense. This implies the sublation of the "Parmenidean difference," a difference tacitly assumed as identity between being and thinking. Between these two, instead, is posited a total permeation. This Hegelian conclusion corrects Platonism, that abstract intellectual thinking that negates the real and concrete world for an imaginary other world. This revision, after all, had already begun with Aristotle and his critique of the world of ideas. With Hegel this revision reaches its fulfillment and takes on the form of a frenzied realization of Platonism itself. To use Hegel's image, the world of ideas came down to earth and took root. However, this revision of Platonic "irrationalism," as we saw, leads to an even more serious "irrationalism." From being abstract, "subjective," thinking becomes concrete, "objective"; that is, it becomes *world*; but this world becomes, then, the realm of meaningless arbitrariness where everything that happens, because it happens, is at the same time "rational" and necessary. And thinking no longer has "being" or truths of its own, and its speech is reduced *"to providing reasons"* for the simple factuality of the world's events.

After these considerations, can we still hold valid that other place of truth in Hegel which claims that every object has as much truth as it has being? Somehow Hegel has tried to salvage *this* truth, the truth of the "path of the world." But even this, looked at closely, is very shaky precisely because of the collapse of the transcendence of God, of absolute being. In fact, it is with reference to absolute and transcendent being, on the basis of its absolute standard, that we can establish the quotient of being and, thus, of truth which pertains to worldly beings. Now, we could say that in Hegel the

47

maximum of being is represented by spirit (*Geist*). But since spirit is nothing more than the self-interpretive movement of all the "shapes" of reality, every one of them both "errs" and is at the same time true, *i.e.*, is in the spirit's truth. How can a "norm" be derived from all this?

All the same, Hegel also distinguishes in his famous triads between Idea, Nature, and Spirit, separating the latter into Subjective, Objective, and Absolute, and finally the Absolute into Art, Religion, and Philosophy. In all these divisions Hegel undoubtedly defends the place of truth and its specific "rational" nature. But its defense, if we could get to the bottom of it, to its extreme consequences, would likely appear as a suicide of reason. (In much the same way, Massimo Cacciari speaks of the suicide of the middle class in Hegel's *Philosophy of Right*, which is incapable of absorbing, conceptualizing, and grounding rationally the fortuitousness of the proletariat.)[35] We have only to think of the different directions taken by Marx, Nietzsche, and Freud in order to have before us the concluding stages of the suicide of Hegelian rationality in contemporary culture. But the real conclusion is marked above all, and for many reasons, by Heidegger. It is with Heidegger that we will take the second step into the abyss: the destruction of that residual place of truth which, according to tradition, identifies being with being true, quantity of being with quantity of truth.

To this end, I would like to turn now to Heidegger's 1930 essay, *On the Essence of Truth* (*Vom Wesen der Wahrheit*), a lecture revised many times and then published in 1943.[36] The theme is the *essence* of truth, that is, as Heidegger explains, "the one thing that in general distinguishes every 'truth' as truth" (p. 117). Heidegger takes his starting point from the current definition of truth, but even in the simplicity of the exposition and by the examples he employs, we see that he has very much in mind what we have called the two places of truth in Aristotle:

> What do we ordinarily understand by "truth"? This elevated yet at the same time worn and almost dulled word "truth" means what makes a true thing true. What is a true thing? We say, for example: "It is a true joy to cooperate in the accomplishment of this task." We mean that it is purely and actually a joy. The true is the actual. Accordingly, we speak of true gold in distinction from false. False gold is not actually what it appears to be. It is merely a "semblance" and thus is not actual. What is not actual is taken to be the opposite of the actual. But what merely seems to be gold is nevertheless something actual. Accordingly, we say more precisely: actual gold is genuine gold. Yet both are "actual," the circulating counterfeit no less than the genuine gold. What is true about genuine gold thus cannot be demonstrated merely by its actuality. The question recurs: what do "genuine" and "true" mean here? Genuine gold is that actual gold the actuality of which is in accordance [*in der Übereinstimmung steht*] with what, always and in advance, we "properly" mean by "gold." Converse-

ly, wherever we suspect false gold, we say: "Here something is not in accord" [*stimmt nicht*]. On the other hand, we say of whatever is "as it should be": "It is in accord." The *thing* is in accord [*die Sache stimmt*]. However, we call true not only an actual joy, genuine gold, and all beings of such kind, but also and above all we call true or false our judgments about beings, which can themselves be genuine or not with regard to their kind, which can be thus or otherwise in their actuality. A judgment is true if what it means and says is in accordance with the thing about which the judgment is made. Here too we say: "It is in accord." Now, though, it is not the thing that is in accord but rather the *proposition*. The true, whether it be a thing or a proposition, is what accords, the accordant [*das Stimmende*]. Being true and truth here signify accord, and that in a double sense: on the one hand, the consonance [*Einstimmigkeit*] of a thing with what is supposed in advance regarding it and, on the other hand, the accordance of what is meant in the judgment with the thing. (pp. 118–119)

Incidentally, let us say first of all that the last remarks are not very convincing at all. In speaking of "supposition" and earlier of what we "*mean* by gold," of "wherever *we suspect*," etc., Heidegger practically raises the question of the "subjectivity" of judgment. Looking at it more closely, here Heidegger is avoiding the question of representation, of imagination. Plato, in the *Sophist*, was more sly. But let us return to the main question. Following common usage which, after all, is that of tradition, Heidegger posits two meanings of the word "truth."

1. The true is the actual and the false is mere appearance (appearance and non-being, Plato says in the *Sophist*); but reality, as "actual in itself" does not sufficiently guarantee the truth (false gold or apparent gold is also "real"); more appropriately, therefore, we should say that truth is the thing in *accordance* with itself.

2. Truth and falsehood, however, pertain also and first of all to our "judgments" on beings; and a judgment is true whenever it *accords* with the thing.

Truth, therefore, whether we are dealing with a true thing or with a true proposition, is *the accordant*. To be true and truth signify *accord* of the thing with what one supposes it to be, and between what is thought in the judgment and the thing. This is how we derive, says Heidegger, the traditional definition of truth: *veritas est adaequatio rei et intellectus*, i.e., the correspondence of the thing to knowledge and of knowledge to the thing, even if what is really meant is *intellectus ad rem*, namely, the correspondence of understanding to, toward the thing. It is important to note, however, that the truth is *adaequatio, concordantia*, conformity. But "conformity" in what sense? How can *res* and *intellectus* be in consonance, asks Heidegger; how can they "con-form"? Heidegger recalls the medieval solution whereby the thing is an *ens creatum*; it accords, is true, insofar as it corresponds to the idea in the mind of God, the creating entity or the *summum ens*. This idea in God functions practically as a "norm" (we call it unit of measure) on whose basis it is possible to establish the truth of everything which is actual, *i.e.*, worldly beings.

This shift, although unproblematic from an "historiographical" point of view, is not without interest. Let us put Heidegger's argument aside for a moment and let us digress briefly. This will enable us to get both a general sense of where we are heading and of where Heidegger's point of view fits in, even if this will mean anticipating certain aspects that can only be clarified later.

Heidegger is essentially saying that the world acquires reality and, thus, truth only with respect to a "*transcendence*." Truth is the actual since it is measured by means of a *supreme* actual which *is beyond*. This supreme and this beyond constitute the standard to which all the actual con-forms. However, this view, which in the Middle Ages assumes the name of God and its creative power, has essentially already been established by Plato. What is beyond is the *model*, the archetype, from which the demiurge draws inspiration in fashioning the universe. What is beyond, in the final analysis, is the *idea*. The idea is the intelligible *transcendens*, super-sensible, and as such, it is the *essence* of the actual, its ultimate truth.

This Platonic premise is the unquestioned foundation of the entire philosophical tradition, which remains such even in the most radical critiques of Platonism. In other words, the idea is neither just a philosophical doctrine nor just the first. The idea, independently of how tradition develops this notion, is the very place of philosophy and its truth. Aristotle and Aquinas still think in these terms, and it is the same with Spinoza, Leibniz, or Kant, with all due exceptions for the obvious doctrinal and cultural differences, which moreover are the "logical" outcome of the Platonic idea. Thus, to the extent that Hegel sublates the Platonic difference between the intelligible and the sensible, idea and world (the two *topoi* of the *Republic*), we can see very well how everything falls apart. The same, it must be said, is true of Heidegger. But whereas Hegel sublates this difference starting from the judgment (*intellectus, intellectualismus latens*), Heidegger, instead, sublates it from being (what we have characterized as the second step toward the abyss). In fact, as we know, Heidegger's general theses could be summed up as follows: highest being and beings are equal (they are "beings" after all); the *being* of beings has never been thought by metaphysics (being is the unanswered question of thinking); as a result truth is neither *adaequatio* of beings to being, nor of the intellect to beings. Let us reflect on this twofold and converging Hegelian and Heideggerean practice.

1. Both Hegel and Heidegger, in spite of everything, accept as valid the Parmenidean relation being-thinking. They continue to believe this relation

as the *original question*. In some ways it is the question of "historical man," as Heidegger says. But historical man is then defined by Heidegger as the man (humanity) to whom is revealed the question of being. That is, man is defined starting from and on the basis of the positing of the question of being, which leads to a mere tautology. The essence of "historical" man (or of "man," if man as a whole is "historical") is not in any way made clear. That is to say that historical man is assumed on the basis of what he says *to be* his essence (namely, on the basis of being), not on the basis of what he *says* (of his *logos*).

2. In spite of everything, both Hegel and Heidegger think within the parameters of the "Parmenidean difference" between being and thinking; and inasmuch as in their own way they sublate it, they both arrive at no longer being able to think. In Hegel, this is the case, since thinking entails placing in evidence the movement of understanding in things or, which is the same, of things in understanding. Or, putting the world into words, translating everything into the dialectical circle of the concept which it already is; or, translating the world into a "public thing"—as we shall see later—and into the chatter of the *logos* that can and must say *everything*, endlessly, and that only in this infinite telling of stories can be "true." Here thinking is saying the already occurred; is lying in wait to ensnare "facts" with words in order to show that they have occurred because, potentially, they have "already been thought." We could call this Seneca's strategy: "You ordered me to die and I will kill myself but not to obey you, but because I had already *thought* of it myself." Nietzsche's reply is similar: "This is the way *I want* it to be." Heidegger, on the other hand, arrives at no longer being able to think, since thinking entails *letting-be* the event, is the occurrence of being in beings, in the presence, in the total silence which renounces *speaking* the event. Both for Hegel and for Heidegger thinking is dwelling in the Parmenidean model or, better, residing in its simple closure.

3. Both Hegel and Heidegger take for granted the two terms of the Parmenidean relation: *being and thinking*, even though they also distort them (the two steps toward the abyss). Hegel distorts thinking and Heidegger being. But neither of the two puts truly into question the origins and the foundations of the "revelation" of being and thinking. To conclude: they complement each other in the inevitable nihilistic collapse of Western *ratio*.

After this digression, let us return to Heidegger. We said that the thing (as *ens creatum*) is true since it accords with the idea of God the creator. But the *intellectus humanus* too is an *ens creatum*. It is a faculty granted to man by God; therefore, understanding too, as any other being, must conform to its own idea. Now understanding conforms if it adjusts its propositions, its judgments, to the thing, which in its turn must conform to the idea. Consider the classical question of the difference between active, divine, creative intellect and passive, human, receptive intellect. God is the intellect who creates the norm to which the entire creation must conform. But God also creates man's passive intellect which, on the basis of the *lumen naturale*, dispensed last by God himself, adjusts to the idea of things, *i.e.*, "knows" them in their essence, even if with all the limitations of its constitutive and human finitude. Heidegger says,

> If all beings are "created," the possibility of the truth of human knowledge is grounded in the fact that the thing and the proposition measure up to the idea in the same way and therefore are fitted to each other on the basis of the unity of the divine plan of creation (*convenientia* of the created to the creator). (p. 120)[37]

This is what the Christian Middle Ages believed. The modern era, however, does not base its knowledge of the world and of its beings on a creative divine transcendence. Nonetheless, the traditional concept of truth does not change. Heidegger proves it by clearly alluding to Hegel:

> The theologically conceived order of creation is replaced by the capacity of all objects to be planned by means of a worldly reason [*Weltvernunft*] which supplies the law for itself and thus also claims that its procedure is immediately intelligible (what is considered "logical"). That the essence of propositional truth consists in the correctness of judgments needs no further special proof. Even where an effort is made—with a conspicuous lack of success—to explain how correctness is to occur, it is already presupposed as being the essence of truth. Likewise, the truth of a thing always signifies the consonance of something at hand with the "rational" concept of its essence. (p. 121)[38]

Heidegger's attempt to refer to Hegel is not without its problems. Hegel, it would be fair to say, is Heidegger's bête noire about whom, here and elsewhere in his writings, he seems to lose his critical acumen. In fact, one cannot speak lightly of "immediate intelligibility" in the case of Hegel's rational process, because the Hegelian "immediate," as we saw, is the result of the most complex and radical mediation. Furthermore, the fact that "the essence of propositional truth consists in the correctness of judgments and needs no further special proof" is at the same time a judgment that leaves us perplexed, especially when we recall the Hegelian attempt to ground judgment in the syllogism and this same formal syllogism in the concrete concept (disjunctive syllogism). This is one of the most important and most profound chapters in the history of Western thought. Nonetheless, it is true that in Hegel the concept of truth as *adaequatio* reappears: the accord of the object with the concept and of the concept with the object. (We have called attention to this earlier on, and more should be said about Heidegger's hasty assimilation of this Hegelian passage to tradition, but we will come back to it later.)

From Aristotle to Hegel, then, adequation (*adaequatio*) is understood as the essence of truth. Heidegger does not see at all that the "rational" in Hegel is not *sic et simpliciter* equal to the "logical," the formal logic of tradition or logic of the understanding; or that God's immanence in the world posited by Hegel is already the Nietzschean "death of God" (of which Heidegger speaks so much). In fact Hegel, instead of carrying on the tradition of the Western *ratio*, really brings it to an end, undermining it precisely by bringing it to fruition.

However, Heidegger's insistence on *adaequatio* is not without reason. In some sense it turns out to be a good move that makes it possible to sum up the entire tradition with a few strokes, namely, that truth has always been defined as the accordance of understanding with the thing. Even Hegel says it:

> Under the domination of the obviousness which this concept of truth seems to have but which is hardly attended to as regards its essential grounds, it is considered equally obvious that truth has an opposite, and that there is untruth. The untruth of the proposition (incorrectness) is the non-accordance of the judgment with the thing. The untruth of the thing (non-genuineness) signifies non-agreement of a being with its essence. In each case untruth is conceived as non-accord. The latter falls outside the essence of truth. Therefore when it is a question of comprehending the pure essence of truth, untruth, as such an opposite of truth, can be put aside.[39] But then is there any further need at all for a special unveiling of the essence of truth? Is not the pure essence of truth already adequately represented in the generally accepted concept, which is upset by no theory and is secured by its obviousness? Moreover, if we take the tracing back of propositional truth to the truth of the thing to be what in the first instance it shows itself to be, namely a theological explanation, and if we then keep the philosophical definition completely pure of all admixture of theology and limit the concept of truth to propositional truth, then we encounter an old, though not the oldest tradition of thinking, according to which truth is the accordance (*homoiosis*) of a judgment (*logos*) with the thing (*pragma*). What is about judgments that here remains still worthy of question—granted that we know what is meant by the accordance of judgment with the thing? Do we really know that? (pp. 121–122)[40]

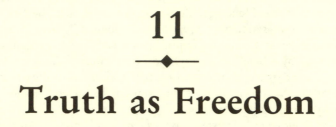

11

Truth as Freedom

"We speak of accordance in various ways," says Heidegger.

> We say, for example, considering two five-mark coins on the table that they are in accordance with one another. They come into accord in the oneness of their outward appearance.... Furthermore, we speak of accordance whenever, for example, we state regarding one of the five-mark coins: this coin is round. Here the judgment is in accordance with the thing. . . . But wherein are the thing and the judgement supposed to be in accordance, considering that the relata are manifestly different in their outward appearance? (p. 122)

How can there be accord between beings, say, and the *flatus vocis*, or the *intentio animae*? We are clearly dealing with things that are different and unlike. What kind of accordance can there be between a sequence of sounds made with the mouth (this is literally how Plato puts it in the *Theaetetus*) and the round shape of a coin? Thus by employing a very simple, if not banal, example, we have reproposed what we earlier called the "original difference" whereby Parmenides could assert, surely creating scandal among his contemporaries, that being and thinking are one and the same. If we had time we could show how the echo of this scandal is present in Gorgias. He was the first to raise Heidegger's objection and to conclude, as we know, that being is not, and that even if it were it could not be thought, and that even if it could be thought it could not be expressed given the essential heterogeneity between words and things. But let us not digress further.

The judgment, says Heidegger, can accord with the thing since it represents it. (*Vor-stellung*: representation. In the sense of positing in the presence, of making present; therefore it can also be translated "presentation.") The judgment lets the thing stand "counter," "such-as" it is in itself. But it is not the act of representation as such that brings about the thing and its correctness to the thing; it is the thing itself that reveals itself *as such* ("such-as").The representing, the presentation, in the precise meaning we

54

indicated above, is more properly a comportment regarding the thing insofar as this, of itself reveals itself. The presentation does not reveal the things; rather, insofar as the things manifest themselves, the presentation is disposed toward them. What is this comportment to the thing? This comportment, says Heidegger, is a dis-posing in the *open* so that beings as such (the things) can be disclosed: "Comportment stands open to beings" (p. 124). In Aristotle, to which Heidegger is always and fundamentally referring, this is the original unconcealed character of *aisthesis* and *nous*, "open" to the world, to beings. We ought to say, then, that beings in revealing themselves in the open (in the openness, *die Offenheit*),

> present themselves along with the presentative judgement so that the latter subordinates itself to the directive that it speak of beings *such-as* they are. In following such a directive the judgement conforms to beings. Speech that directs itself accordingly is correct [*richtig*], *i.e.* true [*Wahr*]. (p. 124)[41]

The judgment, therefore, the understanding, takes its norm from the openness (*das Offene*) of comportment insofar as it reveals itself or is revealed. It is from the roundness of the coin, insofar as this roundness reveals itself, that the judgment derives its norm. And it can because, even before the judgment, there is an openness, an availability, of comportment to beings such-as they are revealed, that makes it possible to present them such-as they are. But if this openness of bearing (*Verhältnis*) makes possible the correctness (truth) of judgments, it is this openness which is the "essence of truth," not the judgment. "Thus the traditional assignment of truth exclusively to judgements as the sole essential locus of truth falls away. Truth does not originally reside in the proposition" (pp. 124–125). Rather, it resides in the original unconcealedness, in the "phenomenality" of beings. In so doing, Heidegger arrives at a conclusion similar to Hegel's: the abolition of one of the two classical places of truth, the one pertaining to judgments, but by following a different path. Let us briefly reflect on this point.

Essentially, Hegel sublates judgment by refining it, *i.e.*, by raising it to the level of the syllogism and "making it true," which meant transforming formal logic into "concrete" logic. All this, as we have seen, makes the foundations of the Western *ratio* highly problematic. Nonetheless, the Hegelian undertaking does not escape what we earlier called onto-logy, the identity of being and thinking, or even pretends to remain in it (the absolute is "rational" and thus "can be thought"). Heidegger, instead, takes the point of view that the unconcealedness of being is more original than the judgment of logic and, generally, of the *logos*, so that the identity of being and thinking is put into question. Parmenides' "truth" begins to fall apart.

In very general terms, the event of the world cannot be explained by thinking because it is not "rational," and it cannot "be thought." Looking at the issue from another angle, both Hegel and Heidegger identify the phenomenon, the revelation of what is revealed, with the thing (what Kant calls the "thing in itself," *i.e.*, the thing is what it is since it reveals itself or, as Husserl puts it, *just as* it is revealed). But the manner of these revelations are very different.

For Hegel the revelation of the phenomenon, the *movement* of this revealing, is the very foundation of truth. In fact, it is the movement which is rational, which *makes it right* and gives it foundation. Behind the movement of the phenomenon, therefore, there is nothing else. All that is left to com-prehend is that this is the very movement of reason, of the "concept," *i.e.*, is the movement of truth.

For Heidegger, instead, the becoming phenomenon of a phenomenon, its truth as unconcealment (*a-letheia*), points to a dimension of concealment (*lethe*) that remains as such, "concealed." Here, too, there is "movement," a presenting of the phenomenon in its unconcealment, but this presenting is at the same time a withdrawing, a presenting by concealing. This presenting, in providing the *ratio mundi* (truth as unconcealment, cause as ground of the presenting of things), withdraws it, at the same time throwing it into a vortex of unintelligibility and unthinkability. Thinking is possible only on the basis of this movement of presentation-unconcealment, but the movement itself cannot be thought since it remains hidden, beyond its manifestations and reasons. One could also say that both Hegel and Heidegger attempt a "phenomenological" solution of the Kantian dualism between phenomena and things in themselves, moving, however, in two opposite directions: Hegel in the direction of a total immanentism, Heidegger in the direction of a radical transcendence. Let these brief remarks, which should be more closely examined, suffice for now and let us return to Heidegger's text.

The openness, not the judgment, therefore, is the essence of truth. But how does "the openness of comportment" occur? How does the openness open, on what grounds? "To free oneself for a binding directness is possible only by *being free* for what is opened up in an open region" (p. 125). Here is a simple example. Only if the infant to begin with is freely open to the word, *i.e.*, is disposed to language, can he comprehend language and present it to himself, by directing himself to its binding and to its rules. Only in this freedom for the openness of the word will the infant be "open to the word" and speak. In simple terms, we can say that the infant learns to speak because, as every son of man, he is "disposed" toward language. Being free, therefore, is the ground of the openness of comportment in which the essence of truth is disclosed. From all this we can conclude, then, that "the essence of the truth is freedom" (p. 125).

The phrase has a nice ring to it, with its use of a classical terminology laden with highly "moral" sounding words such as "freedom" and "truth."

But do we really understand it? And what is meant here by "freedom?" Perhaps by relating truth to freedom, one means to entrust truth to man's arbitrariness, to his "caprice"? To be sure, this is not Heidegger's intention. In fact, he says that to surrender truth to this "wavering reed" which is man is equivalent to destroying it. Even tradition knows very well that truth is not a "subjective" affair and that its essence and origin are imposed on man "from above." "How then can the essence of truth still have its subsistence and its ground in human freedom?" (p. 126). This conclusion seems absurd. And yet, "Resistance to the proposition that the essence of truth is freedom," says Heidegger, "is based on preconceptions, the most obstinate of which is that freedom is a property of man. The essence of freedom neither needs nor allows any further questioning. Everyone knows what man is" (p. 126).

To counter these entrenched "humanistic" prejudices, Heidegger proposes a "a transformation of thinking" (p. 127). Simply put, freedom is not a property of man, one of its possessions; on the contrary, it is man possessed by truth. As we have seen, freedom is "freedom for what is opened up in an open region" (p. 127). What are opened up are beings. Then, "Freedom for what is opened up in an open region lets beings be the beings they are. Freedom now reveals itself as letting beings be" (p. 127). "Letting be" does not mean, however, a sort of indifference toward beings, having nothing more to do with them. "Letting be" means, instead, "to engage oneself with beings" (p. 127); it means "to engage oneself" with its essential openness, being open to the fact whereby beings are essentially the unconcealed (*ta aletheia*) and, therefore "true," if we go back to the original meaning of the Greek word "truth" (*a-letheia*) no longer current today. In fact, in the word "truth" we no longer hear, as in Greek, the unconcealment of beings, their nonlatency, but rather the accord and the correctness of judgments to the thing. But this goes to show that our concept of truth is not original but derivative. For this reason the judgment is not the original place of truth. The judgment, in order to function and to express its "correctness" to beings requires *first of all* that beings be revealed, that they not be concealed in the *lethe*, in their concealedness, that they be *alethes*, unconcealed.

The differences between Hegel's phenomenology and Heidegger's are even more clear now. For Hegel the word "phenomenology" has its essential emphasis on the "logic" of phenomeno-*logy* because what counts is the "rational" character of the revelation of what is revealed. Heidegger, on the other hand, emphasizes the *phenomenon* aspect of *phenomeno*-logy since the emphasis is placed on the unconcealedness of beings, *i.e.*, of the phenomenon, since "what is revealed" is the *phainomenon*. For Hegel, phenomenology is the "science" of what appears; for Heidegger, instead, it is the original unconcealedness of beings to the judgment or *logos* that is the ground of every "science" and, therefore, cannot be grasped by "science" or by the *logos*. "Letting-be," therefore, is "engaging oneself." Heidegger writes,

> To engage oneself with the disclosedness of beings is not to lose oneself in them; rather, such engagement withdraws in the face of beings in order that they might reveal themselves with respect to what and how they are and in order that presentative correspondence might take its standard from them. As this letting-be it exposes itself to beings as such and transposes all comportment into the open region. Letting-be, *i.e.*, freedom, is intrinsically exposing, ek-sistent. Considered in regard to the essence of truth, the essence of freedom manifests itself as exposure to the disclosedness of beings. (p. 128)

The exposing is the ek-sistent, the ek-sistence. These are the constitutive traits of the being of man. Man is always a being-there (*Da-sein*). Being-there means being ex-posed and dis-posed in the openness, to be always already in the truth, that is, in the manifestness of beings, to echo Aristotle. Man "is," or, has an essential relation to being, to the being of beings, which is the unconcealedness itself; man is "there" or is placed in that openness that makes it possible for beings to be disclosed; he is open to beings. The word *Da-sein* admirably characterizes the essence of man to which man is always engaged. In his "there" (*Da*), in his openness, "Being" (*Sein*) is disclosed, *i.e.*, that *transcendens* which is at the same time "there," which "is announced there" as the unconcealedness of beings.

Being-there (*Dasein*) is the peculiar trait of human existence, which is always *ek-sistentia*, ex-position to the transcendence of being. By virtue of this trait, man is not a being among beings, but is the place where beings are disclosed. Transcendence, the relation to being, pertains to man's ek-sistence, which is to say that truth as the unconcealedness of beings pertains to man. These are, as we know, the more general theses of Heidegger's "existentialism."

All this requires reflection. The possibility of the relation between being and being true, we said, rests on transcendental being, on supreme being, since it is the standard to which all other existent beings are referred and in whose terms their being is to be determined. Heidegger, as we saw, employs in this regard the expression "idea-norm." This idea-norm is now shown in its immanence to the being-there of man, as *transcendens* which is also "there," which is announced in the unconcealedness of beings to man. Heidegger too, then, like Hegel, makes transcendence immanent, but in a completely different way.

In Hegel, the finite is raised to the infinite (*i.e.*, to "reason"); for Heidegger, instead, the finite (the finiteness of *Da*, of "there," of *Da-sein*, of the ek-sistence of being-there) cannot in any way be connected with the infinite.

The Heideggerean transcendence is no longer the thinking in the mind of God, the idea to which human understanding must be adequate in order to conform to the thing, *i.e.*, that "thought of God" (the Idea, in the terminology of the *Science of Logic*) that Hegel makes immanent to the world, to nature, and then to history as "path of the world," thereby situating the finite in the infinite.

In Heidegger the transcendence of *Dasein*, of ek-sistence, also goes beyond beings (man is not a being among beings) but essentially lets them be, *i.e.*, engages their disclosedness. This engaging is an attuning toward the being of beings, toward the movement of its unconcealedness; even so being is not "reached." Being, says Heidegger, is *purely and simply the transcendens*. Its transcendence transcends the very transcendence of man's ek-sistence. It finds expression in it, as the movement that presents beings but is not expressed in it. Finite human thinking and thinking of the finite are not equal to the infinite, which is essentially a withdrawing in the disclosedness within finite thinking. The finite cannot, as in Hegel, rise to the infinite; rather it pro-ceeds from the infinite. The *ek* of ek-sistence names just this place of origin, this essence, as proceeding from an unattainable dimension. It is the "thrownness" of being-there of which Heidegger speaks in *Being and Time*.

There is always an unresolvable "residue" which is the *lethe*, the concealment of being from where being is disclosed to man, that is, unconcealed to man in the beings that are. Heidegger, we could say, has gone deeper than Hegel in thinking how being becomes phenomenon, how it is disclosed as the original and radical difference which cannot be reconstituted dialectically in any "knowledge," in any phenomenological "science." Hence the Heideggerean "silence" before the event of being (*Ereignis*). This does not mean, however, that Heidegger truly frees himself from "knowledge" (from the *ratio*), *i.e.*, from that mode of thinking or "investigation" that always thinks the difference with relation to and against knowledge. But this will become clearer only at the end of our journey.[42]

Let us turn now to the openness and its ground. This ground is to be recognized, for all that we said, in that same "there" of "being-there." To sum up, man is ek-sistence; his mode of existence, of being, is to be always and constitutively "there," a determined being-there, "finite"; this "there" is that openness that lets beings be; it is the openness of the open region in which and for which beings are revealed. The finiteness of existence and of beings are in correspondence. To the finiteness of human existence corresponds the finiteness of beings that is disclosed in the determined "there" of being-there. They occur in correlation as event and movement of being. Being makes suitable one for the other—the finite disclosedness of beings *for* the finite openness of man—while at the same time withdrawing from what is unconcealed. But how does the "there" of being-there, the openness to the being of beings, occur?

The ek-sistence of historical man begins at that moment when the first thinker takes a questioning stand with regard to the unconcealment of beings by asking: What are beings? In this question unconcealment is experienced for the first time. Being as a whole reveals itself as *physis*, "nature," which here does not yet mean a particular sphere of beings but beings as such as a whole, specifically in the sense of emerging presence. History begins only when beings themselves are expressly drawn up into their unconcealment and conserved in it, only when this conservation is conceived on the basis of questioning regarding beings as such. The primordial disclosure of being as a whole, the question concerning beings as such, and the beginning of Western history are the same; they occur together in a "time" which, itself unmeasurable, first opens up the open region for every measure. (pp. 128–129)

The openness to being, the "there" of being-there, occurs then as "historical" event, as event that characterizes "historical" humanity. Historical humanity is that which posits the question of being, *i.e.*, the question of truth. This is also "Western humanity." We have already remarked at the beginning this somewhat disquieting aspect of the question of truth when we discussed Aristotle (see point 5). We remarked that the question of truth does not characterize man as such but only Western and historical man, whose essence is rooted in that type of knowledge that is philosophical "science," the "science" of truth, as Aristotle says. Heidegger alludes here to the original disclosure of the pre-Socratic thinkers and particularly Parmenides. They were the first to account for being as a whole, *i.e.*, for being; for the meaning of the truth of its disclosure, of the truth *as* its disclosure. This is how "historical time" begins, on which basis we measure the time of the "path of the world" which, therefore, cannot be measured by any other time of the world. Historical humanity posits the question of being and its truth. Or, to be more precise, we should say that this humanity "is caught" in the question of being, that it does not depend on an act of free will. This humanity, from Parmenides on, finds itself ex-posed to the problem of being and truth.

This is how the freedom of the openness ought to be understood. Man does not choose by his own free will to ex-pose himself to being. On the contrary, he finds himself ex-posed, caught in this ex-position, and thus open, free *for* the unconcealedness of beings as a whole, attuned to being and to truth. In this sense freedom is not a property of man. Rather,

freedom, ek-sistent, disclosive Da-sein possesses man—so originally that only *it* secures for humanity that distinctive relatedness to being as a whole as such which first founds all history. Only ek-sistent man is historical. "Nature" has no history. (p. 129)

These are very serious assertions. How should non-ek-sistent or "non-historical" man be conceived? Is there a non-ex-istent man? And *where* and *when*? And what should we understand by "nature?" Here Heidegger seems to be caught in the most radical contradictions of his thinking. But this does not concern us now. Let us instead try to recapitulate this last stage of our journey.

Freedom consists in letting beings be, in being dis-posed and ex-posed to the care of its unconcealedness. But unconcealedness, the "disclosure of beings," is just truth understood in its original sense. "*Truth* is not a feature of correct propositions which are asserted of an 'object' by a human 'subject'" (p. 129). Insofar as man, being-there, is disposed freely to the unconcealment of beings, he derives from this his *measure* of truth, the "idea-norm," in order then to accord his own judgments to beings, the "accordance" of thinking to the being of beings. The "idea-norm" is thus made immanent to the "there," to the openness of man, to his freedom. The *mode* of its becoming immanent corresponds to the *mode* of openness. This, to be more precise, is the "historically destined" character of man, of historical man precisely. Heidegger writes, "The rare and simple decisions of history arise from the way the original essence of truth essentially unfolds" (p. 130). Truth, therefore, has different *modes* of disclosure. It exhibits from time to time different "idea-norms." (Just as being is from time to time the disclosure of these or those beings, or in these or those beings, all the while holding itself back in its unity and in its final and ineffable meaning for the disclosure of other beings.) That is why truth is "historical," correlative to the historical being of the man of truth. For instance, if being (the ground, the cause, the meaning of beings) is disclosed as the God of Christian revelation, then every particular truth, every truth of beings, accords with such disclosure and with its "idea-norm." All medieval science depends on this original disclosure and revelation of God the creator as cause and foundation of the world; it is with reference to the "idea-norm" of this God that Aquinas was able to posit the truth of physics, anthropology, ethics, psychology, *etc.* Within these truth-parameters one can debate the truth of the judgments that affirm the unity or nonunity of human reason or, as Dante does in *Paradiso* II, one can ask for an explanation of the moon spots that seem to contradict the general theory of the heavens. If the meaning of beings, *i.e.*, of its being and truth, are conditioned by the revelation of God the creator, by the supreme being of Christian Revelation, it is from this disclosure that every "idea-norm" and every accordance between judgments and things is derived.

So instead, if the meaning of being is disclosed as mathematics, as Galilean mathematical reason understood as nature's universal *writing*, all the particular beings and their particular truths are reduced to this mode of disclosure. The whole of modern science depends on this mode, and it is in the light of this disclosure that Newtonians and Leibnizians can debate whether or not the law of universal gravity is sufficient to explain Nature; that Cartesians and Hobbesians can debate whether or not thinking is a spiritual substance or an affection of the brain.

From Parmenides to Hegel the disclosure of being and truth has this "historical" character. This character is co-essential to the truth because it is the "finite" unconcealedness in the "there" of being. Being appears as these or those beings, as angels and demons, as triangles and circles, to stay with the two examples above. In his openness, or freedom, man is open to receive and judge them, to make judgments *in accordance* with them; he is open from time to time, this way and that, as he lets beings be disclosed to him such as beings from time to time are.

In this sense his freedom and his truth are "historical." It does not depend on his will whether he meets nymphs or elves, universal gravity or the atomic table, the evolution of the species or the law of relativity. These particular truths depend on the simple *modality* of the disclosure of being which imprints its "idea-norm" on every historical "epoch." Truth is written now in the Book of Revelation, now in the "Book of Nature," or now the truth is a product of Technology. However, if the disclosure of being and truth is understood in its historical "movement," this means that every truth is "finite" and "relative" and, finally, that truth cannot but be entangled somehow with untruth. Heidegger remarks that, "untruth must derive from the essence of truth. . . . truth and untruth are not *in essence* independent from one another, but rather belong together" (p. 130).

We have reached a crucial point. The discussion relative to the untruth and the non-essence of truth, of which we can follow here only the bare outlines necessary for our own investigation is, says Heidegger, "the decisive step toward an adequate posing of the *question* concerning the essence of truth" (p. 130). Thus the initial question comes up again: "What is the essence of truth?" It has reached its *bottom* (*Grund*) through the discovery of the "historical" character of being-there. (Even here Heidegger seems to be closer and at the same time radically different from Hegel.) What then is the essence of truth? Now we begin to catch a glimpse of the abyss (*Ab-grund*).

12

◆

Truth as Mystery

According to tradition, truth is what in the judgment says the *being* of something, that is, that beings *are* this or that. But, as we now know, judgment is not the original place of truth. Judgment establishes an accord, an accordance or a correctness; it says the beings that *are* such as they *are*, since judgment is a comportment (*Verhältnis*) to the open (*das Offene*), to the unconcealedness of beings. This unconcealedness of the place of truth is more primal than judgment or proposition. But unconcealedness requires the freedom of the openness; thus freedom is the original place of truth, the letting-be of beings in their unconcealment (*aletheia*). Since man is the being of truth, "historical" man, man ex-poses himself freely to the openness of the unconcealment or non-latency of beings.

The ek-sistence of "historical" man, however, is not characterized by the possession of freedom. On the contrary, it is freedom through the ek-sistent being-here which possesses man. This being possessed, this being caught by the unconcealment of beings as a whole, *i.e.*, of their truth, is what determines the historical character of "being attuned" of historical man. Man is engaged to history (*Geschichte*). This is to be understood as *geschehen*, the occurrence of the truth of being. This occurrence is a mittance (*schicken*) of destiny (*Schicksal*). Man's historicity is a destined mittance. By history is not meant simply the "historiographical" succession of epochs. There are "epochs" because being is disclosed now in one manner, now in another, destining man to a meeting with these or those beings. But this same movement of being remains concealed behind the epochs, remains in *epoche*, suspended, kept on hold behind its very own disclosedness.

The ground of judgment, of its "accordance" to beings is thus historical. Judgment can establish the correctness of the word to the thing only because there is already a prior accord as "engagement in the disclosure of beings as a whole" (pp. 130–131), an engagement that is precisely historically destined. "Historical" humanity, humanity caught in the destiny of being and its truth, has always already decided for the investigation of the truth of being, i.e., for the "knowledge" of truth. It has always already asked: What *are* beings as a whole? And even earlier: What *is* the being of this "is"? This is how the journey began with Parmenides and then continued with Plato and Aristotle all the way to Hegel and beyond.

As already attuned to the disclosure of beings as a whole, historical man "is always engaged in being attuned in a way that discloses beings as a whole" (p. 131), is already attuned to the knowledge of being and truth. Historical man *lives* this situation without even feeling the need of revealing its essence to himself. He lives it directly in his "scientific" undertakings, in the "theoretical" glance that turns the world into the object of his "rational" activity. Thus, says Heidegger, Western man, historical man *par excellence*, the man of the destiny of being, can be *naturally* "logical" and entrust himself to logic as the only "human" way to live. In fact, he entrusts himself all the more when his yearning for knowledge increases and when, forgetting the metaphysical origins of his own history, he adheres to a technological and scientific conception of existence.

> The openness of being as a whole does not coincide with the sum of all immediately familiar beings. On the contrary, where beings are not very familiar to man and are scarcely and only roughly known by science, the openness of beings as a whole can prevail more essentially than it can where the familiar and well-known has become boundless, and nothing is any longer able to withstand the business of knowing, since technical mastery over things bears itself without limit. Precisely in the leveling and planning of this omniscience, this mere knowing, the openness of beings gets flattened out into the apparent nothingness of what is no longer even a matter of indifference but rather is simply forgotten. (p. 131)[43]

Thus, Heidegger characterizes the last phase of the historical destiny of the man of the truth of being. Being itself and its question are forgotten. Philosophy is translated entirely into the technological and scientific domination of beings. Beings as a whole lose "meaning," and nihilism appears as the last form of the already forgotten being. In this extreme form of the destiny of Western *ratio*, i.e., Logic, the formal logic of the understanding as Hegel would have said, reigns supreme. But what makes possible this domination is always the prior engagement of historical man in the "totality," in the disclosure of beings as a whole, guaranteed to him ever since the beginning of philosophy. He is engaged, however, without realizing his own engagement, his own attunement, within the truth or unconcealedness of being, within that knowledge that was once philosophy and today is science.

It is this place of historical man within the "totality," within beings as a whole, which now has to be questioned: *how* is man placed in totality, in the disclosedness of beings as a whole? Says Heidegger, "from the point of view of everyday calculations and preoccupations this 'totality' appears to be *incalculable* and *incomprehensible*" (p. 132) [Sini's italics]. This is the case both for that totality we call "nature" and for that totality we call "history." The man of truth organizes his life according to "logic." This is possible because he considers beings within the framework of a *rational* totality, *i.e.*, as disclosedness of being and of its "logical" thinkability. But this same totality, which makes his knowledge possible, escapes knowledge. This "totality," says Heidegger, "although it ceaselessly brings everything into definite accord, still remains *indefinite* and *indeterminable*" (p. 132) [Sini's italics].

With all his "logical" calculations and with all his techniques, the man of truth can always be assured of the knowledge of new beings, of new particular truths, but never of the totality within which these reside and reveal themselves. Nature and history remain unattainable, indeterminable, and incalculable in their totality. That is why one must conclude that the totality is precisely "a concealing of beings as a whole" (p. 132).

> Precisely because letting be always lets beings be in a particular comportment which relates to them and thus discloses them, it conceals beings as a whole. Letting-be is intrinsically at the same time a concealing. In the ek-sistent freedom of Da-sein a concealing of being as a whole comes to pass [*ereignet sich*]. (p. 132)

It is as if we had said that we can com-prehend the part because of its prior accord with the whole. But this whole cannot be comprehended. (This was already the problem of dialectic in Kant's *Critique of Pure Reason*, and it would be interesting to see how Hegel and Heidegger have differently treated and "resolved" this problem.) To disclose beings according to a particular mode of comportment is equivalent to concealing beings as a whole, being and its truth. One thing cannot occur without the other. One can have these or those beings (mathematical being, psychological being, *etc.*) but at the price of *not* having the totality of beings. Beings can be had at the price of their being. Thus, letting-be beings, attuning freely to accept them, entails necessarily not letting being be, not grasping it. For this reason Heidegger says more than once that the entire Western tradition, which has posed the problem of being, has never thought being and its truth.

The posing of the problem of being is at the same time the condition of thinkability of beings and the condition of unthinkability of being. One has to pose the question of being in order to be able to "think" "logically." But since every thinking is thinking of *something*, "intentional" thinking, *i.e.*, attuned to its "object," it necessarily thinks beings, this or that, and leaves being in the dark, the being of beings which he thinks. This means accepting the movement of being that beings give and, therefore, removing the very same movement, leaving it unthought.

Unconcealment and concealment, therefore, go together. Concealment, says Heidegger, is an essential trait of unconcealment (*aletheia*). There is no *aletheia* without *lethe*. Therefore, there is a non-disclosedness, an untruth, which belongs to the essence of truth and which, moreover, precedes it, so to speak: "The concealment of beings as a whole, untruth proper, is older than every openness of this or that being. It is also older than letting-be itself which in disclosing already holds concealed and comports itself toward concealing" (p. 132). But what is being concealed and somehow preserved in this concealment? "Nothing less than the concealing of what is concealed as a whole, of beings as such, *i.e.*, the *mystery*" (p. 132) [Sini's emphasis].

The pre-essential (*vor-wesen*) essence, *i.e.*, that which is anterior to the unconcealment of truth, is the "mystery." But the characteristic trait of mystery, its curious domination at the time of the spread of nihilism, that is, in the epoch of science and technology which epitomizes the destined journey of historical man, is that this very mystery remains concealed, unthought. It holds sway precisely because it is concealed.

This bearing toward concealing conceals itself in the process, letting a forgottenness of the mystery take precedence and disappearing in it. Certainly man takes his bearings (*verhalt sich*) constantly in his comportment toward beings; but for the most part he acquiesces in this or that being and its particular openness. Man clings to what is readily available and controllable even where ultimate matters are concerned. And if he sets out to extend, change, newly assimilate, or secure the openness of the beings pertaining to the most various domains of his activity and interest, then he still takes his directives from the sphere of readily available intentions and needs.

However, to reside in what is readily available is intrinsically not to let the concealing of what is concealed hold sway. Certainly among readily familiar things there are also some that are puzzling, unexplained, undecided, questionable. But these self-certain questions are merely transitional, intermediate points in our movement within the readily familiar and thus not essential. Wherever the concealment of beings as a whole is conceded only as a limit that occasionally announces itself, concealing as a fundamental occurrence has sunk into forgottenness.

But the forgotten mystery of *Dasein* is not eliminated by the forgottenness; rather the forgottenness bestows on the apparent disappearance of what is forgotten a peculiar presence (*Gegenwart*). By disavowing itself in and for forgottenness, the mystery leaves historical man in the sphere of what is readily available to him, leaves him to his own resources. Thus left, humanity replenishes its "world" on the basis of the latest needs and aims, and fills out that world by means of proposing and planning. From these activities man then takes his standards, forgetting being as a whole. He persists in them and continually supplies himself with new standards, yet without considering either the ground for taking up standards or the essence of what gives the standard. In spite of his advance to new standards and goals, man goes wrong as regards the essential genuineness of his standards. He is all the more mistaken the more exclusively he takes himself, as subject, to be the standard for all beings. The inordinate forgetfulness of humanity persists in securing itself by means of what is readily available and always accessible. This persistence has its unwitting support in that *bearing* by which *Dasein* not only ek-sists but also at the same time *in-sists*, *i.e.*, holds fast to what is offered by beings, as if they were open of and in themselves.

As ek-sistent, Dasein is insistent. Even in insistent existence, the mystery holds sway, but as the forgotten and hence "'inessential' essence of truth" (pp. 134–135).

Therefore, since historical man by ek-sisting insists in turning to beings to derive the norm for his judgments, he is removed from the mystery. The two movements are really one and the same. By assuming beings as norm, man forgets the mystery of truth. But only by forgetting the mystery of truth can man turn with confidence to beings and place in them all his hopes and beliefs, as is done most exasperatingly in this age of science and technology. Now, since this turning-to beings, which is a turning-away from the mystery, is a losing of bearings whereby being-there is caught in the restlessness of everyday life, always running after new beings—caught, that is, by the presence of "current reality" with its "objects," the infinite machines and gadgets of technological society; of its millions or, better, billions of printed sheets, records, reproductions; of its rivers of words and so on—*i.e.*, caught in this "ontic" restlessness, man eludes the mystery, *silences it*. But this eluding, says Heidegger, is essentially an "erring."

Man errs. Man does not merely stray into errancy. He is always astray in errancy, because as ek-sistent he in-sists and so already is caught in errancy. (. . .) Errancy belongs to the inner constitution of the Da-sein into which historical man is admitted. (. . .) Errancy is the open site for and ground of *error*. Error is not just an isolated mistake but rather the realm (the domain) of the history of those entanglements in which all kinds of erring get interwoven. (pp. 135–136)

Historical man, therefore, is in error since he is removed from the mystery. In so doing, however, he persists in the mystery. But, properly speaking, what kind of mystery? Of the truth of being and thus, also, of the essence of particular truths. The particular truths are grounded on a mystery, that is, on an absence of ground. Beings themselves have their being, their coming into being, their unconcealment in this groundless ground, in this unfathomable destiny. *How much* being they possess, in their unconcealment and concealment, remains a mystery. How much being have angels? How much being has atomic energy? There is no answer. With scientific and technological hegemony the question does not even arise. This absence defines and completes the experience of the abyss.

PART II

◆

From Sign to Symbol

13

◆

The Truth of the World or What We Must Consign to Silence

Every true philosophy changes the meaning of the entire history of philosophy, just as T. S. Eliot used to say that every new poem changes the history of poetry, *i.e.*, alters our ways of interpreting and relating to it. If we now turn to Parmenides again in the light of what we have learned from Heidegger, we can say that in Parmenides, thinking (*noein*) corresponds to being, to that being which is not "coming into being and perishing, change of place and variation of bright color."[44] Parmenides, therefore, "keeps in store" being, withdrawing it from non-being, from mere *doxa*, from the everyday and "inauthentic" running after beings, making calculations and projects with them. In this sense, therefore, for Parmenides being is already the *transcendens* pure and simple, the original place of truth. Heidegger, by going back to the Parmenidean *aletheia*, closes the circle of Western thinking, save that for him being can no longer correspond to thinking, because being is the *mystery*.

In more analytical terms, one should say that the Heideggerean position encompasses within the unconcealment of being the great journey of the Platonic-Hegelian dialectic. Being, for Heidegger, *gives itself to view* in its "being and perishing, [in the] change of place and [in the] variation of bright color." That is, to Being the "destined historicity" is co-essential. But the giving-itself-to-view is then also and above all (*first* of all) a concealment *in* beings.

For Heidegger too, as for Aristotle, man is rooted in the unconcealedness of Being. Man and his speech are always already in the truth; they partake of it. The same distinction between the two places of truth in Aristotle contains implicitly the Heideggerean conclusion that the truth that is in us (*en dianoia*, as *pathos tes psyches*, as *synthesis* and *diairesis*) does not pertain to Being as such. Being is disclosed in contact (*thigein*) and in assertion (*phanai*), which is neither affirmation nor negation; thus Being is by itself the truth about which it is not possible to be in error. (It is only possible, Aristotle would say, to think or not to think Being, to know it or not to know it.) However, this thinking and knowing is, for Heidegger, a continuous and constitutive "error." Aristotle, one could say, proceeds on the basis of the original unconcealedness of Being encompassing within judgment the Platonic dialectic; Heidegger, instead, encompasses within it Hegel's dialectic and history. All of this makes very clear the rigid and "fatal," "destined," continuity of traditional metaphysics in Western thought.

Truth continues to pertain to its onto-logic place: *what* Being *is* is the original truth ("onto-"); *how* Being *is* (as unity, cause, reason of its manifold manifestations) is the truth deduced by judgment ("-logic"). For this reason Aristotle says that it is easy to attain the general, but it is difficult to grasp the truth in its particulars. It is easy to say something about the truth, since speech is already "in agreement" with it, but it is difficult to express it in determinate and particular statements. For this reason truth requires an investigation, a "theoria," whose character is "historical" (social-progressive). And it is in this latter sense that philosophy is the "science" of truth. With Hegel the investigation of truth and philosophy as science take the crucial step in which the Parmenidean identity between being and thinking reaches its fulfillment and, at the same time, the beginning of its undoing. In contrast to tradition, which opposed (*intellectually*) being and thinking (in order to put them together again in a "beyond," *i.e.*, *in mente Dei*, as Heidegger has shown with regard to the Middle Ages), Hegel affirms (*rationally*) their identity. This is possible only by resorting to a third, "middle," term: the middle term of the syllogism, which becomes less and less abstract to the point of acquiring the concreteness of being in the disjunctive syllogism.

Heidegger, too, resorts to a middle term, but since he does not understand that Hegel had also understood it, he takes him to task for having limited his definition of truth to the traditional concept of "agreement," which is only superficially true. In Heidegger, as we indicated, accordance entails an original belonging-together of man to Being, namely, that freedom of letting-be which is the openness for the unconcealment of Being. In Hegel, however, this middle or third between thinking and being is the very movement of reason in its giving-itself-to-view as intellectually divided and then being put together dialectically in a unity. This is how being and thinking are the same, and this is how judgment can unite them and distinguish them, taking its starting point from a deeper unity. However, since this identity and unity are the identity *of* and *in* appearances, the specificity of Parmenidean being, its refusal of non-being and becoming, falls short (being is really becoming and in union with non-being). Analogously, the specificity of thinking also falls short since it is no longer limited to truth but is also constitutively open to error and is no longer restricted to mere intuition (*noein*) but turned instead to an infinite process of mediations in which the same being is involved (everything is a syllogism and vice versa). The Hegelian middle says, therefore, that being is the *history* of being (movement of the *Wirklichkeit* which is at the same time movement of knowledge, *concept*). In this sense all the real (the movement of the real, its history) is rational and the rational is real. The real, therefore, is the very same "Dionysiac" revelry of the phenomenon, without residue, so that there is no meaning beyond the becoming of meaning, no stable (and thus "rational") foundation under the surface. But this is as much as saying that the rational is the sense-less (*insensato*). This inherent determination of the Hegelian "essence" is not, then, very far from the Heideggerean conclusion which says that the middle is "mysterious," without reason and without meaning, since from the middle every reason and every meaning first originates only to always again conceal itself in them.

To the Hegelian rational totality, Heidegger could oppose the Leibnizian question (which in fact he makes his own): "Why are there beings rather than nothing?"[45] *What* Being is, in the form of truth (that is, of unconcealedness), is pure event, "excessive," "incalculable" and finally "unthinkable." The "path of the world" contains every reason of the world and, therefore, is itself without reason. Or, in Heideggerean terms, it is the movement of the unconcealment of Being which gives, from time to time, the "standard" (the "idea-norm" of truth), that is, the "rational" parameters in whose light truth and falsity can be measured. But for this reason, this movement can be neither measured nor comprehended. It comes from the dark, from the nothing (*nulla*) of beings, and persists in the dark.[46]

As we know, however, this experience of the dark, of the abyss and of the mystery, is constantly being removed. The *what* of Being, insofar as it *is* (befalls) falls into oblivion. It is no longer the object of thinking. According to scientism and neo-positivist philosophy this is the end of metaphysics. Thinking, investigation, are concentrated instead, always more spasmodically, in the will to know and always-only-to-know-more, on the *how* of phenomena through experimental technology and logical-formal calculations. But this is how the removed and forgotten mystery, as Heidegger has well observed, dominates our time (indeed *precisely because* it is removed and forgotten).

The dizzy acquisition of many types of knowledge about beings (of particular and instrumental truths) is obscurely accompanied by the radical non-sense of these truths. But since a thinking of meaning is no longer possible (of the *what* of the event of being) because metaphysics has totally "expended" itself by turning into science and, indeed, into technology (into the computing and programming praxis), the obscure meaning of non-sense, as derived from the mystery of the *what*, has become "psychological" and has been confined to the "private." (This has occurred for key reasons that we will only be able to understand much later.) And it has been left up to the *individual* (supposed real) to decide for himself the sense or non-sense of the world, life, death, God, man, *etc*. The individual can *think* as he *pleases*, even though nobody knows on what grounds he can *think*, nor, indeed, *what* the individual is. But, in the last instance, all this is not necessary, because the question is precisely "psychological." As long as he has the "impression" of thinking, for instance, on some talk show, which has chosen as one of its topics to "resolve" the question of God, the individual trusting his "feelings" asserts that God exists: "One *can feel* that God exists, *I* feel it."

We should add that this is the real basis, the destined sense, of the modern "tolerance of expression," which consists in transforming issues that at one time were "public" (when thinking one way or another was not *indifferent* and could mean risking the Inquisition) into "private" issues or, at best, into issues that are "newsworthy": *liberum arbitrium indifferentiae*. Thinking now dwells in tolerance, in the house of tolerance.[47] The reasons for the dis-orientation of "historical" man in the age of science and technology are inherent in the character of his experience. This is ruled by the very same hypothesis that drives the entire scientific inquiry, namely, that there are no limits to what can be known of beings and that the unknowable does not exist. To be and to be known are the same, as Peirce says.

Let us suppose, therefore, that we possess much more knowledge than historical man possesses today. For example, we know what *will be said* of the cell and of galaxies in a few centuries (if these will still be spoken of then as objects of knowledge) and so on for innumerable other "things." But could this increase in knowledge, this richer understanding pertaining to this or that "state of things" acquire the meaning of an ultimate truth? The cognitive act, founded on judgment (energy is this, ether is that, and so on), cannot produce ultimate truths, *i.e.*, truths relative to the *what* of the event of being, to the *sense* of this event. Judgment, in fact, is not the original place of truth, but every knowledge of the *how* is rooted there. Even though cognitive truth, the aim of scientific investigation, actually alters, even radically, our life, it never has anything to do with *sense* and, in this sense, does not concern us.

This discrepancy is a key reason behind the dis-orientation of "historical" man. He knows and understands a great deal more than any other man, present or past, but has no answer to the question: "Why are there beings rather than nothing?" We can translate this loss of which we speak into some definite questions. We can say: "There *is* truth"—but what is the meaning of this sentence? Can we doubt that it has a *sense*? The sentence, "It is evening now," for instance, *has* sense, and likewise an infinity of other sentences. Thus, since a great number of truths, which we call particular truths, have sense, can the word "truth" not have sense? We do not know what the "essence" of truth is (at best, it can be "mystery"), and yet *are there* truths? Isn't this a dis-orienting situation? And yet, who is not affected by it?

We can also say: "If there *is* truth (somehow, whether we know it or not) then truth has being"—but what does this sentence mean? What does "being" mean? Undoubtedly, there are "things," beings that *are*, but not being, the essence of beings. *There is* no being. To assert the opposite is to get lost in the meanderings of metaphysics, of a useless knowledge good only for philosophic manuals and in itself useless, outdated, and archaic; of a knowledge which is no longer up to date and no longer measures up to the *needs* of "modern" humanity. And yet, to say that there *are* beings but that their being is a question without answer leaves us completely dis-oriented. Finally, we can say: "There is *the world*." But what is "world"? Has the world being and truth? But what sense can the phrase "The truth of the world" have? *Is* there a truth of the world? And *how* is it or *how* could this supposed "truth of the world" be?

Let us briefly reflect on this last phrase, which obviously also implies the others. If we name the truth of the world, of the universe, we have already presupposed a few things. For instance: (*a*) that the universe is a fact, or a totality of facts, which are (truly) this way or that and not otherwise; (*b*) that a "universal" consciousness (one infinitely adequate to its object—the universe) contemplates the universe, *externally*, and can say how it is made, "truly." Anyone can see how absurd and nonsensical these hypotheses are, and yet we always accept them as *obvious*, as obviously true, in our discussions on truth, the world, and on all other things in the world and their particular truths.

A further nonsense is the belief that the vision of the supposed infinite consciousness, which observes the universe and its facts from outside, can be transmitted to "finite" human consciousness and, particularly, to the "scientific," "investigating" consciousness. This is precisely what science presupposes: an infinite process (a "social" process, as we find already in Aristotle) that gradually conforms to the infinite truth of the universe. Peirce has expressed all this impeccably when he says that truth is an infinite "public" process, a "being" *in the* thinking of single consciousnesses. The path of truth is the same as the path of "scientifically" investigating thinking. And he added, correctly, that there cannot be "science" unless on this basis, on this premise. But this premise is still that of metaphysics (and remains as such, whether one knows it or not, or says it or not): being is thinking, its "historical" unfolding, its becoming "public" thinking and "public" truth.

At this point, however, the reasons for this nonsense become clearer. It is plausible that "historical" man may have forged his concepts of knowledge, truth, and world by means of an improper reversal. He may have imagined an infinite consciousness (or one disposed to infinity) and his vision of the universe as model of truth, by simply transforming his finite consciousness, cognitively standing *against* the world, his "public" world, into infinite consciousness. On the basis of *this* cognitive consciousness he has modeled *the other*, the consciousness that sees the whole universe and its truth. It is clear, then, that the truth that philosophy and science seek is nonsensical, since it epitomizes an ultimate vision (or gradually tends toward it, which is the same) whose object, ultimately, would be an explanatory state of affairs.

There is no view outside the world, nor is the world a fact (a chain, or a series of facts) that can simply stand as an object to be viewed. What vision could *not* be an interpretation, based on previous interpretations and refer- ring to future ones? What fact or state of affairs could be "explanatory" (explanatory of *sense*, *i.e.*, ultimately explanatory)? The explanatory schema based on judgment, on what Hegel called "understanding," but which more generally we can call "rational" judgment, cannot lead to a sense of truth, to self-contained *sense*.

As an example, let us use the well-known Kantian hypothesis.[48] Kant argues that if God appeared to man in person in all His majesty and reality and revealed him the truth, *etc.*, man could no longer be *free* and could no longer act morally. In fact, who could act *against* the truth after knowing it and seeing it with one's own eyes? Who could sin anymore or choose to do good, of *his* own free will, if he had come to know *de visu* how things would be necessarily in the end and what awaited him in eternity as the result of the choices he made? Therefore, if God does not reveal himself, one can always speculate that it is in order to leave man his well-deserved freedom.

This is how Kant reproposes, implicitly, the classical alternative of the entire history of metaphysics to which Plato had given the name of the hypothesis of "sons of the earth" and the hypothesis of "friends of ideas." The former say that the world is senseless matter, the latter that the world is governed by an intelligence or ultimate purpose. This is the alternative. But even though this pleases common sense, the alternative does not make sense. It pretends, in fact, to be speaking of the world and its truth on the basis of those assumptions that were indicated earlier—that the world is a thing that stands over there, with all its facts or events, and that a consciousness (perhaps a divine one) contemplates it externally and discerns or reveals its truth. But let us leave this problem aside for now and let us continue with Kant's hypothesis.

Let us suppose, therefore, that in His majesty and mercy, God really lowers himself to speak to man: "You see, atom of the universe, this is how things are, this is the sense and reason for everything, of which you are the smallest, alas, most restless part." If the atom, because of divine goodness, was not yet annihilated and could still speak, would he keep quiet? At this point, two alternatives present themselves:

(a) *The sense of everything can be translated into human discourse.* If this is the case, then, it is subject to communication, clarification, discussion and so on. We can almost see him, the atom, retorting: "Why did you make this choice and not another one?" "Why couldn't you do better?" But every "better" implies a relative evaluation: better *for whom*? And *for what*? And still: "On what grounds can a truth be 'true'?" "Is 'being' true because it *is* or because it *has to* be according to Your Will?" And, "Why were we not consulted? Because we would not have been able to see the 'justice' of the whole?" "But is this justice a 'being' or, again, is it what Your Will has decided is just?" We are back where we started, and so on. The good Lord may well regret his goodness.

(b) *The sense of everything cannot be translated into human discourse* (as Kant believes after all). What hope is there, then, that everything has *reason* to be? But is not a world without "reason" precisely the hypothesis of the "sons of the earth"? We could put this alternative also in these terms:

(i) We can speak to God, as very gladly we would speak to Parmenides hypothetically brought back to life (even Plato had this "itch" in the *Sophist*), perhaps after having gone down on our knees but also very determined to "understand": "What of the *doxa* if it *does not exist*, has no being?" "Why do things *seem* many and in motion if being is one and motionless?" "What does *seem* mean?" "What do you *really* mean when you negate becoming?" and so on. But does this hypothesis really make sense? Could we really speak to Parmenides in the "modern" sense of the word? Could we carry on a "philosophical dialogue" with him? Would he be open to a "discussion" the way we intend it, or would not his idea of discourse and truth be so totally foreign to our mental sets that it would be really impossible to "understand" one another? Maybe we could try with his disciple Zeno: "Is Parmenides a man who gives answers or just 'asserts'?" After all, Parmenides is no Socrates, who already seems one of us. Even Plato would say that he could not understand at all what Parmenides meant. How many problems with Parmenides! Can you imagine with God!

(ii) The second alternative is that we cannot speak to God, that we cannot have a dialogue with him. In the first instance, as far as we know (*i.e.*, in the light of our knowledge—who else's?) not even God could escape the "historicity" of dialogue, that is, its infinite interpretive nature; nor could he escape, in principle, the possibility of *changing one's mind* (*i.e.*, of changing His mind entirely!), since it is for this reason, precisely, that there is dialogue, and when the participants are not influenced by the words of others there is no dialogue. (In fact, there is no dialogue *unless* there is this influence but only listening.) In the second case, God's reasons would be for us, for our "reason," nonsensical, without "reason."

In conclusion: Either: The "truth of the world" can be translated, expressed in the *logos* (*i.e.*, in the form of the statement "*a is b*") and, then, we must keep in mind that the statement is made of signs that refer to things or events that in turn are signs that have to be interpreted by other statements and so on, *ad infinitum*. For instance, the statement "It is evening now" refers to the signs of the evening, each of which implying a statement: "It's dark," "The sun has set," and so on. We must remember that everything is a syllogism. The chain of signs and interpretations extends to infinity, as Peirce says.

Or the "truth of the world" cannot be translated or expressed in the *logos*. This is Gorgias' anti-Parmenidean hypothesis which is already implicit in Hegel and is made explicit in Nietzsche, for example, in *On Truth and Lie in the Extra-moral Sense*, and then in Heidegger.

In the first case we have what has already been described. The truth of the *logos* entails an infinite increase in types of knowledge relative to the "how" of phenomena—an increase and, at the same time, a transformation, given the "historical" character of truth-parameters. (In actual fact, it is not a question of a path or of a simple linear accumulation, as even epistemology at the instigation of the history of science is beginning to admit today.) But this increase of the "how" does not allow for any access to the "what" of phenomena. Being or rather the nothing of the world, are becoming equivalent, as is already evident in Leibniz' question, "Why are there beings rather than nothing?," which foreshadows the end of Parmenides: the end of defining being as what is opposed to nothing and safeguarding it from the possibility that being may be equal to nothing. The nature of "logical" knowledge, that is, of knowledge based on the *logos*, depends, in fact, on the establishment of being. Its propositional and judgmental structure, or semiotic structure, aims at determining the premise of being without ever being able to justify it in its "whatness," that is, without ever being able to define its "sense" (the meaning of being that Heidegger was looking for).

In the second case we have a situation like the one observed by Wittgenstein, namely, that there is nothing to be said about the world. Let us be reminded of how Wittgenstein expressed this conclusion with a brief excursus through some propositions of the *Tractatus Logico-philosophicus*.[49]

1. The world is all that is the case. 2.063. The sum-total of reality is the world. 6.3. The exploration of logic means the exploration of *everything that is subject to law*. And outside logic everything is accidental. 6.37. There is no compulsion making one thing happen because another has happened. The only necessity that exists is *logical* necessity. 6.371. The whole modern conception of the world is founded on the illusion that the so-called laws of nature are the explanation of natural phenomena. 6.372. Thus people today stop at the laws of nature, treating them as something inviolable, just as God and Fate were treated in past ages. And in fact both are right and both wrong: though the view of the ancients is clearer in so far as they have a clear and acknowledged terminus, while the modern system tries to make it look as if *everything* were explained. 6.373. The world is independent of my will. 6.41. The sense of the world must lie outside the world. In the world everything is as it is, and everything happens as it does happen: *in* it no value exists—and if it did, it would have no value. If there is any value that does have value, it must lie outside the whole sphere of what happens and is the case. For all that happens and is the case is accidental. What makes it non-accidental cannot lie *within* the world, since if it did it would itself be accidental. It must lie outside the world. 6.522. There are, indeed, things that cannot be put into words. They *make themselves manifest*. They are what is mystical. 6.53. The correct method in philosophy would really be the following: to say nothing except what can be said, *i.e.*, propositions of natural science—*i.e.*, something that has nothing to do with philosophy.

Wittgenstein means that philosophy is not interested in the being-so, in the simple event, the "how" for us, but is interested, precisely, in the "meaning of the world," in the "what."

And finally he concludes, "7. What we cannot speak about we must consign to silence." What Wittgenstein is saying here corresponds to that proposition in Heidegger that says that reasons and foundations are *in the* world, occur in the world and with the world. The world, therefore, can have neither reason nor foundation. The world and the truth of its event are "mystery," or "mystic"—what one cannot and must not speak about. The world, therefore, is without sense. Nihilism is the only "sensible" conclusion.

14

◆

The Meaning of Nihilism in the Age of Being

Is the view of nihilism really "sensible"? To many today it *seems* very "sensible." This is how civilized man reasons. After having left behind the ghosts of superstition, Max Weber says, rational man has proceeded to the "disenchantment" of the world through logic, science and industry.[50] He has discovered, then, that the world has no meaning. Only man *gives* it meaning out of need and desire. So-called values are a *private* matter of every society and, in more civilized societies, of every single man. But the moon is indifferent to the lovers' plight and the sun to the undertakings of conquerors. This is how the majority of men think today, including those who do not even bother to think but want to appear modern or even "postmodern."

However, what nihilism says when one tries to analyze it seriously is completely nonsensical. First of all, on what authority does nihilism base its claims? Why is it not also an interpretation? How, and on what basis, can the proposition "The world has no sense" claim to have absolute truth? Second, the statement of "non-sense" belongs in any case to a logic of "sense." It is as if we were to say, "The world has no flavor." The example sounds strange if not ridiculous, and yet it is absolutely of the same type as the sentence, "The world has no sense." The fact that we are not aware of the congruity shows to what extent we are "fooled" by our metaphysical prejudices. To ask if the world has *sense* is just as extravagant and absurd as it is to ask if it has *flavor*; but this will be made clearer later.

Therefore, if we say that the world has no sense, clearly we know what "sense" and "non-sense" are. We are inevitably employing a logic competent to judge sense, a thinking capable of evaluating the truth of "sense," whether *there is* sense or not. That is, we are using a logic of the "what" and not solely of the "how." But how is that possible? Has nihilism not explained that the only possible logic is that of the "how"? But, then, how can *thinking* claim "non-sense"? How can the question even be raised? If the only logic at our disposal is that of the "how," we are limited, in fact, to observing *how* things are. Not only can there not be a place for any "what," but the question or the need for it should not even arise. Any computer can reply correctly to the question of whether the temperature is above or below zero; its "logic," however, could never ask: "Why do you ask?" and, above all, "What *sense* can my answer have?" Nihilism rests on a paradox. Its conclusions, among the many metaphysics has historically contrived, are the most nonsensical. Furthermore, as we shall see later, nihilism contradicts common experience and the very structure of experience. But for the moment, we should ask ourselves what the hidden premises of nihilism are.

These premises, once again, are none other than the Parmenidean identity of being and thinking as *fundamentum veritatis*. In the attempt to correspond to being, thinking has entered into an "historical" vortex in which nothing else is left of truth as essence and foundation, and nothing else of being. Nihilism simply says "no" to what metaphysics for centuries has said or tried to say "yes" to, but always on the same premises. What is the sense of these premises? What is the secret of the Parmenidean identity between being and thinking? In this regard, we raised earlier a suspicion and a specific question. We asked: "What is Parmenides' truth?" and we suspected that it might just be the opposite of what he says. It is not because being absolutely is, and is thinkable, that truth consists in speaking it (in speaking that being is) and in thinking it as it is; it is rather because we speak and judge that truth consists in a being that can be thought and judged. The original place of truth, therefore, is not the being which is and is revealed in judgment. The original place is really the *logos*, judgment. It is the institution of this "logical" *logos* that produces being and the question of truth as correspondence to being. This is how on the basis of a public *logos* a public being and a public truth are formed.

Furthermore, we speak of a truth of the world by presupposing a universal consciousness and point of view in whose presence the world and all its events occur. But how are we able to make such a presupposition? On the basis of what model? We asked earlier whether man had imagined a universal consciousness, modeling it on our particular consciousness, a consciousness already "cognitively" disposed, that is, posited "against" the world as its object. But if this is what happened, we must ask, how *could* it have happened? The question opens up a path that perhaps it is time we took.

The question that opens up this path asks essentially: "How did the world of being originate?" "How did the world of 'historical' man come about, of man caught in the revelation of being, beings, beings in totality, with all the consequences, in large part known to us, which have derived from it?" Among these consequences is the total reduction of truth to scientific knowledge whereby the infinite investigation of the *how* entails the abandonment of the *what* to the "mystery," or its reduction to the illusory fatuity of the "private" and to the oblivion of *sense* in the purely existential restlessness of the "last men" expediently and hedonistically disposed. Let us try to get to the root of these questions. Maybe the *impasse* of thinking does not belong to the "nature" of thinking but is only the result of a thinking not sufficiently radical.

"How, then, is the question of being constituted?" "What is its sense?" "What does it mean that the question of being has its foundation in the *logos* (and not vice versa)?" The answer to these questions can be found in the fragments of Parmenides' great contemporary, Heraclitus the "obscure." In these fragments is displayed, for those able to discern it through a radical questioning, the constitutive movement of the *ratio* in its earliest stages. The movement of thinking between Parmenides and Heraclitus, therefore, is complementary—a single parallel event that has marked *the age of the logic of the world* or the age of the logic of being.

15

◆

The Thinking
Common to All

Let us listen, then, to the voice of the solitary of Ephesus to discern the sense and the image of truth that it still generates for us. Let us begin with Fragment 1B, which scholars, on the basis of testimony from Aristotle and Sextus Empiricus, are sufficiently in agreement is the exordium of Heraclitus' lost work.[51] It goes like this:

> Of the *Logos* which is as I describe it men always prove to be uncomprehending, both before they have heard it and when once they have heard it. For although all things happen according to this *Logos* men are like people of no experience . . . but the rest of men fail to notice what they do after they wake up just as they forget what they do when asleep. (§197)

The first remark to be made is that the first word that resounds in the fragment and, presumably, in the entire work is the word *logos* (*tou de logou*). To be sure, this is not accidental. The writing style of the ancients, and even more so of Heraclitus, aimed at a plastic conciseness of expression. We know that "books" (a term rather inappropriate for their works) had no titles as they have today. The first line indicated, therefore, in the most concise and precise way, down to the very careful arrangement of words, the topic and the basic thesis of the work. It should be possible to conclude, then, that Heraclitus' topic, its "novelty," its "revelation," is the *logos*.

What is said about the *logos* is of exceptional importance, which at the time must have been *unprecedented*. (Whereas for us, inevitably, it reminds us of Hegel, which could be a further topic of reflection, since Hegel was well aware of his "Heracliteanism.")[52] What is said, then, is that all things occur in accordance with this *logos*. Clearly, this is not so simple to understand.

According to most interpretations of the passage, it can be said that the word *logos*, in this context, points at least to four things: (*a*) the *logos* as the profound nature of things; (*b*) the law of their occurrence; (*c*) the doctrine of Heraclitus, which expresses this nature and this law; (*d*) the verbal discourse, which signifies Heraclitus' doctrine and the reality of how things are, or, to put it in terms of Heraclitus' general doctrine, of how things come to *pass*. Another important point is the claim that men have no understanding of the *logos*, that they are *axunetoi*. We will examine this question later, just as we will clear up shortly the statement that what men do after they wake up is hidden from them, just as they forget what they did while asleep. It is hidden because they do not understand the *logos*. The meaning of this last statement is clarified by the so-called second Fragment (2B), which also makes ulterior specifications in other very important directions. "Therefore it is necessary to follow the common; but although the Logos is common, the many live as though they had a private understanding" (§198)

The word for *common* in Greek is *koinos*. Heraclitus, however, uses the Ionic form, *xunos*, in which, as far as we can tell, he must have heard echoes of the etymon, *xun nooi*, i.e., "in thinking." For Heraclitus, what is "common" is to be *in thinking*. Gabriele Giannantoni, in his commentary on the fragments, comments as follows: "The world of understanding and truth, thus, is a world both public and common."[53] This is an admirable sentence that seems written just for us. The men who do not understand the *logos* (and are thus not awake) are men *a-xunetoi*, who are not in thinking, in the *nous*, in the *noein* of which Parmenides also speaks. (We are reminded of Peirce's saying that the "rational" nature of man consists in that men are "in thinking," and not thinking "in men.") Since men are not thinking, or do not know that they are, they are asleep while awake. They nurture their "private" dreams, their own particular "wisdom," or their "beliefs" (the *doxa* that Parmenides opposed to *episteme*). We could say that men nurture the fables of myth in which the common truth of the *logos* does not yet exist. From these already conclusive premises, Heraclitus draws all the conclusions we could ever hope for. Heraclitus the "obscure" is being extraordinarily "clear" here.

"To those who are awake, there is one ordered universe common (to all), whereas in sleep each man turns away (from this world) to one of his own" (Freeman, §89).

"The thinking faculty is common to all" (Freeman, §113).

"Those who speak with sense must rely on what is common to all, as a city must rely on its law, and with much greater reliance" (§253).

"The wise is one thing, to be acquainted with true judgment, how all things are steered through all" (§230).

"Listen not to me but to the Logos," says Heraclitus (§199).[54] (To listen just to me would be sheer *idiosyncrasy*, Peirce would say.) What is wise, therefore, is none other than the common *logos*. It inhabits the soul (here begins the rule of the "strategy of the soul") and is liable, as Aristotle says, to a continuous "public" increase (truth is a "social" fact). In fact, says Heraclitus: "The soul has its own *logos*, which increases itself" (Freeman, §115). A similar theme is found in the famous fragment §235: "You would not find out the boundaries of soul, even by travelling along every path: so deep a measure does it [the *logos*] have."

In Heraclitus' fragments, thus, we have the beginnings of the notion of a world both common and public. A *koinos* world since it is *xunos*, "in thinking," in that "thinking common to everyone" that is the *logos*. As Giannantoni says, "the world of understanding and truth is a world both public and common." This is the world of men "awake" ("historical" men, Heidegger would say), that is, of men awakened by the *logos* but also by Heraclitus' discourse (but not by his private *logos*, his personal and idiosyncratic wisdom), by that discourse that reproduces the universal *logos*, that truth common to everyone which, as Heraclitus says, is like the sun that "never sets." The men who are awake, "historical" men, are the men of truth, of the *episteme historike*, of historical science, as Plato says in the *Sophist*.

Now on these bases, we have to show how the world, which earlier we defined as "onto-logic," is reconstituted step by step. This occurs essentially with Plato, in the *Republic* and in the *Sophist*, through the analysis of the question of truth and image. In fact, in the *Sophist*, the division between the public world of beings (*onta*) and the private world of *images* (*phantasmata*, *eikones*) takes place, never to be discussed again. And still in the *Sophist*, the theme of the *logos* as "common" investigation of "*historical* intersubjectivity" is developed, which must establish at the same time the science of being, *i.e.*, essence (*ousia*), *eidos*, beings *in-themselves*. The *logos*, situated in judgment (*dianoia*), establishes then the possibility of truth and falsity, and this, as we know, is the starting point of the Aristotelian investigation from which we began. Clearly, this theme cannot be developed here. Let us try, instead, with a more general discourse to identify the essential structures of that world "awake" in whose dazzling light we historical men, as participants in historical intersubjectivity, still live, now more than ever.

"The events of the world both common and public," Heraclitus says, "occur *kata ton logon*, according to reason."[55] (Much the same is said by Hegel who, as we said earlier, is aware of repeating Heraclitus.) This "unprecedented" statement is actually sufficient by itself to determine the identity of historical man. But what is the deeper sense of this statement? What is it really saying? Or more to the point, what process must be tacitly at work so that a man can assert such "unprecedented" words, which for us, however, have been entirely "obvious" for a long time? Heraclitus' saying entails rising to a particular type of *vision*. What is being said is that the events of the world occur (or, it is as if they occurred) *in the presence of the logos*. "All things occur in accordance with the *logos*," says Heraclitus (§197). It is as if the saying were a finger pointed to the heavens. This pointing shows the place of truth, the place of the *logos*. It considers the facts *sub specie logica*, that is, in accordance with (their) truth. Namely, one should assume the point of view of the *logos*, *i.e.*, the universal point of view (neither mine, nor yours, nor his), the "pan-oramic" point of view that has everything before it.

This implicit movement, this pointing, sets the limits of the panoramic place of truth. It is what constitutes the birth of that universal consciousness, of that universal interpretant which is always pre-supposed every time the truth of the world is involved. And, it is what produces the very notion of world, of world both common and public, of *the* world, in short.

The pre-Socratic age has left us a further example, or confirmation, of the occurrence of this movement. It is easily recognizable in Xenophanes' god *who sees everything whole with the strength of the mind (nous)*.[56] To be sure, it is not an accident if Xenophanes is reputed to have been Parmenides' teacher or, according to others, his disciple. The two great and revolutionary innovations of Xenophanes' saying are very important for us. He insists on the uniqueness of the divine against the *idion* of the "false and lying" gods, which he judges, significantly, to be "anthropomorphic." Second, the peculiarity of the divine consists in moving everything with the mind ("using the mind," as Heraclitus says). Therefore, historiographical questions aside, we see delineated between Heraclitus, Parmenides, and Xenophanes, in a short span of time, the essential physiognomy of the *ratio* and its truth. This is not to imply that historiographical questions are not important but only that their very possibility and truth rest on a movement that takes the panoramic place of public discourse and its public object to be the discriminating factor between truth and falsity, science (*episteme*) and opinion (*doxa*).

16

◆

The Public Eye

Let us try to understand with an example the significance of the constitutive movement of pan-oramic truth and its presupposition, the universal interpretant. The obvious reference to the universal interpretant and its truth (to the truth of *its* public world) is so familiar to us, has been for us for so long the absolute equivalent of reality, that it is difficult for us to recognize it as just a *presupposition*, that is, in the last instance, as *one* interpretation and not as the only possible and "sensible" one. Let us go back, therefore, to what we normally understand by "historical reality." We shall see easily that it is entirely dependent on the presupposition indicated above, even if we will have to limit ourselves to very general, brief, and concise remarks.

The historian aims, as is well known, at *reconstructing* a "historical" event. For instance, he wants to reconstruct the political crisis that plagued Athens during the famous dispute between Aristides and Themistocles. Aristides, a traditionalist and representative of the conservative landowner class, wanted Athens to assemble a great army in order to fend off a possible attack by the Persians. Themistocles, the spokesman for the entrepreneurial and merchant class, supported the construction of a great fleet. He said that if the Persians came, the people of Athens would take refuge on the ships and to hell with the city, its lands, and landowners. Themistocles won out, and Aristides was ostracized. The fleet of the Athenians defeated the Persians, and Greece was saved. All this we know from "evidence," that is, from documents and monuments. These are the primary instruments of the historian, who begins with the *facts* in order to reconstruct the events and not to invent stories. Consequently, the fundamental questions every historian asks are essentially two: "*What* happened?" and "*Why* did it happen?"

The first question, "What happened?" presupposes an "ideal": to reconstruct the network of all the events within a definite unit of meaning. Naturally, this is necessary because at every instant billions of things occur in the world, or even in the smallest part of the world such as Athens. What was happening in an anthill outside the city is of no interest to the dispute between Aristides and Themistocles. It is extraneous to its unit of meaning. In the same way the marriage mishaps of the Athenian Corisco are equally of no interest, unless of course he votes against Aristides just because his wife, having met him once in the street, was very taken with him. Thus, given a unit of meaning (the dispute between Aristides and Themistocles), the historian aims at gathering the complete series of facts.

What lies hidden behind this otherwise very sensible and praiseworthy ambition? It hides the belief that *there are* "facts" that occur. And is this not "true"? Is there a more "sensible" belief? Is it not "self-evident" that in every instant "facts" occur which then, put together in a chain, give way to *events* and so on? Yes, but how do we and the historian think these *facts* occur? He thinks about them as if they occurred in the presence of a "public eye" that is always there ready to record them. This is how facts can be said to occur *in truth*. For the historian, in short, it is a question of "making known" the event "objectively," in the way it would have been observed or would have appeared to anyone if everyone or anyone had been in the place of the public eye.

The public eye does not take part in the dispute between Aristides and Themistocles. It is not even a witness of flesh and blood. Naturally the historian, just as any judge, must make use of flesh-and-blood witnesses since he was not there to witness the event himself. And as any judge, the historian weighs carefully the trustworthiness of the evidence. The witness is that much more trustworthy when he is "disinterested." Unfortunately, the witness is never *entirely* disinterested, and his senses, besides his judgment, are fatally "subjective." To be sure, this is a "scientific" limitation of history, which can never be as "objective" as the natural sciences. (Even these, however, have been having problems, since discovering that the instrument which records the electron does not leave it alone, does not let it occur *in itself and for itself*, but modifies its path fatally, making it occur *for it*.) The witness, therefore, would be perfect if the "public eye" could speak, purely and simply, through him; that is, in the same way that it does for the historian when, in his turn, he makes the effort to speak and to *make known* the facts. The public eye is like the god of Xenophanes. He has no body and records everything with the force of his mind. Thus, he cannot be "subjective." Furthermore, he has no point of view since he is panoramic. He resides neither on Acropolis nor on Pireus. He is everywhere. Moreover, he has no idiosyncrasies. He sides neither with the aristocrats nor with the democrats. He neither likes nor dislikes Aristides, whether he tries to seduce the wives of others or is happy with his own. The public eye is the eye that sees neither the world of Aristides nor that of Corisco but the world common to everyone, *i.e.*, the world *one sees*. In other words, the objective and impersonal world where events occur as *they are*, that is, objective and impersonal, *i.e.*, *true*.

Maybe we begin to doubt now the good sense of the historian's premises and of our own when we say that *there are* events that occur. What does "there are" mean? We *make* an event known and then, inadvertently, assume it as *known*. I mean that we look at events through the public eye and its public truth (as if everything occurred in the presence of the ubiquitous and panoramic "public eye") and then, forgetting we have done this, we say that the *being* of these events is public and, for this reason, they are *in the truth*.

The events that occur to Themistocles, Aristides, and Corisco are not true, or are not entirely true, because their public eye is clouded by private idiosyncrasies, and political and conjugal passion—namely, by "self-interest." The true event can be grasped only by looking at it from outside, with a public eye. But is it after all so unproblematic to equate the being and truth of events with this hypothetical public eye? Is it really without flaws? But there is another, more disturbing question. What happens when we put into question the *absolute* "good sense" of this public eye, of this universal interpretant? Does not this very same public world, the world *one sees*, risk disappearing altogether? Once the vision is gone, does not the object of this view also disappear? And are we not, then, deprived of "reality," of that which we commonly think it to be and in which we confidently trust? It may be useful to reflect that it is precisely the contemporary world, where the techno-scientific organization of beings triumphs, that tries to guard itself from the danger of such questions by trying to steer the meaning of everything that occurs toward its public truth, reviving in great style Heraclitus' project of the *logos*. The world common to everyone, the world *one sees*, is today literally the world of the "video," to say nothing of telecommunications. It is also the world of spy satellites, which see the whole of what occurs below among us mortals. It is the world of missiles that "see" the mobile target and unfailingly reach it.

Let us consider now the historian's second question, "*Why* do events occur?" We are witnessing, so to speak, "the fate of Xenophanes," that is, the consequences of the anti-anthropomorphism of his truth. For Homeric man, the "why" of events is in the last instance ascribed to gods. It is a god who gives strength to Achilles' arm and through whom Hector's fate is sealed. In actual fact, things are not so simple, because the gods themselves are subject to fate, which they can delay somewhat but cannot change entirely. Xenophanes sees in all this an anthropomorphic "projection." Homer's gods are moved by passions and self-interest just as the superstitious men that worship them are. Xenophanes' god, instead, is disinterested, governs only with the mind and according to justice. With time, however, this God becomes more and more "detached." The Christian God intervenes with his "providence," but the God of Voltaire's *Philosophy of History* no longer does anything. He neither leads armies into battle nor causes nor prevents earthquakes. Thus, Xenophanes' fate consists of two complementary and correlative aspects: (*a*) psychologization (internalization) of ends, which become "feelings," *i.e.*, motives and motivations. The ends are only *human*; and (*b*) liberation of the movement (of events) from any teleology. The increasing popularity of this view is responsible for the *why* of historical events coinciding more and more with their *how* (*i.e.*, with the simple modalities of their occurrence). This is how "meaning" leaves the world, as Wittgenstein says. Every "why" is nothing more than the series of events as they occur.

Let us consider more closely those two complementary and correlative aspects (the psychologization of ends and the liberation of movement from any teleology). These two moments reflect each other, respectively: in the public world of public truth (the intersubjective truth that constitutes the "knowledge common to everyone") and in the private world of individuals with their (private) psychological truth. For this reason we have, on the one hand, the natural sciences of pure "public" *movement*. (From Aristotle's *Physics* to Galileo's and Hobbes's *De motu*, to Einsteinian relativity, except for the obvious "historical" differences that have to be taken into account. However, it should not be too difficult to show that in this itinerary of our scientific culture, its movement increasingly frees itself from any "end.") On the other hand are the psychological sciences of the "private" (sciences of images and intentions). Bacon, D'Alembert, and the modern encyclopedia of knowledge all reason in the same manner.

History can be situated between these two scientific modalities, since its *events* are *res gestae* in which the intentions of the agents, *i.e.*, of men, have some weight. The head of the governor of the Bastille falls with the same gravitational acceleration as the weights Galileo threw from the tower of Pisa or Newton's apple, but the sword that severs the head does not move accidentally but rather with precise intention. All the same, it is well known that the common vocation of all sciences and of all knowledge is to come as close as possible to the model of the natural sciences, that is, to a concept of pure movement as pure "how." This is not so strange if we consider that the premise of "rational" knowledge, as we have discovered, is unique and common, namely, the "video," the universal vision that objectifies the world (makes it into an "object") and that, in fact, establishes it as *the* objective world. The sciences of nature and those of the mind rest on this profound unity. They are not at all "two cultures," as is naively believed.[57]

Let us consider this situation, which is basically incoherent but whose principle is coherent. Let us examine first the incoherence. The constitutive movement of the *logos*, as we saw, consists in a sort of other-worldly position (the "public eye"), that is, in the taking of a pan-oramic position. More properly, this is equivalent to instituting a disembodied "pure mind" (*nous*). For this "pure mind" all the world becomes *object* (of vision). This is what I have called the "strategy of the soul" engendered by discourse (*logoi*).[58] The *dialegesthai*, the *dia-logos*, institutes the souls and their internal vision. They succeed in "seeing" both common and public truth. That is, by overcoming their reciprocal idiosyncrasies, the souls raise themselves to the point of view of that universal soul (as in Plato's *Timaeus*) that faces the world, the common world with its public truth. These dialoguing souls can gain access to the "true" vision because they possess within themselves a fragment, a spark of the universal or divine soul. Or, to rephrase it in more modern terms, it is because the *logos* of every single human being is *in* public thinking, as intersubjective-social activity.

But this is the incoherence or the "paradox," as Husserl says. The public truth of the common world, the "objective" truth, passes *for* a vision that in principle *is not* objective. In fact, it is the very principle of subjectivity, of consciousness. The scientific ideal is objectivism, but the truth and the *sense* of this ideal cannot be objective, because every "objectivity" presupposes a constitutive subjectivity (what Husserl calls "transcendental" subjectivity). As objective sciences (sciences of the pure "how"), the European sciences lose all *sense* (all reference to the "what"), *i.e.*, all final purpose. This is the "crisis" of the European sciences and, more generally, of Western civilization of which Husserl spoke.[59]

This crisis emerges clearly where science pretends to take possession of the subject "objectively" (in the sciences of the subject, *i.e.*, psychology). But the subject by definition is not an object; in fact it is that for which there are "objects" in general. Every objectivist approach to subjectivity, therefore, is not only nonsensical but is also destined to failure. The "subject," of which empirical psychology speaks, and which *issues* from its techniques of "objective" measurement, is not properly the "subject," but its ghost. This, then, is the incoherence and the paradox. Yet in all this there is also a more profound coherence of which Husserl was not aware. For example, this coherence is evident in that "making known" that is transformed fatally in a "*being* known." Public truth can only aim at the common objective being, that is, at *being*, since this is what the *logos* has to assume as its own foundation and guarantee.

The coherence of which we speak is inscribed from the beginning in what we called the truth of Parmenides' truth: establishing being in order to found the truth of thinking. The very "soul," then, the very universal consciousness *must* be assimilated to the model of objective truth, lest one risk the demise of all "sciences," of all "logical" knowledge. Empirical psychology is caught in paradoxes, but no other "knowledge" of the soul is possible that does not model itself on the empirical-objective knowledge of the natural sciences. Husserl's defense of transcendental subjectivity does not lead, *cannot* lead, to a possible "knowledge," to a "science." This defense cannot prevent science from going its own way with a coherence that is stronger than any paradox. Husserlian phenomenology, in fact, does not offer alternatives to the will to knowledge of science and, what is more, by defending subjectivity metaphysically (transcendental "subjectivity") it is incapable of comprehending the profound nature of the scientific project and its assumptions. Husserl's complaint on the crisis of science produces neither a new science nor an authentic understanding of science's paradoxes starting with the one, for example, that Enzo Paci has defined as the paradox of subjectivity.[60]

The journey of modern science, in its coherent avoidance of every finality, can only aim at a single model, at a unity of knowledge that has its objective in "making known." This is exemplified by computer science and, in general, by the sciences of communication, where the object is increasingly reduced to *quanta* of information. It is symbolic that this occurs also with reference to the experience of death. More and more, the man who is dying in a hospital is "attached" to a monitor, the function of which is to "make known" death, the *event* of his demise, its *having occurred*. And indeed, a large part of modern medicine is founded on the instrumental technique of "looking within" the organism to bring it "out," to make it "known." This coherence leads to Wittgenstein's thesis in the *Tractatus* that *sense* is not of *this* world, whose *being* is to be known, to be public sign.[61] "Sense," in fact, has no being, since it is not an "event" that can be objectively recorded.

At best ("fundamentally," as we shall see), *sense* becomes a "private event." On the one hand, one declares the sanctity of its principle; the respect for *privacy* is the foundation of civilized living in advanced societies. But on the other, not even the "private" is left alone. The sciences of the soul (depth psychology, sociology, *etc.*) probe it objectively, wanting at all costs to make it known. Their techniques of in-formation attack it from every angle (techniques of "persuasion," "advertisement") con-forming it to models (television, "show biz"). Even politics appropriates the "private," as its essence also depends on "information." All this leads to another ambiguity that should be also pursued: the profound unity between logic and rhetoric, that is, the revaluation of the latter removed from the traditional opposition with the former and somehow assimilated to it. The philosopher-scientist, become "post-modern," no longer refutes the sophist, but rather assimilates him. After all it is a "family affair," as Plato already says in the *Sophist*.

The techno-scientific organization of beings repeats and demonstrates in all possible ways that there is no truth other than the public truth of science, but it also adds that the "private" can continue to think about "sense" as it wishes (of course, for as long as this "thinking" remains "private," *i.e.*, without consequence for "public life," for its organization and institutions). At this point, however, it is necessary to know more about the public-private distinction.

17

◆

How One Thinks
(in Private)

The "private" (the "individual," the pride of the West) is a formation of the "public." A private truth can only exist, or can begin to exist, from the point of view of public truth. The mythic world, the societies founded on myth, ignore the opposition public-private. Myth speaks constantly of fathers, mothers and sons, men and women. Sex, love, hatred, and daily work are at the center of its images and its tales, all of which, for us who live *after* the division between public and private, sounds very much "private": the realm of individual affections, sentiments, passions, drives, and needs.

In actual fact, public man hides his "private life" because it is "unbecoming." The President cannot speak in "public" about his sexual preferences or make obvious his personal dislikes. He must speak with a public voice, in the name of the "institution," which is impersonal and disinterested. There is a public eye and a public language—hence the feeling of hypocrisy and the conventional character of public discourse; hence the fact that any allusion to the private (*i.e.*, to sex), besides appearing "unbecoming" in public, produces at the same time irony, hilarity, and ridicule. Myth, on the other hand, can speak of sex all it wants (as often as modern man, after all, "thinks" of sex) without having to worry about being serious, with a frankness that is disconcerting.

Let us now consider more closely the opposition "public and private," which is modeled and conforms, or goes along with, other typical oppositions which are at the basis of ontology, *i.e.*, *episteme* and *doxa* (Parmenides, Plato); awake and asleep (Heraclitus); light and darkness, *nous* and *aisthesis* (Plato but also Parmenides); divine and anthropomorphic (Xenophanes but also Plato, who analogously distinguishes between *theia techne* and *anthropine techne*—divine art and human art). Now, the important point to understand is that, in the beginning, this opposition excludes a dimension of

93

experience that is not really "private," since the private does not yet exist. It is true, however, that this "removed" dimension is displaced in the "private" by the institution of the *logos* and its public truth. Something originally different from the private is subjected and absorbed under the sign of the *logos*, *i.e.*, is distorted in the dimension of the private and assimilated to public truth, which is the condition, the unit of measure of all this process.

On the one hand, we have the thinking common to everyone; on the other, we have private thinking, which is mere opinion, mere imagining. The first element is more and more identified with the soul (Xenophanes, Parmenides, Plato), the second with the body. Hence, we have the removal of the affective and the sexual from public man, differently from myth, which speaks of nothing else. But this opposition also determines the peculiar character of individuality, *i.e.*, of the concept of individual. The gods, instead, are not individuals, are not people; they are not even abstract symbols, or generally forces of nature. And yet every god is well fixed in its character; he is highly concrete *without being an individual*. Hence man has difficulty "thinking" of gods after the division public and private; hence their enigmatic character for rational man, as well as the great amount of nonsense that has been said and written about the gods of mythology.

The "private," therefore, is he who on the one hand has a soul that partakes of universal thinking and public truth, and on the other, has a dreaming and nocturnal psyche, that is, an imaginative faculty that characterizes him as empirical man and not as public man. This is how psychology's hegemony originates with all the paradoxes we have seen. For instance, this is how the problem of the "parts" of the soul in Plato, Aristotle, Aquinas, and so on originates, until we get to Freud's typology and the notion of the unconscious.

At the same time, the individual has a body. (The psyche is the mediating element between him and the soul, the brute and the angel, as Pico della Mirandola says.)[62] The body is his opaque individuality, his "inertia" (says Sartre).[63] If we look at Plato, we see clearly how philosophy is born essentially as a struggle against the body. The philosopher can think with a "pure" mind only if he can remove the body and its "passions." It is natural that at the time of the waning of metaphysics, *i.e.*, of philosophy, there is a reaction aimed at vindicating the body and its "rights," for instance, with Feuerbach and Nietzsche. This vindication, however, is entirely ambiguous to the point of becoming altogether contradictory when it expressly takes on the appearance, as is the case today, of a vindication of the "private." The private, in fact, is a formation of the public, and its naive vindication ends by achieving the opposite result of justifying the rights of the public and its foundations.

Thus, it is not by vindicating the "rights" of the body that the private becomes less private. The body experienced (*esperito*) by the private is precisely its being constituted as private by the public. Furthermore, the reversal of a dualism always confirms the dualism and its "logic." Thus, the "public" crisis we are living today, the frenzy of the body, nudity, sex, *etc.*, is nothing more than the despair and disorientation of the private, the last degree of its non-sense and not at all its "liberation." This is suggested by the mere fact that there is nothing more public, more conformist, more exploited by the strategies of the mass media than the celebrations and ostentations of the private, its daily and nightly carnivals, its "popular" spectacles and infectious "feasts," namely, its mass snobbery and operetta-like travesties.

But the question to ask is: Of what is "the private" *deprived*, insofar as it is the other side, *alter ego*, of the "public"? Or to put it another way: What is removed and hidden (by confining it to the private) by the light of the *logos* and its public truth? The issue is too complex to give a cogent, theoretical reply here, which, at this point in our inquiry, could not be fully comprehended. To arrive at an answer, in the briefest time possible, we turn to an example that can show us the way. Let us suppose that a man is walking down a street on a windy day. He is headed for the bank, where he has some business to do that is essential to the daily survival of his family. What does this man do while walking? Naturally, he "thinks." Let us focus on this "thinking."

We all know what and how "we think" while we walk and, in general, while we go about our many daily chores, that is, while we live. We know it, naturally, without really "knowing it." We have never "paid attention" to it. For this reason James Joyce's *Ulysses* still creates amazement in most of its readers. Heidegger, too, has observed that man always speaks, day and night; in him "one speaks" always. But what kind of language is it? Even if we just observe it superficially we notice that it is very different from the language of everyday "public" communication. It is neither a completely verbal language, *i.e.*, expressed in words and sentences, nor completely non-verbal. It proceeds in an erratic, confused, discontinuous manner and is made up of many layers at once, some more important than others, some going completely unnoticed unless the effort is made to focus on them. One could say that there are different levels of "silence" in the silent man who thinks and speaks to himself or, to be more precise, who lets "one speak" within himself.

But where does this language come from? Truly, we know as little about it as we know about dreams. To say, as one usually does, that it is a language of "images" makes the issue even more complex and paradoxical, since we know even less about images. But let us see how we would describe the situation of our example in the light of common sense and common knowledge. We would certainly say that there is a *real* man walking along a *real* street in a *real* day with *real* wind. Meanwhile, "within" his (*real*) head, a private "movie" takes place: fantasies, reflections, remembrances, plans, images, emotions, *etc.* This is what we would say. You will have noticed, however, that at a certain point our language became metaphorical. When we say that "within" the head of the man a "movie" takes place, we cannot add the word "real." In fact, it is not "properly" speaking a movie but only "so to speak." And were we to open our man's head we would not "see" at all, in the proper sense, his images, fantasies, heartaches, and not even his perceptions. And what is most extraordinary, he himself does not really "see" all this in the way, for example, that he sees the trees shaken by the wind.

Our man of the example is the sole witness to all we have called his internal and private world. This private experience is his and his alone, which is to say that it has no public reality, but does not mean that it is not "real," in its own way, real for him and for us who have similar experiences all the time. But in what way is it "real"? We are aware that the description of the example given by our common sense (*i.e.*, the "sense" common to all of us since we are all part of it) is entirely obscure and even absurd, if for no other reason than we know very well that "real" things (man, street, wind, *etc.*) are constituted *for us* through that invisible experience and *not in that same real way*, for instance, as perception. There is man and there is wind, but where is the perception of the wind?

Let us look closer at *what* the man is thinking, or at what we suppose he may be thinking. To simplify, let us say that he thinks, more or less at the same time and at different levels of attention, awareness, and relative continuity, about five things: (*a*) his daughter, who at this moment is away in another city; (*b*) the wind, which is bothering him but also refreshes him; (*c*) the bank and the street on the way to the bank; (*d*) his wife; and (*e*) an approaching car on which instinctively and prudently he is keeping an eye. Once again, common sense says that these thoughts "correspond" to real things, associated, however, in his head, with "states of mind," *i.e.*, with fear (of the car), annoyance-pleasure (at the wind), nostalgia (for his daughter), and so on. Common sense reasons as follows: there is a big real world with real objects, such as cars, banks, streets, and cities—all objects that are in a real space, at rest or in motion. But in this world there is also "man," a real object in a world of real objects, who is also in motion and at rest within the common and public space of the world—billions of men in motion and at rest. But in the heads of these men, of these small and strange animals, there is a never-ending turmoil, as tumultuous as it is silent, of moods, thoughts, images, desires, remembrances, sensations, and so on.

Clearly, this is a typical pan-oramic or "public" description, which presupposes and requires a universal eye, both external and public. In describing our example at the level of common sense, it is practically as if we were telling a "story." Our description takes the typical standpoint of the omniscient narrator. Like a novelist, we take up the position of a universal and privileged observer. The novelist knows everything and sees everything. He looks here and there, now following this character, now that character. He only needs to turn his head and there he is in the street with his man and at the same time within his head but also in the car and in the head of the driver, and so on. Then, suddenly, he changes cities and observes the daughter, her movements, her words, and can even listen to her thoughts and even know things that are in her soul and that she herself ignores. There is one thing only he cannot do: violate the laws of time beyond a certain limit. He can run ahead and double back in time, but he can only observe things and narrate them sequentially, one after the other, according to the laws of the word, as de Saussure says.

This look is essentially metaphysical. It is the look that posits being (public reality) and time; that *gives* being and *gives* time and presents them as gifts to rational man. This look is "psycho-historical," as I have explained in *Beyond the Sign*.[64] Common sense, offspring of a thinking common to everyone, is completely captivated by it. There is one thing, however, that common sense has not asked and that, in fact, it has specifically "removed" from its descriptions. It has not asked *how* the man of our example lives his experience—that is, how everyone of us would live it in his same situation: in the street, on a windy day, with the daughter far away, going to the bank, *etc.*

First of all, we have to recognize the fact that the man of the example, being one of us, one like us, *i.e.*, a man of common sense, would live his experience the way we have just described. He, too, "sees" himself in an objective public world, in a *real* street of a *real* city, *etc.* He, too, "sees" in image his daughter in another city, at a public distance from his city, just as the bank and the car are meters and kilometers away, if we measure them, or seconds, minutes, and hours away if we travel or walk. And, last, he sees himself "lived," "crossed" by thoughts, intentions, memories, conjectures, whims, emotions and so on. In fact, this man, which we all are, has for a long time now "internalized" the public look and has made it a part of his common everyday experience. This is how, at the same time, he can be a private man, with his personal problems and vicissitudes and with his private dreams, which he would be very reluctant to completely confess in public.

But, on the other hand, what he is experiencing is something else again, or is *also* something else. We will try to express this "something else" in a proposition: he experiences "here" (lives here) what he experiences, but he is experiencing it in conjunction with manifold "theres" which, in their turn, are really "here," just as he, in his turn, is really "there," according to an intricate and complex network of relations that always and continuously interpret *each other*, in a way speak to *each other*, and in so doing modify *each other*.

This proposition is not at all simple. To really understand its meaning (which will be clearer much later in our journey), we must first *destroy* the public objects that we usually consider to be real *in themselves*, in their public character, forgetting that they are instead "constructed" by that public eye and public *logos* in whose light we have been educated, been brought up, and have learned to speak and think. It is not an easy task, since it undermines precisely the most habitual certainties of common sense on which we constantly rely to live and function. Somehow, we have to activate a "counter-vision" that will enable us to understand how "man," "street," "daughter," "wind," "bank," "car," "city," *etc.* are objects with public meaning, in the light of the public eye. These objects *are there* for *this* public eye, strengthened and corroborated by the intersubjective-public language which, in fact, says "man," "wind," "city," *etc.* We forget their public-inter-subjective constitution, which establishes them as "common truths," as truths and realities common to everyone in common thinking and speaking.

The real experience, the real encounter, however, is never *just* with the "man" or with the "street." The man of our example, as anyone in his place, does not walk along the street *just* as a "public" place. To be sure, he makes use of this public knowledge that he has internalized. This is how he *orders* his movements, finalizing them for *public ends*—avoiding being run over by the car and arriving at the bank as quickly as possible. His actions take into account public mental schemes: the car is there, I am here, the bank is over there. But this is not really all of it. He also encounters the street in another way. He lives its atmosphere, is attracted or repelled by it, observes it or not, and so on. We could say that there is always an "emotional" encounter, even if it is only indifference, which is an emotion by default. But as soon as we say "emotion" or "emotional," these words stand for us for something referring or relative to a "private" or "internal" event. The "real" street is so and so (wide or narrow, straight or curved, sunny or shaded), but how our man "lives" it is his business; it is an entirely private matter. But we know now that "private facts" are a formation and a consequence of the public eye and that these divisions are neither original nor unproblematic. Therefore, let us take a point of view different from the obvious one provided by common sense and its public truths.

Let us try to imagine, for example, that the objective knowledge of things, as they are in themselves, does not come *first* and our emotional reaction *second* (or *apart*, in *interiore homine*). Let us imagine, instead, that the "emotional relation" is the original and fundamental approach to things, *on* which the objective world of knowledge is founded and constructed. Heidegger suggests something similar in *Being and Time* when he speaks of "emotive tonality," thus opening up an extraordinarily valuable topic which, however, he never fully pursues. Let us try to understand, therefore, the proper meaning of what we called "emotional relation," being careful not to classify it as a feeling or a state of mind that is added "psychologically," within the man's head, to "real" bodies and to "real" public objects. Let us think of it as that relation that literally "opens up the world" (opens up being-in-the-world). As a first step, let us keep in mind three points.

1. There is no "world" or "man" already constituted, placed one in front of the other, one external to the other, or one within the other. This way of thinking is a "logical" scheme, a "public" point of view in terms of which we interpret experience for certain reasons, but it *is* neither the whole experience nor its first and original manifestation.

2. What there is, instead, which is even more basic, is a *determined* relation, or many *determined* relations. Let us limit ourselves to just one relation, for the sake of simplicity, to the relation of our man to the wind whereby he is *in the* wind and *with the* wind.

3. "Man" and "wind," however, are public objects and effects. If we wish to return the relation man-wind to its basic structure, we must express ourselves, say, as follows: the relation with atmospheric phenomena, of which the wind is a particular case, is constitutive of being-in-the-world.

Even so, this relation is not expressed well; but let us go on and try to clarify the foregoing by correcting it and modifying it as much as possible to suit our purpose. Insofar as man "comes into the world" (in the full sense of the expression) he is ex-posed, thrown into the *open*.[65] He dwells originally in light and darkness, in heat and cold, in silence and noise, in quiet and storm. All these experiences of relations, and naturally infinite others, are originally constitutive of his existence, of his *being-there* as *body* that shudders, feels heat and light, is fearful or is calm, *etc.* Obviously, even here, we must not think that *first* there is a body that *then* shudders or is hot, *etc.* This shuddering, this feeling hot, *etc.* constitute what we call *then*, at the level of public meaning and public objects, "body." If we desist from taking the body as an object in itself, as already constituted and existing in itself; if we stop looking at it from outside (and not even from inside by internalizing an external mode of seeing); if we give up this external objective-panoramic view, then, the body, too, as public object in the public world, will fade away. Let us keep, rigorously, to experiencing *the* body, to the experiencing *of the* body, which in this experiencing is not yet "body," with its public-conceptual-objective unity. That experiencing is precisely the shuddering, the sweating, the breathing quietly or with difficulty, *etc.*—all this *is* progressively the body. There is, in other words, an establishing of relations that place *it* in relation to the world or, better, that open it to the world, to the *how* of the world, to the how of becoming world *for* a body which shudders, sweats, *etc.*—relations that *make* it "world."

The type of relation just described is never lacking. The man of our example, however, takes it very little into account, like all of us men of the techno-scientific *ratio*, after all. We arrange everything under the rubric of public objects and translate these experiences by the public expression "atmospheric phenomena." Nonetheless, we know very well how "atmospheric phenomena" can often "curiously" influence our "moods." The man of our example has noticed the wind well before saying to himself: "It's windy today." In actual fact, he has "felt" the wind and has reacted with annoyance, irritability, but also with a strange pleasure at "being in the wind," with its intimation of a somewhat exciting day, with a vague sense of danger ahead and with whatever "sense of adventure" there is in it. Perhaps he has *felt* a similarity between going against the wind and the events of his life which worry him but which, at the same time, excite his vitality, his capacity to "react" and not to be dismayed. In all these ways, in fact, the wind has influenced his "mood," which does not happen frequently to someone living in the city rather than in the country, where nature is a more present and determining factor. The ancients paid great attention to "atmospheric phenomena," "making them public," in their own fashion, as gods and in their myths. But in all these examples there is one constant, "mood." Every experiencing entails a mood, even if it is just indifference.

"Mood" goes up and down, comes and goes, but in its own way is always there. "Why?" Heidegger asks. Nobody knows. It is such an ephemeral phenomenon that nobody "pays much attention to it."[66] And yet, its presence is the constant of every experiencing. Generally speaking, it has already been "decided" that a mood is a "psychological" phenomenon, *i.e.*, not very "real." But nothing *real* could be encountered without "mood," without fear or attraction, desire or curiosity, repulsion or need. It is in "mood," with "mood," for "mood," that what we have here called "constitutive relations" or "originary relations" are continuously occurring. This is how the relation opens itself up *to the* world and opens *the* world.

To speak of "mood" as a mere psychological phenomenon but not very "real" and to speak, instead, of the wind experienced (*esperito*) by the man of the example as something "real," which has nothing to do with the mood of that experience, is the usual way in which public truth asserts itself and *its* view and confines to the "private" what does not conform to it.[67] Now we know, however, that what is hidden and distorted by the public eye are precisely the constitutive relations, *i.e.*, those we call "atmospheric." Let us try to understand better, then, what we mean by the expression "constitutive relations" and try to see them concretely at work in experience.

18

◆

The Sign-Symbol Relation

Even in this case, we will make use of an example. We shall take our starting point from the famous interviews which the Swiss psychologist Jean Piaget conducted with children. One of these children, when asked to speak of the moon, replied: "When I walk the moon follows me. It's me who moves it."[68] In the example, the child's looking and walking are related to the moon. We can easily imagine that they are also related to many other things such as the sun, the house, the trees, *etc.* Generally speaking, we can say that there is no such thing as "walking" without these or other relations. To be sure, even the man of the previous example encounters the relations of foot and pavement, even if he pays little attention to them and even if he has completely forgotten the original scary and adventurous attempts, bewildering and intoxicating, that he experienced many years ago when he first learned how to walk.

To limit ourselves just to the example of the moon, it must be said that before being taken and made "public" as a celestial body, or as a satellite of the earth, the moon reveals itself and belongs to experiences of constitutive relations, *i.e.*, constitutive of being-in-the-world. There is a constitutive relation between man (child) and moon. This does not mean, however, that there is a man + moon + their relation. The poles, which in public form we call "man" and "moon," are constituted correlatively and together precisely in the relation, never outside or prior to it.

Moon, therefore, occurs in the occurrence of man. But how does it occur? How is it an *event* in the constitution of the being-in-the-world of man? First of all and in general, moon occurs as a sign, as a *sign relation*. In fact, everything that occurs is a sign, a being-for or a standing-for, a referring. For us, there is no relation with events, with "things," if not as sign relations. This sign, however, should not be understood as an object that stands

101

between the "real" man and the "real" moon; as a perception that exists *in the* head but that no one sees except the interested party, mysteriously. What we call "sign" is more properly an "originary sign relation," a relation that posits, precisely at its poles, the child's "look" and what he "looks-at" as moon. Let us try to understand the sign relation using our example.[69] We are really dealing neither with "moon" nor with "child," but rather with a "cosmic" relation of light, a relation of "seeing," or, better yet, of "having-to-see" (*aver-da-vedere*).

If we picture the relation as a triangle, at its three poles or angles we can place the three elements that, generally, play a role in every sign relation: the *Representamen*, or what functions as sign; the *Object*, or what the sign refers to; and the *Interpretant*, or the "interpreting" response that is addressed to the Object by the Representamen.[70] In our example, therefore, the *Representamen* will be a certain luminous radiance of a celestial object (we are really saying too much but only in order to be better understood). The response of the *Interpretant* is the turning toward, via the radiance, to what the radiance points and reveals or, somehow discloses, namely, that *Object* that public language calls "moon." Thus, there is a *being-illuminated-having-to-see* (*essere illuminati avendo da vedere*). This is what happens primordially, described imperfectly and approximately to be sure, between the "look," which *is* the child's (which is "child"), and the "looked-at," which *is* "moon."

However strange it may appear to the already consolidated common sense, the "look" here is somehow reciprocal. The child feels, at the same time, that he is being "looked at" (and perhaps protected) by the moon. To call this a child's "psychological fantasy" is once again to assume "child" as an already constituted "reality" and, naturally, "moon" too as an object in itself. This means being unable to understand the primordial and constitutive character of the relation "moon-child."

Even the adult looks at the moon feeling somehow that he is being "looked at" and perceives this look sometimes as benevolent and sometimes as malevolent; among his most common expressions there is, for example, "to be moonstruck," and so on.[71] Why? Nobody knows. Common sense says that these are just fantasies, oddities. The psychoanalyst says that these are just subconscious "projections." But what "sense" would man's "look" have if, among infinite other things, it could not have as its originary constituent also "looking at" the moon, being-able-to-see *by* its light?

If we have understood the general character of the sign relation we can focus, then, on an essential trait of its structure. As sign the relation stands-for, refers, as-signs a task, a having-to-be, as Heidegger would say. This means that the relation, by positing its two poles, places them at the same time at a distance. The two things are one: positing the poles means positing a (their) distance. The relation, then, in essence, makes the *distance* happen. It can be said, then, that *the experience of the distance is the essential trait of the originating sign relation*. In our example, the child is *turned to* the moon. He is constituted by this being turned to, obviously not because it *is* the moon, but because he "is caught" in the turning-toward (*dirigersi-verso*); he is caught in looking at it as his having-to-see. He sees *himself* looking at it or, to be more precise, he sees *himself* in himself. There is a seeing that only later gives way to a seeing *himself*, to a seeing *himself* looking. Naturally, this goes for all the relational experiences of the child. This is how he is caught by the mother, by toys, by sleep, *etc.* From the totality of these global experiences, he "springs forth," precisely, as "child," as that child he has become and becomes.

To return to our example, then, in the sign relation, and for the sign relation, the moon is always "at a distance," namely is *elsewhere*. But it is "elsewhere" by being *here*, by signaling here its present absence. Naturally, this mode of being "at a distance" also assigns to the child his *where*, which is such starting from the *elsewhere* of the moon. Generally, there is a distance that resides (*di stanza*), is here: the presence of an absence.[72] In the example of the child who pulls the moon along as he walks and, thus, compares himself to it, the child is measuring the distance of the moon and at the same time his relational presence. It is important to note that what happens with the moon or the sun or the lamp in his room also happens to the child with his own body. He observes his hands and feet, he takes them, sucks them. They are at a distance, always *elsewhere* and in a way that progressively also limits the *where* of his grasping, sucking, which constantly has to be reached. This is how he constitutes himself *in the* body and *with the* body and also *as* body, according to originating distances-presences that function always as norms of measurement and placement for all other distances, making possible basic orientation.

"Distance" is the knot of our question, and now we must turn our attention to it. Within the span of this distance, so to speak, we must try to discern two processes that are as distinct as they are simultaneous and describe them in their in-different difference. We can call these two processes the *sign relation* and the *symbolic relation*. The unity or interaction of these two relations we shall call "experience." However, this term should not be understood according to the current, empirical, and more narrow sense of "experience," as something that has to do with sensation as opposed to concept and so on, but only and exactly as the one we have indicated: the unity of the sign-symbol relation.

THE SIGN RELATION

We have already pointed out some aspects of this relation that now must be further developed. The event of the sign, insofar as a relation occurs with it, determines a "polar" space, *i.e.*, a space characterized by a tension in polarity: (*a*) The sign is a having-to, a task or a having-to-respond. The event of the sign does not define a mere passive contemplation but an "emotional" tension, a "practical" or "pragmatic" situation. There is an expectation that has to be corresponded to. (*b*) Thus the event of the sign determines the corresponding pole, *i.e.*, the "who" and the "how" of responding, namely, the interpretant. (*c*) The interpretation, then, by activating the Signified of the sign, brings forth the pole Object, *i.e.*, *what* the sign refers to.

In our example, the radiance of the moon is the sign which, taken as such, posits the corresponding pole, *i.e.*, determines the *here* of responsive looking. Such a sign determines the "here" as the *where* in which it is announced. Thus the sign already places at a distance, since it directs the having-to toward the *elsewhere* (directs the having-to-look-toward, directed precisely by the sign). The sign, we could also say, grasps who-is-looking-on in his *where*, *makes* him looking-on in his where, since the sign signifies to him an *elsewhere* from his where, from that where which is sign-ed (*segnato*) by the sign itself—an elsewhere-to-look.

Therefore, the "elsewhere," that-for-which the sign stands, namely the Object, emerges at one with this distance, this distancing. In our case, moon, as elsewhere of the where of having-to-look, which in the where "sign-als" (*fa segno*). Moon cannot be grasped by the hand or caught in a well or pond.

The Object is placed at a distance that in principle cannot be bridged. This goes for the moon as for any other object of vision, and even for our own body, which we can certainly touch and feel being touched. In every touching and being touched, in fact, the Object, as Husserl says, "conceals itself," vanishes and escapes the "grasp." All we can do is multiply the signs of the Object to infinity. We can keep looking at the moon, photograph it through a telescope lens, even invade its space, walk across it. Every action gives way to many more signs that posit the Object as the one pointed to and as the beyond of this pointing.

In more general terms, we could say that this is how we experience infinite semiosis, the infinite referral of which Peirce speaks and in which every "reality" is caught. In fact, what we ordinarily call reality is only the Signified of this recurrent experience. This, however, is not *everything* we experience (the sign, the distance, the Object, and the infinite referral). From its depths arises a more profound structure of experiencing (*esperire*), which is what we call here "the symbolic relation."

THE SYMBOLIC RELATION

By occurring, the sign institutes the distance and the *difference* (*i.e.*, between child and moon) and at the same time chains them together in an infinite referral ("The moon follows me," says the child). But this is possible for the sign on the basis of a more profound *identity*: moon and child are posited in their difference because together they constitute a *symbolic whole* (a *symbolon*). The identity at issue is what resides [*di stanza*] in the difference, just as the difference is distance of the identity. In Heideggerean terms we could say that there is an originary belonging-together from which every difference takes place, or every judgment, in the Hegelian sense of *Ur-teil*, the original division.[73] But, first of all, the meaning of the expressions *symbolic* and *symbolon* must be clarified.

The meaning of the word *symbol* has nothing to do here with its usual meaning whereby, for instance, scales are the symbol of justice or lion is the symbol of strength; nor are we invoking the traditional theory (entirely unsatisfactory and erroneous) according to which the symbol is a product of the "spirit" of man, of his creative or imaginative faculty. With the word "symbol" we are referring, instead, to the original Greek meaning derived from the verb *sym-ballein*, which means "putting together," "uniting," "bringing together." The *symbolon* was originally the broken half of an object which, when brought together with its other half, could serve as sign of recognition. The *symbolon*, thus, is the fragment of a whole that does not exist or no longer exists. Because of this characteristic, the symbol turns out to be a most particular sign. Above all, it *is* a sign since, as any sign, it refers (the fragment refers to the object not yet broken of which it is a part, a sign), but differently from any sign. The symbol does not refer to an "other," to a "different from itself" but still to itself, to the "same"—*the other to which the symbol refers is still itself*. In fact, the broken whole of the symbol refers to the same whole not yet broken. This also goes for every one of its parts. Each part stands for the whole unity from which it derives and represents. Each one is there to say that it is what it is because it derives its being from that unity that con-tained it, that kept it together. Let this brief explanation suffice, and let us now turn to our example to further clarify the meaning of the expressions "symbolic relation" and "symbol" (or *symbolon*).

We are saying that originally moon and child are *the same* and that this sameness is "symbolic." They are the same just as a fragment, the half of a broken piece, has its sameness, its original unity of meaning in the union with the other half. This symbolic sameness is what determines moon and child as polarities of the sign relation, as poles of *their* distance and sign difference. Thus, we could say that the moment the moon *signs* [*segna*] the child as "child" (child-who-looks-at-the-moon), and the child designates moon as the unreachable Object of his looking, the distance erupts and breaks the whole of the "sameness" "moon-child." The sign of moon posits the child in the presence of *his* "Other" and, in so doing, conceals that this other is still the "Same." The child, therefore, has in the Other his own "sameness." But this Other is really nothing (*nulla*) of what he is.[74] (It is the distance, the absence, and in this sense nothing [*nulla*] of the child, of his presence.) The child, thus, has (is) the Other as Other, *i.e.*, as unreachable Object and not as "himself."

In fact, the original unity of the *symbolon* (moon-child) "is" not *in* experience. Indeed, in its most profound structure, experience *is* really this not-being-there of the original unity (which, all the same, in its own way "is there," as distance and referral, *i.e.*, as sign but not as unitary or unified symbol). That is why we speak of "symbolic *relation*," since what there *is* is always symbol in the sense of being "fractured," "broken," "partial"; in the sense of referring to a totality that is not there, namely, as sign of a totality that has never been. There is no originating symbolic unity unless as *relation*, reference, "intentionality," "sign of nothing [*nulla*]." The symbolic relation is the relation to one's own sameness as to one's own nothing (*nulla*).

In following the moon, therefore (and the moon, the child), the child is following himself. But of that symbolic unity moon-child *there is nothing* (*ne è nulla*). This nothing (*nulla*) resides (*di stanza*) as distance, sign. In fact, the occurrence of the symbolic nothing (*nulla*), of the referral to one's own sameness which is not there, determines the sign-distance with its poles. It follows that every sign is, in the last instance, *sign of nothing* (*segno di nulla*). The child has in nothing (*nulla*) his own sameness. He himself, in looking at the moon, is sign of nothing (*nulla*).

This nothing (*nulla*), however, is not the negation of what he is—a determined child looking at the moon (determined insofar as, since looking at the moon). Nothing (*nulla*) here is not equivalent to nothing (*niente*). Nothing (*nulla*), instead, is precisely what determines the child *as what he is*: "child looking at the moon." He has his own sameness, *is* his own sameness insofar as he is nothing (*nulla*). This means that the nothing (*nulla*) of the originary symbolic unity, its presence in the form of absence or nothing (*nulla*), is what makes possible the child's look, the child-looking-toward the moon, as his own sameness and at the same time as his nothing (*nulla*), as *his* Object or elsewhere of *his* where. Precisely symbolic nullity (*nullità*) makes the child what he "is," *his* "being determined."

With these last reflections something extremely important and decisive has happened, namely, the end of the Parmenidean strategy. Being, determined being, to be precise, turns out in fact to be nothing (*nulla*). Being and nothing (*nulla*) are the Same (a nothing [*nulla*], as we said, which is distance and not nothing [*niente*]). The truth of Parmenides' truth has reached its ultimate sense, since thinking is now being directed toward a new perspective, and a new horizon opens up as sign of a new path. A brief reflection on the concept of "totality" can illustrate, by way of analogy, the "tonality" of the opening toward which we are heading.

The symbolic relation has taught us this simple "truth": the part *is*. The whole, instead, the totality, *is not* (is nothing [*nulla*]). It is true that the whole shines in every part and beginning in every part (as that absence, or nothing [*nulla*], or distance that makes the part what it *is*), but precisely for this reason and *in* this part, the whole *is* not. This not being (there) is the nullity of the part. That is why it is "finite" (de-finite): it shines, (not) having nothing (*nulla*) behind and before itself. It is, in every sense, in-complete. And thus, it is always already complete. Therefore, in this sense, it is "perfect" (*perfecta*).

The traditional metaphysical conception, instead (*e.g.*, the Kantian-Hegelian one or, more generally, the "Christian" conception) claims that the part is imperfect and that only the whole, the totality, deserves the term "perfection"; the infinite, not the finite, is perfect. Instead, just the opposite is true. We have said that the whole that shines in every part and beginning in every part (as nothing [*nulla*] of the part) is precisely what determines the perfect completeness of the part. Why then is the part not simply the whole? Because every part is always a having-to-complete, a response, a lack. The child's look *toward* the moon lacks its Object, to which he responds and toward which he is turned. The part is part because it lacks and turns-toward, but what it lacks and turns-toward is nothing [*nulla*]. It waits. For nothing (*nulla*). This tension is "perfect" since it lacks nothing (*nulla*). This nothing (*nulla*) is precisely the edge that de-limits it and completes it.

There are moments in experience in which nothing (*nulla*) in its most pregnant definiteness, is attained, for instance, in the sense of "having-nothing-more-to-attain" either as a result of a withdrawing from any turning-toward or as a result of an attaining satisfied with the nullity of its possession. In these moments of con-fusion what is properly attained, then, is the full in-difference between being and non-being, between beings and nothing (*nulla*). Any alternative question to "Why are there beings rather than nothing?" as Heidegger after Leibniz asks, would reveal itself to be (if ever such a questioning could take place, which it cannot) what it is: nonsensical, since beings and nothing (*nulla*) are attained together, in their reciprocal ek-stasis, in their indifferent difference, in the common dwelling (*stare*) of their distancing (*distare*). Maybe the words *eros* and *thanatos*, in their reciprocal belonging-together, indicate adequately the tonality of the experience to which we refer. Maybe the play of Art aims, deep down, at this essential place of experience.

19

◆

The Place of Experience

Now we must investigate more closely the knot that holds together the sign and symbol relations. This knot, in fact, is the *place of experience* and, as we shall see, also characterizes the "crucial truth." First of all, let us recapitulate briefly what has been said so far. The sign, we said, occurs as Response. The event of the sign is what *makes way* for the Response; there is sign because there is response. It is the Response, in fact, that re-cognizes the sign as what stands for, as what refers. The "radiance" refers to the moon and becomes "moonlight." This is how the Response cor-responds to the sign, to its being-for, to its referring. This correspondence is the basis and the foundation of judgment. Heidegger glimpsed at this, but was far from being clear about it. By cor-responding to the sign, the Response is what "turns-toward." The pole of this turning-toward is what we call Object. By cor-responding, the Response posits the Object as its Other, as the Other of the sign to which the sign refers. All the relations alluded to here obviously occur at one with the event of the sign. They *are* the event of the sign in its global occurrence; they constitute, in a single movement of occurrence, the taking place of the sign relation, its opening up as "polar space."

Now, the place of this taking place is essentially *ambiguous*. It limits the *where* of the Response (of the Interpretant's response) but only insofar as it stands for an *elsewhere* (Object) that announces itself, "signals" itself in the very same "where," namely, as the presence of an absence, as a distance at which it resides (*di stanza*). This means that the "where" (the Response) has its truth outside itself. The Response is in relation to what is not there and can never be there. The Response, in fact, as we saw, has in an Other its own sameness. This ambiguity is projected and, finally, centered on the Object. The sign is *taken for* the Object (in fact, we say that the sign *stands in the place of the Object*). The sign, therefore, in a certain way *gives* the Object, but by keeping it at a distance and substituting it for its presence. The sign is taken for the Object, which is opened up to the relation, but is also distinct from it, since the sign itself gives the Object in the manner of its infinite withdrawal (infinite semiosis).

The ambiguity of which we speak, however, is more profound than it may at first appear. It pertains first of all precisely to our way of referring to the sign. When we say, in fact, that the sign "gives" the Object but, at the same time, "keeps it at a distance"; when we say that it "substitutes" for its presence so that the Object itself "withdraws"; all these expressions, in short, are indicative of a certain way of experiencing and thinking about experience that makes one believe that beyond the sign *there is* the Object qua "object." These expressions focus on the Object, understood as the unifying pole of common, intersubjective responding. As such, we could say, the Object is "historicized" by the sign, in the sense of the Platonic *episteme historike*.

The possibility of the emergence of "public" realities and truths resides precisely in these operations. In this interpretation of the *logos*, and more generally of the sign, the world of thinking common to everyone takes root. This is how the sign acquires the function of *intermediary* between the responding and knowing pole ("subject") and the known pole ("object"). From here emerges the enigma and the mystery of what the subject-in-itself (or transcendental subject) and the object-in-itself (or transcendental object) may be, and how it may be—what Kant defined as being equal to x, and Maimon interpreted (as did Peirce) as the ideal pole of infinite approximations. On these foundations the cognitive strategy of the philosophical and scientific *ratio* has always been played out, with its enigma or, as Heidegger would say, with its "un-founded mystery."[75]

Now, however, we must cut the knot of all these ambiguities by simply remarking that the sign does *not* give the Object, by keeping it at the same time at a distance, because there is no Object beyond the sign. Instead, the Object *is* in the sign. It is a system of signs coordinated by a unity of meaning, as Husserl would say.[76] To say that the sign "gives" and "withdraws" is equivalent to attributing to the sign the same *kinesis* of Being postulated by Heidegger on the basis of an ontology and, finally, of an onto-theology, even though it is "negative" and thus impossible. This means that this mode of speaking and thinking assumes as implicitly valid, as the sole meaning of experience, the onto-logy of the world and of a thinking common to everyone, even though leading it to the impasse of the absurd and the mysterious.

What we are calling here Object and Interpretant linked by the Response are not the active and perhaps "mysterious" subjects of the relation, but the poles of the space of the sign, the internal polarized directions of the sign relation. Since they are internal to this relation, the poles are not able to constitute any foundation of *sense*. They are affected by an infinite referral that is the essential character of knowledge. (Knowledge, we observed earlier, can proceed in an indefinite manner, can always "increase," without ever attaining the foundation of sense.) The poles of the sign relation are extrinsic to the logic of sense, cannot carry or tolerate it. It is by sheer ambiguity that they are said to be, on the strength of their referring, *i.e.*, of their cognitive logic, nonsensical and mysterious.

This unnoticed ambiguity is behind the contradictory "silence" to which Heidegger and Wittgenstein lead us. This is the contradictory conclusion of the *ratio* (of the "history of being" and its onto-logy), which despite thinking *against* itself (nihilism) is unable to discern in thinking anything other than itself and reduces all experience to itself. Where, however, does the "logic" or thinking of *sense* have its foundation if this foundation has always been misunderstood as logic of the sign and for this reason been declared "mysterious"? Nihilism contradicts itself since it says what on the strength of its logic, conceived as the only possible one, it cannot say. Its "no" is equivalent to the metaphysical "yes" it wants to destroy.

But we still have to ask what motivates that impossible metaphysical assertion, asserted nonetheless, which wants to provide the foundation (*i.e.*, the sense) while being constantly "deferred" in an "historical" process of infinite interpretations, as well as that nihilistic assertion which, once having recognized the inevitability of infinite referral and infinite interpretations, asserts, then, its non-foundation, *i.e.*, its non-sense and mystery? In our terms the problem can be stated as follows: how, on what basis, does the sign pro-duce the distance? Or, in more general and simpler terms, *to what* does the sign refer? In fact, to say that the sign refers to the Object means to assume the point of view of the sign (its "logic") and to be caught in it (to be fooled by it). What the sign refers to, what withdraws in the sign, is shown by the symbolic relation that is at one with its occurrence *in the* sign and *with the* sign. To understand what this means is the knot that now must be unraveled.

The occurrence of the sign, of its characteristic distance, has its visible and essential investment in the Response. The Response, in fact, is what makes possible the unfolding of the space of the sign relation. In terms of our example, the simple act of turning to look at the moon is what makes the child the child-looking-at-the-moon and the moon the child's looked-toward, by means of that presence that is sign of moon. But what is exactly the occurrence of the Response?

1. First of all, it is "perceiving the distance." "Being" is perceived as "having-to-be." This entails being pulled out of, being distanced, *i.e.*, being displaced by the original unity of the *symbolon* (there where, to refer to our

example, moon and child were the same). The Response, we could say, cor-responds, or better, *has-to* correspond, *not* by corresponding but, precisely, by responding (it responds because it does not correspond and yet cor-responds by responding). The Response is essentially ek-static (proceeds). Having to correspond is the *ecstasy* of the sign.

2. Since it is displaced in the cor-responding, the Response is a being-directed-toward, toward what one has been displaced from.

3. This is equivalent to being, not originary symbolic unity (the originary sameness and self-sameness of moon and child), but symbolic *relation*, as *symbolon*, which has its Other, the Object of its Response in the nothing (*nulla*). The being of the Response is the fragment edged (*orlato*) with nothing (*nulla*). Its *where* is the event of the fissure (*fessura*) (the fissuring, the splitting of the original unity) as the place that looks over the nothing (*nulla*) of the *elsewhere* toward which the Response is directed.

All this involves what has been said so far through our example. The child is placed in the presence of *his* Other, which is at the same time his own sameness, his pro-venance. He has in the Other his own sameness which, however, is nothing (*nulla*) of what he is. Thus, by following the moon, the child follows himself, that himself that is not there except as sign, as presence of an absence. This presence-absence determines the child in his "being": the directing-toward of the look looking at the moon. Viewed from a symbolic perspective, the Response is the return, the way back toward the "self" that is not there or has never been there. Hence a very important consequence follows: *every sign response is, in its essence, also symbolic. It is an image of the whole, i.e., of nothing (nulla).* In this sense, the event of the symbolic relation is nothing more than the coming about of the "fissure," which through distancing posits the Response and its Object in a relation of "sameness." The "fissure" keeps at a distance the Object which, however, is the "same" of the Response, and in this sense "is not there." More properly, then, it must be said that the "fissure" (the event of the symbolic relation) *decenters the Response in itself*. The Response, thus, is sent and destined to fall in nothing (*nulla*) of the Object, in that nothing (*nulla*) that is itself. (Let us remember: this is a constitutive nothing (*nulla*) that determines it to be what it is, since nothing (*nulla*) here is not equivalent to nothing (*niente*), but is the very same coming about of the distance within the sign relation; it is the nothing (*nulla*) of the "fissure" that also occurs and, in this sense, *is there*.

If what has been said is clear, we can begin to perceive the contours of the knot that ties together the sign and symbol relations. However, we have not yet reached bottom. Let us, then, recapitulate from the beginning the *situation* explored so far in the light of these last remarks and of what has happened in them.

The symbolic relation is nothing other than the event of the distance *as* sign (or *in the* sign). One could say that it is the fissure of the sign (what determines it in its being sign, *i.e.*, referral). The "fissure" is assuming the presence (any presence) as having-to-be the absence announced in the sign. In the presence the absence *becomes* sign. This is the same as assuming presence as *referral* on whose basis the Other, the absent, is assumed as Object of the sign, what the sign refers to. However, for the symbolic relation the absent, the Other, is still the Same from which the distance is produced. This last point needs further clarification.

Why is the Other still the Same for the symbolic relation? This assertion, so decisive and fundamental for us, must not give rise to doubts, nor should it be seen as a mere "definition" of the concept of symbol (as that unity that splits in itself and thus is a fragment, *etc.*). I will illustrate the point first by asking a question and then by formulating a hypothesis that will turn out to be absurd.

The question is the following: How else could the *original distance* come about (*i.e.*, the event of the fissure or of the place of all possible ulterior differences) if not from the Same? Let us now formulate the hypothesis against the question that the original distance, instead, can come about from the Other. This hypothesis leads to two absurd conclusions, thus confirming the question that the hypothesis meant to deny. (*a*) If the distance and the difference do not come about from the Same but from the Other, then it has already come about and is no longer the original distance. In fact, in the hypothesis the Other has already been assumed with its distance and difference. (*b*) This supposed distance that should come about from the Other, and not from the Same, would require, then, the presence of the sign, of the sign of the Other. How else could the Other come about if not, precisely, as a sign of its distance and difference? But here we are asking, precisely, how this sign could come about with its distance.

The failure of the hypothesis that has just been demonstrated confirms, therefore, the initial thesis. For the symbolic relation, the Other is still the Same from where the original distance comes about. This is the only possible hypothesis. The original distance, whence all distances originate (*i.e.*, all signs), is the fissuring or the fissure of the Same. Thus, the "situation" can be understood only as follows: there is, or occurs, a coming about of the fissure in the Same. This entails the coming about of the distance between Response and Object.

If we consider that the first moment is more properly symbolic and the second is more properly a sign (although obviously they occur *together* and are one and the same event), then we have exhausted the comprehension of the knot that ties together the sign and symbol relations, considered from the perspective of the Response. But now we should ask: How should we understand the Same? Or, in terms of our example, What does it mean that moon and child are originally the Same? The moment the moon becomes Object for the child, *i.e.*, occurs as sign, it takes on the appearance of Other. What does it mean that this Other was originally the Same (unity "moon-child")?

We have already pointed out many times that this unity "moon-child" *is not* in experience. In experience, instead, there is the "fragment," the *symbolon* as broken fragment, the symbolic *relation*. In terms of our example, there is the child who looks at the moon, the child's look turned to the moon. And the moon? Could we reverse the relation, so to speak, and look at it *from the other side*? Could we say, for instance, that the moon responds to the child, that it has in the child its Other, its truth, its Same?

All this is clearly incomprehensible and absurd. Suddenly we find ourselves flung into an abyss that brings our journey to a halt. We find ourselves in an *aporia*. We cannot see how, sensibly, it is possible to reverse the symbolic relation between its two members or poles of the sign, Response and Object. And yet it *must* be reversible since, as we saw, the foundation of any possible relation must come about beginning from the Same and not otherwise. Furthermore, this *is* precisely the symbolic relation, the relation of sameness and indifference between its different elements. If it *makes sense* to speak of symbolic relation, insofar as it is different from the sign relation, the relation of sameness is its condition, precisely what differentiates it from the sign relation. Otherwise, it would have been just as well to stop at the sign relation, declare that it is all "there is," and add that its coming about was simply a "mystery."

Finally, to stop at this would entail the total "humanization" of the symbol and the sign, now understood as products of the "mind." It would mean relapsing into that metaphysics of the sign (so calmly and unproblematically welcomed by semiologists) that takes the sign as an arbitrary intermediary of human communication and the symbol as the product of fantasies and "allegories" of the "spirit" corresponding to *human* "needs" and to *human* "feelings" but not at all to the "world" (to "being"), which is kept at a standstill in its onto-logic extraneousness and, finally, once more, in its "mystery."

To relapse, at this crucial point, into metaphysical and scientific anthropologism and humanism means relapsing into all the enigmas, ambiguities, and absurdities of the *ratio*, namely, into that psycho-historical strategy from which, with so much hard work, and for so many years, one has tried to take one's distance. Thus, the naive and alarming reply of the child, "The moon follows me. It's *me* who moves it," with all its ambiguities, sheds light, for us, on the edges of the abyss in which we have fallen, an abyss that represents for our discussion the greatest of dangers, an abyss whose darkness we do not know how to escape but in which, on the other hand, it would make no sense to dwell, as nihilism wants.

20

◆

The Moon's Looking

Let us go over the situation of *aporia* and let us examine it.[77] The event of the "fissure" is what severs the symbolic whole, *i.e.*, moon-child. Two pieces or fragments are left, the child and the moon. It is impossible to say, however, what the whole was like *before* it broke (the whole "moon-child"); in fact, it must not be said, it is not *to be said*. Only the sign "says," in its occurrence, in its gazing-at (*mirare-a*)[78] and in its catastrophe in nothing (*nulla*) of the Object.[79] Each of the two poles, we have also observed, has in the Other its own sameness, its pro-venance, but the other is for him nothing (*nulla*), absence, distance. This is how it becomes Object of all its Responses, reference of all its signs, their unreachable beyond.

Let us dwell now on the reciprocity of the two poles. Let us suppose, with a different example, that the symbolic relation does not concern a child looking at the moon but a "looking" relation between mother and child. This is a "convenient" example. It allows for the reciprocity and the reversal of its two poles. It is self-evident that the child has in the mother his provenance, that she is his own sameness, namely, the one from whom he *is*, while she is also for him his specific and constitutive Other. The same is true of the mother who becomes "mother" by having in the child her own sameness and, at the same time, her own specific Other. The example of the relation moon-child is, on the other hand, an "inconvenient" example. How can the moon "respond to" the child? How can it have the child as its "Object"? Is the "inorganic" world not "indifferent" to human signification and to human relations, as nihilism claims?

In actual fact, it is precisely the "inconvenient" example that holds back and conceals *its* truth, but the truth is there, waiting to be "looked at," waiting to be thought. And what has to be thought, first of all, is the nature of the error into which we have fallen, inadvertently and fatally, because of the burden of tradition. This error can be expressed as follows. We have spoken often of a symbolic whole and always with a warning that *it is not in experience*. But already the fact that we *speak* of a symbolic whole, that is, of a *before* (even if not chronologically) in which moon and child were the Same, means assuming the poles of the sign relation as having already occurred (*i.e.*, the looking Response of the future child and its Object, the future moon) and putting them together abstractly a posteriori and externally. We are constructing, thus, an "artificial" third element between the two and with the two and projecting it backward to the "before" of the two, as their original unity.

But this abstract, imaginative reassembling is always and still the work of the public eye of the *ratio*. Inadvertently, we have assumed, or continue to assume, this view every time we have spoken of a symbolic whole or even when we have just alluded to it. We have assumed it despite all our critical cautions and warnings that this symbolic whole is not in experience, *is not there*, and so on. So that, speaking of moon, child, and their relation, we have proceeded according to "common sense" which, as is well known, is only the outcome of a thinking common to everyone and their "panoramic" viewpoints on whose basis the (common) world and all the things in it (including moon, child, and all the rest) are posited.

Thus, we have committed the very error we should not have, all the while going after the place of experience and its knot, of going beyond experience and its concrete occurrence. After all, this is what common sense does every moment with its public-private fantasies. And since we *are* people of common sense, it will be better, on the one hand, to quickly forgive ourselves without too many qualms for the mistakes we have committed and, on the other, to consider the whole episode as a useful lesson and a good example of how the strategy of the *ratio* is always lying in wait for our thinking with its infernal traps disguised as "logic" and "good sense." We should be consoled by the fact that the majority of contemporary thought, whose origins are in neopositivism, analytical philosophy, and similar trends, proceeds happily and unawares on the basis of premises similar to (not to say worse than) those for which we are expressing regret, arousing thus the delight of their "sensible" readers and achieving renown for their great "subtlety."

Let us return now to our problem. What really occurs when we experience? The essential point is that what happens, what we experience, is being *distant* being *near*. This is what must now be understood properly. The sign of moon which in occurring produces the Response is the occurrence of a fissure that con-tains *its* difference. To put it in Heideggerean terms, it keeps the distant near and, thus, occurs as a sign of moon. But the Response, as we have already observed, is a de-centering, *i.e.*, an oc-curring from. From what? From that which in its present absence summons and calls. This being decentered is, properly, a having-to-be, that is, having to reach one's own provenance. It is this provenance, then, that summons and calls.

Let us apply all of this to the child's looking as Response. First of all, the child's Response is not an empty looking. It is not as if the child first looks and then sees the moon. We are speaking here of an original situation in which looking *comes into the world*, emerges in a primordial sense, and emerges exactly because, to use our example, it encounters the moon, *is* the moon's looking. In other words, we could say that looking, as any other act or Response, is characterized originally by its *intentionality*, precisely in the sense in which Heidegger recognized in this notion the deepest and still unresolved problem of Husserl's phenomenology. It is looking *at* something. In our case, a looking aimed at (*ha di mira*) the moon which, in this determined aiming (*aver di mira*) and because of it, is a concrete looking. The Response of the child, therefore, is looking *of* moon. This conclusion is to be taken *in all the fullness and richness of the expression*.

At this point, if there is a name that can be given to the symbolic provenance of the child's looking, this name is precisely "moon," since the looking is literally *made of moon*. In a certain sense, it is the moon which looks at *itself*, which becomes vision, or which makes itself "visible." Naturally, the word "moon" is not to be understood here as the name of a "public object," *i.e.*, as the sign of that public object that in fact the "moon" is. It goes without saying that as word, as linguistic sign of intersubjective communication, the term "moon" is also always already this. This ambiguity is inevitable and fatal. We must neither despair, however, nor attempt to erase it, nor resign ourselves. The knot between sign and symbol relations can neither be erased nor *should be* erased. Instead, it should be thought, without falling into the temptation of transcending it or leaving it in its ambiguity, not understood (unthought).

By saying "moon" we are already in the "public" sign and in the "public" world but, at the same time, the very same word "moon" is made of moon and has a symbolic origin, besides an origin as sign. The ambiguous character of the sign, which obviously reflects the same ambiguity of the sign relation, is what we will understand better later. Let us leave until then the investigation of the problem, and let us try, instead, to assess the decisive step we have taken.

The Response looking-aiming at the moon is a decentering *from the* moon, assuming it as the "toward which" of looking. The same should be said naturally of hearing, as provenance from sounds and noises, *i.e.*, from the rustling of trees in the wind, from the singing of birds, from the sound of objects, and so on. In general, we can say, then, that every Response comes from the "world." But "world" is only the public and collective name that summarizes abstractly the concrete encounter and the concrete event of infinite symbolic events. And yet, if we keep in mind the constitutive ambiguity of our speech, it is not meaningless to affirm, as we are now doing, that the responses of the child are made of world since, for instance, they are made of moon; the child (the future child who will emerge from future encounters and experiences) is made of moon.

This is how it is, then, that its Response cor-responds to the moon as Object, as a sign of which "moon" is the "public" meaning. It corresponds having already corresponded as a symbolic event of the Response, *i.e.*, event of the fissure, as the decentering of the Same and from the Same; from that Same that, in our case, is the world with the appearance of moon. The symbolic dimension, therefore, is not a place of original unities in which moons and children are supposedly present in mysterious and ineffable totalities. Neither is it a place where there are such things as symbols, special realities *beyond* the experiencing of the sign. The symbolic relation is the same event of the "world" in the sign relation, an occurrence of moon as looking, looking of moon. The symbolic relation is the event of the fissure that determines the distance, namely, the moon as looking. But the dwelling (*stanza*) of this distance is that same one (moon) that by occurring appears in image. Every Response has the Same precisely in what it corresponds to. The Response, one could say, "cognizes" because it re-cognizes. This is a truth that philosophy has expressed from its beginnings and that since then has carried with it, misunderstanding it. This Same is the "from which" the Response, in responding or, in our case, in "looking," is decentered and edged (*si orla*)—the moon which occurs as child's looking made of moon. The event of this looking, of this edge (*orlo*) or "looking fissure" (*"fessura vedente"*), posits a presence and at the same time keeps it at a distance—this is how it is a *seeing* (of moon).

But insofar as it posits and keeps at a distance, the event is immediately also a relation to the Object, that is, a sign whose *meaning* is precisely "moon," in the objective "public" sense. Thus, we have a relation between (symbolic) *event* and *meaning* (of sign). This relation is the knot that we were investigating and that ties together the symbolic relation and the sign relation, the knot of their different sameness. On this knot, as we shall see, is established the "crucial truth" with its two in-different faces.

For now, let us note the following. For the sign, the Object is in nothing (*nulla*). It is a referring to an absence that will never in principle become full presence. And after all, what could a "full presence" be if not nothing (*nulla*)? Every presence is a distance, a coming from nothing (*nulla*) and heading toward nothing (*nulla*). For the symbol, instead, the Response in its decentering is in nothing (*nulla*): edge and eye of moon, view of the world. Analogously we could say that for the sign, the meaning, *i.e.*, the public meaning "moon," is nothing (*nulla*) of the event or what erases the event by translating it into an Object always sought after and deferred. For the symbol, instead, the event is nothing (*nulla*) of meaning, what by occurring annuls meaning and keeps it in nothing (*nulla*). It follows that the crucial truth of the knot between event and meaning will appear as a relation between two nothings (*nulla*), reciprocally *determined*. We shall return to these formulas later on to analyze them in greater detail.

21

◆

Being Distant and Near

Now the time has come to go back to our first example of the man walking to the bank. We are now able to analyze it in its more complex signification. We said that the man experiences *here* what he experiences in connection with multiple *theres* which, in their turn, are here as he is there, by virtue of a set of relations that continuously interpret *one another*. The meaning of what is being said is, first of all, that the man and the distant daughter (for brevity's sake we will consider just this aspect of the example) are "really" in a relation that is unfolding. They *take along* one another, in a continuous interpreting of their distance, which is also their proximity. From this interpreting (or "coming to mind," as common sense has it) they are co-originally and then continuously constituted. Now, this interpreting *one another* by being *together* in one's own and for one's own distance is properly a "real" experience. This event, which continuously occurs, is the reality of the experience in its proper and original sense and not a simple "manner of speaking." This is despite the fact that the "public" places of their bodies are *elsewhere*, which obviously has its "weight," a "reality" of *its own*, as we shall see.

The situation of the example, however, is not how common sense imagines and expresses it. Their bodies are, first of all and really, "here" and "there" and, furthermore, have within their heads images and feelings of reciprocity. We commonly think that the man and, above all, the daughter are far away, from a "real" and "objective" standpoint, and that they think about each other and feel each other's presence in their "private" fantasies. We do not think, at all, that they are "really" in a continuously present relation, even if at different degrees of presence, which makes them be what they are, notwithstanding the fact that their bodies are elsewhere.

But their bodies, which are also in a "public elsewhere" of public and objective distance, are what they are precisely for those constitutive relations of reciprocity (father-daughter, man-street, child-moon, *etc.*) *besides* being

119

in two cities, in two different public places. Their being constituted in that relation of reciprocity (father-daughter) and their continuing to be constituted according to a destiny that never stops interpreting itself in an itinerary of always changing distances determines precisely the *reality* of the relations that the man has with the street, with others, with his life, and, generally, with the world—just as the daughter, from that relation, is determined to "choose" in a definite way and not in any other her friends, the things of the world, and the world.

Now, it is of this relation (as well as of many others) in the man of our example that *one speaks* while he finds his way in a journey that sees him as public (and private) individual, in public (and private) places and situations. The problem is just in our ability to comprehend such a complex situation, *i.e.*, this plot, this knot of sign (or public-private) and symbolic realities. Undoubtedly, there is a "public" walking of the man, a way of measuring public distances in kilometers, hours, and minutes in compliance with public goals: the bank, the oncoming car, the shortest way, *etc.*; and in compliance with private motivations: his hopes, desires, fears, *etc.* But these relations are only a part of his "reality," of his experience. They are a small, abstract part, selected in accordance with the conventional concepts of public and common knowledge which, then, are judged to be *the reality tout court* according to a mentality typically informed by metaphysical or objectivistic prejudices.

Besides this public and abstract "selection," the public-private walking of the man is yet another. It is also a continuous symbolic *self*-interpreting on the basis of constitutive distances with the daughter, with the street and, generally, with the world; distances that he *is* and takes with him, from always and for always, that make him the man he is, that make up his concrete experience. There is in him a continuous occurring, a taking place, an eventuating (*evenire*) of the sign; a continuous "speaking" which is not *in* the man, but *is* the man. With him, one could say, walks the entire world of his experience with its typical distances; all the paths already taken, even the walking with the head up looking at the moon of which he has no conscious recollection, as well as his first steps as a child taken around his parents' "big house," *i.e.*, the experiences that constituted him in the world and as the one whose having-to-be is the world as his deepest sameness.

To be sure, the public distance between the man and his daughter (and the bank, the oncoming car, *etc.*) has also its symbolic base and truth, and it is starting from this that even that distance is in its way real. Even the physical presence of the "other," the chance to see it, to listen to it, to touch it is in its turn a symbolic relation that makes the distance occur, in peculiar and typically lively ways. As we all know, it is one thing to look at the moon, to see it with one's own eyes brighten up the night with all its radiance, and another to have it present to us by evoking it through the interpretive signs of words and memory.

The spatio-temporal definiteness of bodies is the liveliest and most powerful ingredient of what we call "reality," that is, our experience. In the last analysis, this emerges from that primordial distance from our own bodies, as our first and closest Other, of which we have already spoken. But to translate this primordial experience into the *absolute reality* of pure bodies in motion in *absolute space*, bodies that in addition would contain "psychological" phenomena (thoughts, memories, images), is a fiction of the metaphysical *ratio* and its public hallucinations.

In concrete experience, there are constitutive symbolic relations (*i.e.*, the occurrence of constitutive distances) that are translated into sign relations and on which, then, the entire public world of public truths is established. It is because of this primordial distance (first of all with regard to their having and experiencing a perceiving corporeity and, then, with regard to their reciprocal perception) that father and daughter can also experience, consequently, a public distance, measurable in kilometers and in travel hours. All public distances are rooted in symbolic distances and have in them their condition of possibility.

The "real" experience of the man who walks along the street, then, is that of a primeval being distant from the daughter by being near to her. On this basis, he can also establish a public measurement of the distance that separates his public body from that of his daughter. And since this is equally true for the daughter with respect to him, they are really, and at the same time, here and there; they have, here and there, a world of experience on the basis of this contemporaneity and, in addition, conventional public coordinates and relations that can be translated abstractly in kilometers and hours. (Even though the corporeal distance, which makes them non-visible, non-perceivable, anxious or indifferent because of the distance *etc.*, is not at all abstract, but symbolic.) Similarly, the event of the moon in looking is a symbolic being distant and near, on which the possibility of public measurement of the moon's "objective" distance, as object of intersubjective public knowledge, is based.

Symbolic relations, however, move *across* what we call "individuals" (considering them "real"), move across them rather than "occur" to them, as common sense is led to believe since unswervingly it *believes* in the reality of individuals. The individual, in fact, is a public formation, a product of public linguistic intersubjectivity and nothing more than that. The symbolic relation does not belong to the individual, but he belongs to it. It would be an equivocation to say that it is the most fundamental and most profound truth of the individual. On the contrary, the individual, this public-abstractive formation, is constantly being pulled out of himself (from his public-private) by the symbolic relation and thrown into the "open" of the world, that is, returned to the world, to the place of his provenance and destiny. The child is thrown into the moon, proceeding from it as the decentered edge of the Same. Thus, he has his truth outside himself as well as the mobile presence of his past and his future, which accompany him in a continuous self-interpretation.

22

◆

The Im-perceptible
Difference

We examined the place of experience (of what we mean here by "experience") and its characteristic sign-symbol knot. This examination has opened up for us the possibility of posing some important questions. For example: What is the relation between experience and truth? What role does truth "play" in experience? How do these two "places" intersect? And, finally, what is the meaning of "truth"? The terms of these questions and the issues they raise are typically "metaphysical" ("experience," "truth," *etc.*), but the *manner* of these questions is for us "beyond" metaphysics (if by "metaphysics" is meant the theory of beings as such, of beings "in totality," *i.e.*, "truth of the being of beings"). Let us clarify this last assertion.

By re-positioning ourselves in experience (after many difficulties, errors, and misunderstandings), we have returned to *its* constitutive "finiteness." We have demonstrated the original and "partial" (as a "part") character of experience, but, we also added, *as its "perfection."* This qualification signals the *non*-metaphysical character of our argument. The partial character of experience, in fact, has always been asserted; this is a "commonplace" of philosophical thinking. But philosophical thinking claims that experience is partial in relation to the supposed totality of being. Being is everything, everything that "is" or is "real." Experience, instead, is always the appearance of a "part," in accordance with "finite" viewpoints and coordinates. Thus, experience is only partially "being" and only partially "real." Hence, the often stated "finite" character of man, "limited" by his perceiving body (the Platonic opposition between *soma* and *psyche*), which, in essence, is placed "in situation," has a partial "point of view," is "de-finite," "limited," and, therefore, erroneous or never *"entirely" true.*

We, on the other hand, have defined precisely these same traits of experience as *its perfection*. We have illustrated this aspect by referring to the classical relation of part-whole. The part stands as an image of that whole of which it is a part, but the whole is *not*, is nothing (*nulla*). It follows that in its having-to-be, in its turning-toward, the part *lacks* nothing (*nulla*), *waits for* nothing (*nulla*), *is attuned to* nothing (*nulla*). Therefore, this tension is perfect since it lacks nothing (*nulla*). The nothing (*nulla*) alluded to here is that edge that delimits the part and makes it complete, *perfect*. Thus, not the infinite but the finite is *perfect*. The same goes for our example where the looking *of* moon is perfectly what it is, since it is decentered in its distance, which makes the hypothetical whole (look + moon) impossible to grasp.

We should note that a hypothetical grasping (*afferramento*) would mean, precisely, the end of experience, which is relation and difference beginning from the Same. In fact, there cannot be an original relation beginning from the Other, as we saw, since in order to respond one must correspond; one must occur as decentered from one's own provenance or from one's own Same. Experience is not the "Same," *i.e.*, the "total" grasping, but the deferring and the distancing of the Same and in the Same.

We could say that grasping is hypothetically possible only with a divine eye "which sees and thinks everything whole," but this hypothesis is, precisely, the expression of *that metaphysical alienation of truth* (of "public" truth) that is unduly assumed to be the ideal standard on the basis of which the truth of our "finite" looking, not at all "whole" but always "partial" (and, indeed, for this reason, capable of "experience") can be measured. This assumption of an ideal truth ("public" and divine or, which is the same, objectively scientific) is what leads experience to nihilism, to the devaluation of finite experience (*i.e.*, experience) and of the finite world (*i.e.*, world). This nihilistic devaluation occurs, as we indicated, whether we assume that the divine eye "is there" or whether we assume that "it is not."

To all this we countered that what occurs in the place of experience is not the "world" in its public and total sense but, on the contrary, the sign-symbol relation occurs to the world insofar as it is world *determined* by this relation, *i.e.*, world in countenance of moon, of moon's looking. But metaphysical strategy and its nihilistic conclusion *do not adhere to* experience and to its "perfection." Instead, they *envision* or imagine the world as totality, as beings in totality (which in reality are nothing [*nulla*].) Already the first proposition of the *Tractatus* quoted earlier, "The world is all that is the case," is ambiguous and corrupted by metaphysics. All that is the case ("world" in *this* sense) is a metaphysical reverie that presupposes an eye that sees everything that happens, a pan-oramic eye. To appropriate this presupposition is to have already opened the doors and windows to metaphysics, to its fundamental assumption. Whatever conclusion we may draw from this premise (mystic, nihilistic, atheistic, materialistic, *etc.*) it will be in any case "metaphysical" and, therefore, "psycho-historical," with all the resulting absurdities we have observed.

But "metaphysical" is also stopping to remark that the revelation of beings in totality, in their co-essential concealment, is "mystery." This statement, too, continues to employ the public eye, *mysteriously* unintelligible and ineffable, by going beyond the finite and perfect reality of experience. The insistence of thinking on the "finite" character of experience, understood as its "imperfection," and on the unimaginability or inconceivability of a totalizing view (of a "divine" view, whose inconceivability is affirmed both by the "existential" atheist and by the religious one, by Sartre but also by Barth) is precisely what constitutes nihilism as the last image or form of metaphysics. Even more generally, we could say that nihilism insists on the interpretive, perspectival character of truth. This leads to three typical *dissolutions*, all related to one another: the dissolution of the Hegelian "totality" (the "infinite"); the dissolution of the subject-substance and of the supremacy of consciousness; and the dissolution of the concept of truth (which becomes "lie" in Nietzsche).

The wave of these dissolutions, as destroyers of the enchanted castle of the *ratio*, permeates completely our contemporary culture. It is so "self-important" that today it implicates even the sciences to the point of widespread "historical" revisions of the concept of science. Contemporary epistemology has even accepted the perspectival-interpretive relativization of every possible truth in the sciences. Thus, "public" certainty in scientific knowledge is undermined. All the same, these dissolutions still rest on entirely metaphysical bases. Let us take as an example the dissolution of the subject-substance, certainly one of the most important and decisive events in contemporary culture if we think of the triad Marx-Nietzsche-Freud. This dissolution, nonetheless, leaves intact the *place* of interpretation and of the sign (in this perspective we do not have as yet an actual "going beyond the sign"). The subject-substance is replaced, and it is no small matter, with the impersonal and anonymous subject ("one" interprets), *i.e.*, with the Interpretant (see Peirce's triangle of the sign described earlier).[80] In this case the Object (the Object of the sign for the Interpretant) also remains intact (the "beings" which from Plato onward hold the onto-ontologic record of truth), even though this Object is, then, posited as an "unknown," as an x. These relations, desecrated and disenchanted, are finally assumed to be the last ground of experience, enigmatic and mysterious.

Thus, the categories of the *ratio* are brought to the dissolution of their meaning, of their having meaning, and, yet, they persist and impose their thinking strategy, reducing every vision, every "experience" to *their* vision, letting it be understood that there is nothing else to see and think and that in them the whole of experience (or, to be more precise, the concrete sense of experiencing) has always been resolved. In general, we could say that nihilistic thinking confuses nothing (*nulla*) with nothing (*niente*) or, in its most profound manifestation, *i.e.*, in the exceptional Heideggerean investigation, it unduly confines the nothing (*nulla*) to the mystery, thus confusing it with the Object (which is always withdrawing). But nothing (*nulla*), as we have seen, is neither "nothing" (*niente*) nor the Object posited to infinity (infinite semiosis); rather it is the simple revealing of the distance in the sign. Let us return to this point, which is so sensitive and crucial for us.

The event of nothing (*nulla*) of Sameness in the symbolic relation is not the occurrence of the "moon" as public Object but rather is the placing of the distance that is at the same time the dislocation of the Response: distance *of* moon as *symbolon*. We know that the Response responds because, even before, it cor-responds. We must not posit, on the one hand, abstractively, looking (as an empty *ability* to see, an empty "potentiality" of vision) and, on the other, moon, as possible Object of vision. This general ability to see (and the correlative positioning of the world as an objective place for the potential encounter of "visible objects") is a point of arrival and not of departure. The original seeing (the original responding) is always a concrete seeing, a seeing *of* something. If the seeing would keep originally to one side and the Object of vision to another, as two Others and different origins, they could neither ever encounter one another nor, more precisely, ever "be" in any way, since they could not even be posited as "different."

Thus, the responding *comes from the world*, is decentered from the world, is a distancing of the world even if our "common sense," used to reason "after the facts," finds it difficult to understand this "evidence." The Response responds to the world, *i.e.*, in the countenance of moon, because it cor-responds to the world beginning from the fissure (in our case from the fissure of looking), which corresponds by *no longer/never* corresponding. The fissure con-tains and, thus, separates. The Response takes aim at the distance, *i.e.*, has the Same in image (*i.e.*, already as sign) and, therefore, goes after it in the nullity of the Object.

To sum up, we could say that the event of the moon as moon's looking (distance, in image, of the world in countenance of moon) is the Same as the "moon," as public meaning (as system of signs, as Object). This Same, however, does not mean "equal to." There is, so to speak, between the two moons an *im-perceptible* difference. The knot of experience (the ground of *perception*) is this *im-perceptible* in-different difference. We have shown their two incongruously congruent faces with two parallel pairs of propositions:

—For the sign, the Object is in nothing (*nulla*). (Nothing [*nulla*] *of the* sign, its infinite referral; nothing [*nulla*], which is not nothing [*niente*].)

—For the symbol, the Response, in its decentering, is in nothing (*nulla*). (Not nothing [*niente*], but nothing [*nulla*] of the distance.) Edge and eye of moon, perspective of the world.

And still:

—For the sign, the Signified is nothing (*nulla*) of the Event. (The Signified annuls the Event, does not "have" it, since meanings do not grasp it, never speak the Event, the event of the fissure which for the Signified has always already occurred.)

—For the symbol, the Event is nothing (*nulla*) of the Signified (annuls the Signified; making it occur also makes it fall and annuls it because the Signified is always inadequate to the Event).

We have thus summarized the knot of the symbol-sign relation insofar as it de-fines the place of experience. The "crucial truth," already announced some time ago, is established on this knot. The crucial truth expresses that dimension that goes beyond, or begins to go beyond, metaphysical thinking. It exemplifies that *mode* that goes beyond metaphysics and of which we spoke at the beginning of this chapter. We should add, however, that the crucial truth also goes beyond metaphysical thinking mainly because it contains that thinking within it.

23

◆

The Crucial Truth

Since it is founded on the knot of experience (*i.e.*, on the inseparable entanglement of symbol and sign relations) the crucial truth is not "absolute." In fact, it is faithful to experience as partial "perfection." After this general indication, which needs to be elaborated, let us ask first, why is this truth "crucial"? To what does the expression refer?

The expression, first of all, alludes to the "experience" of truth, to which the crucial truth is faithful. Now, the experience of truth can be located at a crossing, at the knot between Event and Signified, between symbol and sign relations. Let us imagine two perpendicular lines and call the horizontal "Signified" and the vertical "Event." The crucial truth is at the point of intersection of these two straight lines. This is the image; now let us see its "sense."

The crossing of the truth is naturally two-faced, *i.e.*, it says the two *senses* of the perpendicular lines at the same time. We can express this crossing with two pairs of propositions. Every pair is a unit, an event in unity. Speech, in other words, distinguishes between these two faces, but the truth and the meaning of speech is the occurring together of these faces, since they are true at the same time and in the same sense.

— Event of truth (occurrence of truth).
— Truth of Event (*i.e.*, meaning of Event).

Or:

— Event of interpretation (occurrence of the distance or fissure, that is, occurrence of the symbolic relation).
— Interpretation of Event (the Event posited as Object for the Response, *i.e.*, as sign relation).

Any crucial knot, therefore, is an interpretation, both as Event of interpretation (interpretation which occurs, by taking *its* distance) and as Signified of interpretation, as its translation into sign. The crucial knot is located, then, between nothing (*nulla*) of the Response (the decentering in nothing [*nulla*] of the distance, distance *of* the world) and nothing (*nulla*) of the Object (infinite moving of signs and through signs toward the Object, which is not there). The crucial knot passes from the nothing (*nulla*) to nothing (*nulla*), that is, posits in relation two nothings (*nulla*), as we said earlier.

In the terms of our example, the Response occurs beginning from nothing (*nulla*) *of* moon (distance, which is a having-to-be, having to be corresponded to, to re-cognize). The Response, then, follows the countenance of moon (image, sign) in an Object that, in its turn, is nothing (*nulla*). This is how every interpretation goes after the truth or *experiences* its own truth. But what is the *sense* of this experience? We reach here the point that is truly "crucial." Every interpretation *goes after the truth of its own untruth*, in other words, experiences its not being "true." William James, in adopting Peirce's thesis for his own purposes, claimed in a now famous phrase that "Truth means becoming true."[81] What we are saying, instead, and what *must* be said is precisely the opposite: *truth means becoming false*. Analogously, we could quote an even more famous saying by Nietzsche, who says, "Become what you are." We are saying exactly the opposite: *one cannot become what one is*, namely, one cannot become one's nothing (*nulla*), one's own interpreting distance. This hypothetical becoming, if it were ever possible, would be equivalent to the end of experience, since to be in experience means to be in *one's own* unbridgeable distance.

With these two examples, we have meant to show how our journey has led us to a point of extreme radicalization of nihilism where truth and falsity, being and nothing (*nulla*) are identical. But this extreme point is also a turning point, or crucial point, from which we can bid farewell to nihilism and its metaphysical premises. On the basis of what we have demonstrated, we can say, then, that the experience of truth is also the experience of the non-identity of one's own identity. In this sense, the experience of truth is the always repeated experience of the "catastrophe," in the literal sense of the term, namely, the catastrophe of one's own identity and of the identity of any truth.

In other words, to experience is to go after the truth (make space for it), which, however, is equivalent to going after the catastrophe of one's own identity or the identity of one's own interpretation. But since we *are* our interpretations and nothing more than this, the catastrophe of our interpretations (of our being-in-the-world and of our having-the-world) is our very own catastrophe. Going toward, going-through (*tra-scorrere*) has always been in evidence in infinite semiosis. It is the "erring" of truth, to use a Heideggerean term, but an "erring" that depends on "error," on the "being-in-error" of every interpretation. Thus, whereas the terminology is Heideggerean, the meaning is precisely the opposite. We are not in error because we err, as Heidegger says, but we err because we are in error. This im-perceptible difference, naturally, is not casual, as will be seen later.[82]

Any interpretation, therefore, is in-error and thus *gives way* to erring, to infinite interpretation. It is in-error because of the ek-static character of the sign, as we said already, since the sign, any sign, *takes place* in the displacing fissure of the symbol. In these formulas, doubtless abstruse to an ear trained in good common sense, is inscribed and described, however, precisely the most common element of our most common experience, namely, what is always and continuously happening, what happens or happens *to us* but that we never see, sheltered as we are by the metaphysical categories of common thinking.

We shall try to illustrate this point once again with a simple example, and since we have to count on common sense to make ourselves understood, we will make use of its conventional categories of "public" and "private." Our example is a typical "private" story of a relationship, of a "romantic affair," as it is called. The situation, roughly, is the following: A and B were lovers; then they broke up. The "usual story." After some time, A and B still ask themselves "privately," in a sort of "search for lost time," why were they in love? Why did they break up? What "really" happened between them? This kind of question is asked of any event of our lives, of the entire "story" of our lives. What is typical of this kind of questioning is that *there is* no answer. And there cannot be an answer because the question is not formulated correctly. There is, in fact, no absolute truth, nor can there be one, outside the *finite* concreteness of the relation, outside the concrete experience of the relationship. And yet the question, this type of question, which we ask ourselves so often, expects precisely an absolute truth independently of the way the relationship is determined from time to time, this way or that.

In expecting an answer, the question imagines implicitly the existence of a "third" party, an "objective" eye, which by looking at the relationship from on high can determine its objective essence, what it actually was, in truth. This is what A and B are trying to do with their private questions, by going over their lost time and trying to raise themselves to an "objective" view, almost assuming the viewpoint of a "third" party. But even the viewpoint of a third would be at best only another relation, with *its* interpretation. In fact, this is just what happens: the girlfriend C and the friend D interpret the relationship of A and B. One says that it was all A's fault, and the other that it was all B's fault and that anyway, "it was obvious that it could not work," which is what *A* and *B* could not see at the time and had no reason to see.

What happened between *A* and *B* was the crucial experience of *their* truth, which is never translatable into an absolute or definitive truth. Every occurrence of that "event" was a dis-posing of *A* toward *B* and vice versa. For *A*, as for *B*, this disposing meant assuming a perspective whereby *A* became *involved*. *A*, then, saw himself constituted as the one who had in *B* the Same of his passion, the provenance of his desire and love, of his sub-sisting (*sub-sistere*) as one who desires and loves. He assumed, then, the identity of "*A* in love with *B*": a love aimed at B and which cor-responds to him. All this occurs, of course, with all its infinite nuances and "magic."

The manifold and variegated occurrence of these nuances is the event of the truth of that love. It translates immediately in the presence in *A* of *B*'s semblance, *i.e.*, in the interpretation of that truth or event of that truth that has *B* as the always unreachable and sought-after Object. The lovers look for each other, their passion speaks up constantly in them; they never have enough of the physical presence of each other, the more of which is offered, the more it recedes, renewing its enchantment and mystery. Naturally, in all this are at play all the most essential structures, recalled many times, of the original relation with one's own body in which are rooted the modalities of the sexual encounter. But this crucial passionate knot between *A* and *B* is essentially mobile and indefinite. *A* and *B* dispose themselves in numerous ways, attracting but also rejecting one another, exciting and deluding. By reducing that knot to a single element (passion, *i.e.*, sexual attraction), we are unduly simplifying the experience, which is made up instead of a knot of knots, of a plot of plots (as is clear from the example of the man walking to the bank who is disposed to numerous relations and places that interact among themselves in many ways). *A* is so many other things besides "being in love with *B*," and these things he is and becomes enter in different ways in his love, just as for *B* the presence of love modifies all her other modes of being. It is not an accident that *A*'s relatives and friends "do not recognize him any more," ever since he fell in love with *B*. And even *B*, who thinks she knows him well because of their love relationship notices, day after day, that she does not know him at all and almost never discovers what she had expected to find.

The crucial event of the truth, we could say, is a "historial" (*istoriale*) event, a "historized" (*istoriata*) form made up of a myriad of crucial points, of events that occur continuously.[83] Perhaps we can express all this with the image of the mosaic. Every piece of the mosaic is like the minimal occurrence of a crucial event. Every little piece, in every sense, is in-significant, but by occurring it makes possible the overall meaning, the interpreted figure that is being formed. In fact, we have to imagine our mosaic not as already completed and fixed on a church window but as a kind of mobile mosaic that is forming by itself, as a kind of filmic mosaic, a mosaic in motion. The fragments, the little pieces, as they occur time after time, design within partial wholes (the progressive interpretations of the occurrence of the little pieces) images and shapes, which at first are uncertain and faded but become ever more precise. But while these images become more precise others fade into nothing, while others change appearance and identity.

From these small collocations, and their precarious and neither univocal nor stable shapes, A continuously experiences the event of his love for B, i.e., the truth of his being dis-posed to cor-respond to B, as his own sameness, as the Same of his passion: the place of provenance where the passion feeds itself. From the event of these small units, A continuously interprets the Object of his passion in the attempt to reach it, to "make his own self his own," in the attempt to make his "where" of man in love coincide with the "elsewhere" that designates him as such, since from the very beginning, it is this very correspondence that is at issue, even though its elusive ecstasy escapes every interpretation at the very moment it is provoked. The event of meaning and the meaning of the event confront and "refer" to one another (si inviano) at every turn, i.e., they correspond to one another and yet "are there" precisely because they do not identify with each other.

The crucial truth is this center of mobile light: pieces that continuously occur and whose shapes are constantly being re-interpreted. This truth lights up the mosaic in motion without ever "fixing" itself. From the crucial truth, in fact, there is no way out toward an overall truth, definitive and absolute. There is never the finished mosaic, still and completed, so that it may be contemplated "objectively" from outside. A and B are with the mosaic and in the mosaic. They are the continuous occurrence of new fragments in whose light A imagines (si figura) B, the Object of his love, and vice versa, continuously achieving losses, recoveries, confirmations, betrayals of his previous interpretations, which are always again re-interpreted in the light of the occurrence of new fragments or of other events of crucial truths. Naturally, this also means that the identity of A (A in love with B) is also being continuously modified. The identity of his passion for B changes. This historizing (istoriarsi) of the truth is a history of catastrophes. They maintain a relative identity and overall meaning, to the extent that they do maintain it. Then, there is nothing (nulla), with its truth.

If we now move from the "private" to the "public" sphere, we could say that the great "historical" catastrophes occur in much the same way. This is how the Assyrian empire crumbled and how the Ptolemaic system declined; how the biblical age of the world or the doctrine of fixed species turns out to be false. The difference, in all these cases, is only in the greater complexity of the elements that come into play, not in their essential dynamics. If we had space to give more examples of this kind, we could show what a petty lie the "historical truth" told in books often is, whose main purpose (in its own way important and influential) is to make way for "public truths," truths about things and events that have never happened to anyone.

24

◆

Truth as
Being-in-Error

With the help of these examples, we can now draw some general conclusions. As we have seen, the crucial truth (which is crucial precisely because it is at the crossing of two senses) occurs in two ways: (*a*) The first sense of truth is the event of perspective, *i.e.*, of symbolic distance, of having the distant near (*event of truth*), for instance, the event of the moon's looking or that first troubled look in which *B* revealed herself to *A*, attracting him toward his new and unknown self. Truth, here, is the very same occurrence, the very same event. All that happens, in fact, is truth, the simple truth of the event and as event. This event is a fragment of world that occurs in countenance. Everything, Aristotle says, has as much being as it has truth. This truth, translated in the experience of nihilism and its overcoming, now says that everything has truth since it occurs, be-comes (*eviene*). This occurrence *makes way* (*dà luogo*) for "sense" but "in itself" *has* no sense. It is like a little piece of mosaic that by itself does not form any definite shape. (*b*) What occurs, however, is also and properly an interpretation (the old Aristotelian place of judgment), namely, a countenance, an image, and a sign.

The first sense of truth is the *fact* that interpretation occurs. The second sense of truth is that this event *gives itself as sign* (*dà segno di sé*): *the truth of the event*. Here, we enter in the place of meaning and sense, of the sense of the event. These two moments of truth are distinct *for us*, but in actual fact they are a single event. The symbolic relation, as we said earlier, *is simply the event of the sign relation*, of the sign. There is no tiny piece of mosaic that occurs without *its* interpretation occurring at the same time, *i.e.*, its collocation in a shape and in a form, in an image and in an identity. *This* is experience, which does not occur as something-nobody-knows-what but always as something *defined* by *its* interpretation.

The symbolic relation, we also said, is the event of the fissure that determines the distance. But the dwelling (*stanza*) of this distance is that same one that in occurring appears in image or countenance (as sign), namely, the event of looking made of moon that has the moon outside itself. Thus, what we are calling "experience" is the knot of the manifold that we "are," having-to-be-it.

After these specifications, we are finally able to observe fully the truth of this knot that we have called the "crucial truth." The crucial truth, this knot between Event and Signified, *takes place* essentially "in error." Every Response is a blunder, a revealing by concealing. Every Response is the ek-static placing, *i.e.*, dis-placing from the Same in order to have it as *one's own* Other, *i.e.*, as Object. For this reason, the interpretation is led to a continuous "erring." It is precisely in "erring," in the wandering of interpretation, that "error" is revealed: being Other from one's own Same (*symbolon*) and being the Same of the Other (Object, *sign*).

The symbolic relation is "in error" since it distances itself and "absents" itself from the Same, *imagining* itself as Other from itself. The sign relation is "in error" because it looks behind the signs for what it already "has" or "is," namely, the Same, precisely, in the form of Other. *A* looks in *B* for the Object (for the definitive confirmation) of his love; but he is already this Object from the moment in which it occurred that *B* was the Same as *A* (as *A*'s love cor-responded to by *B*). But he could not be the Same, other than by imagining himself in the countenance of Other, that is, as the one who, having and being the signs of B (looking, talking, touching as event of passion), looks for B endlessly behind the signs, *i.e.*, looks endlessly for himself, going after the Same of his being Other.

But if this is "being in error," then, it is the same as saying that in interpretation truth is revealed, if truth is indeed going toward the untruth, "erring." To go after the untruth is equivalent here to going toward the nullity of the Object starting from the nullity of the Response. The Response is, in fact, nothing (*nulla*) of the Same, of which one says, in responding, Other. But this responding entails, then, looking for himself in the Object, that is, in one's own Other, which once again is nothing (*nulla*). Truth and error *annul each other* in the Response, by coinciding. This is the reason for the duality of the sign and the word, observed earlier. The word, especially, always has two faces: from the point of view of the sign relation it is conventional, while from the point of view of the symbolic relation it is not.

In fact, insofar as it is not turned to the Object and is itself the simple event of the fissure (the identity of the event, *i.e.*, of the mother's face and the word "mother"), the word is made of world: it is the word *of the* mother or the word *of the* moon. The original con-fusion between words and things, which ethnologists and psychologists attribute to children and to "primitives" under the heading of ingenuousness, ignorance, or superstition, conceals a more refined knowledge as well as experiences without which not even ethnologists and psychologists would be able to utter a word, although they are very far from being aware of it, "captivated" as they are by metaphysical and scientific "good sense." But the word, although made of world, is also and at the same time turned always and already to the Object. It is always and already "public" or on the way to its conventional and "public" character. In "moon" resounds or echoes the moon as event of the world in countenance of moon, but in so resounding "moon" directs the community of speakers to the public and intersubjective object "moon." The sign and the word are, thus, always already caught between ecstasy and mystery.

But let us return, after this brief parenthesis, to what we said earlier, namely, to the reciprocal "annulling" of truth and error (untruth). This "annulling" is posited within an ambiguity that will be clarified later; but first we must clear up a possible misunderstanding. If every interpretation "errs" because its being in perspective from and toward nothing (*nulla*) is already a "being-in-error," we could be made to think, then, that every interpretation is negligible or indifferent, that it does not matter *how* we interpret, and not even *what* we interpret, since every interpretation is in error anyway. The sign and the interpretive word, thus, would be abandoned and left to themselves, *because not-true*. A similar attitude, very much widespread today, reveals one very simple fact, namely, that those who assume it still believe *absolute truth* to be valid, whether they hold and assert that absolute truth exists or whether they nostalgically, playfully, or nihilistically assert that it does not. In fact, the devaluation of interpretation and of the sign, because "not-true," has "sense" only if we start from a conviction of what they ought to be but are not, that is, "true" and absolutely capable of expressing the truth. But those who abide by this belief reveal simply their inability to think the truth in any other way than in the form of absolute truth, that is, in the form of metaphysical and pan-oramic thinking, and not in the concrete form in which *one experiences* it and of which one is not aware. After all, the disenchanted nihilist, who gives up on the sign and on interpretation, is also not aware that although he thinks he is free of every metaphysical illusion he continues, comically, to live them.

Now, the crucial truth has shown itself, precisely, *not* to be *absolute*, namely, free of the sign, of meaning and of infinite interpretation. The event of truth is at the same time truth (interpretation) of the event. This indifferent Sameness and difference must now be grasped. The event of truth, as we said, is the fact that interpretation occurs. The truth of the event is that the first fact *gives sign (dà segno)* of itself. The experience of truth lives on this *giving sign (dar segno)* of itself and never outside. If this were not so, the event of truth, in its simple event, would become an absolute truth. But what becomes (*eviene*) is not *the* (absolute) truth but its interpretation, as the experience of truth constantly demonstrates.

Thus, this movement or *kinesis* of truth (between its event and its interpretation) is itself constitutive of truth and there is no truth, no truth can be given, without it. Any interpretation is true since it occurs. But *what* occurs in the interpretation is not *the* absolute truth; it is, rather, the becoming untrue of the interpretation. To interpret *B* as Object of love was a "true" event for *A*, but *what* was then so interpreted in its event had already signed (*segnato*) a destiny of its own which, in any case, was going after its own untruth, even if *A* and *B* had decided to marry.

The *sense* of truth is, precisely, in this belonging-together of the untruth of interpretation which, since it befalls, also "falls" with respect to its eventuating truth (*verità evenemenziale*). In fact, in experience there is no dimension that is non-interpretive, not a sign. And every interpretation, insofar as it occurs, has all the truth that it can and must have. This means that every interpretation is *on the way* toward the untruth of *its* truth. This "being on the way" is, precisely, the *experience* of the truth.

What has sense, therefore, is precisely the experience of this journeying, of this befalling and falling. More succinctly, we could say that it is the *distance* that "gives sense." However, the sense of this "sense" is not yet completely clear. In order that it may be attained, it will be necessary to take a further step, a further radical step, which will enable us to dispense altogether with the question of "truth," as a question that has its "place" in "public" being, but outside of which is nothing (*nulla*).

25

◆

Four Corollaries of the Crucial Truth

Before taking the last step, however, it is only proper, for the sake of completeness, to establish four corollaries of what has been said so far.

FIRST COROLLARY

We have mentioned the question of the individual. What we call individual occurs precisely in the crucial truth. It throws him into the openness of interpretation, *i.e.*, in the erring. The individual, therefore, is fatally bound for the catastrophe that he cannot avoid. And why should he? The individual is an abstract formation of the "public" immersed, whether he likes it or not, in the stormy waters of the symbolic relation, in the ocean of "events." The individual can in fact dispose himself to accept as he goes the untruth of his truth or truths. *A*, for instance, can resign himself to acknowledging that he does not love *B* any longer, or not in the same way, and that not even *B* loves him anymore. In so doing, to be sure, he has not avoided the catastrophe of his individual identity as "lover of *B*." He has, in fact, accepted the crucial truth modifying his identity, *i.e.*, letting it end in nothing (*nulla*).

But the individual can also rebel. He can pretend not to accept the untruth or he can "insist," as Heidegger says.[84] He can do this in two ways. One is by not entering the relationship, since every relation is a nullifying relation with an impossible Object. (*A*, then, becomes a misogynist and avoids all women. As we know from Verdi's *Rigoletto*, the woman is "fickle" and deceitful, although we often forget that the opera character who gives this well-known damning judgment is the libertine Duke of Mantua—another case of the pot calling the kettle black!) Or, alternatively, he can rebel by changing the relationship to a total will to mastery in a supposed domination over the impossible Object. (*A* does not marry *B* but *C*, and avenges on her his previous delusion by oppressing her life, at least for as long as he can.)

138

But this presumption to insist on *one's own* interpretation, which *must* either give us the impossible Object or autistically keep us entirely away from it and from any danger of "loss," runs into the risk, as we all know very well (although always too late), of propelling us forward to the most terrible catastrophes, the worst dangers, and greatest suffering, including that of refusing to live (for fear of dying, which proves the ineluctability of the experience of the crucial truth, which *occurs* regardless). Faced with the crucial truth, the individual, having to cor-respond to the absence of the Object (having to correspond to nothing [*nulla*]), cannot in any way withdraw, even if disillusioned. He *is* in the journey of his destiny; in fact, he is this same journey, this "erring." He cannot avoid traversing it, just as he cannot avoid speaking simply, because he has discovered, as Hobbes says, that *verba sunt meretricula*. And even if he were to do so, to stop and be silent, this would be the most tragic catastrophe the individual could ever fall into, in every sense, as he would be losing his public, private, and social identity. All that is left to the individual, therefore, is to "per-sist," accepting to "stand *for*" his own destiny and remain faithful to the nothing (*nulla*) of his destination, a nothing (*nulla*) that is not nothing (*niente*) but from which he continuously makes the experience of *sense*, the sense of his own destiny.

SECOND COROLLARY

At the beginning of our journey, following Aristotle, we asked the question, what is man? We will certainly not give here a pan-oramic answer. We will say, instead, that a typical trait of man, as he has revealed himself to us, is his being "decentered in himself" (*i.e.*, his being distanced Response, ek-static Response). The symbolic nature of man does not dif-fer from his public nature, unless by an indifferent and imperceptible difference. One has to conclude, in the last instance, that the symbolic is the same as the public (interpretation of the distance) and without residue (*i.e.*, it has no other "being") and is also the continuous catastrophe of the public.

Naturally, the nature of the "public" changes. The public, after all, is nothing more than the constant changing of interpretation. The "public" of the ancient Egyptians is not the "public" of the Greeks. The psycho-historical interpretation of the public character of experience, which characterizes us as Western men (initiates into the metaphysical-scientific *ratio*), is, perhaps, the most radical attempt to carry out to the very end the decentering of man in himself. At issue is what many times has been referred to as the "strategy of the soul," to which the correlative non-sense of the world and the nihilistic conclusions of our civilization correspond. Perhaps for this reason the psycho-historical interpretation discovers, at the end, the "return to the world," that is, the return to its own "removed."[85]

This could be illustrated by the "scandal" of Freud (to which we can only allude here). Freud created (and creates) scandal because he said (*a*) "what" man continuously thinks about day and night (like the man of our example who walks down the street), thus revealing that what *is thought* continuously in him are things that cannot be uttered "publicly," in the presence of society ladies or, more generally, "in public"; (*b*) that the *logos* of the unconscious strangely resembles the *logos* of myth; (*c*) that the "soul" has an irrepressible tendency to return to the world, that is, that *eros* and *thanatos* are inseparable in their enigmatic *giving sense* to existence.

THIRD COROLLARY

The "public" consolidation of the distance (essentially by means of language and its intersubjective use), namely, its spatio-temporalization, gives way to public measurement. Thus, the way is open to the quantitative measuring of the distance, as the walking man of our example was doing. These "objective" measurements are "objectively" true. They embody objective meanings and, in this sense, are true. Our man "knows" that it takes ten minutes to get to the bank, and this is objectively true; furthermore, there is no doubt that it is very useful and important for him to know it. To disregard the value of these truths (and today one is well aware of this tendency, not without its dangers) is as absurd as it is foolish. Often it is also ridiculous. The "private" European *petit bourgeois* masochistically goes around as a barbarian while at the same time not renouncing at all to the "public" use of the technology of his civilization, which after all is very convenient to him.

It is another story, however, when public measurements pretend to be absolutely "true," *i.e.*, independent of symbolic relations and concrete experience. But they, as any other thing, inevitably pay the price for their arrogance. Public measurements, too, and the scientific truths that are based on them, go after their untruth and at the same time err "historically," that is, they also experience their crucial truth. It must be added, however, that the mode of occurrence of scientific measuring, of "quantification," is also subtended by *its* own symbolic distance (which has its roots, as we have already pointed out, in the original experience of the body's distance). Even scientific measuring has its own way of originally experiencing the distance, with its own destiny of truth.

Every interpretation, since it occurs, we said, has a consistency of its own, its own truth. Why then should science, with its theories, its hypotheses, and experimental proofs not have a truth of its own? Even myth and any other public interpretation has it, and science is no exception. Even technology, we could say, refers to nothing (*nulla*) in a way all its own. Therefore, our "technological" times achieve their own experience of truth, an experience of its crucial truth, with its destiny of good and bad catastrophes.

Faced with the catastrophes of our time, it *makes no sense* to either desist or insist. One can only per-sist in order to measure up to the *sense* that accompanies us, in any case. A way of per-sisting (certainly not the only one on which to insist blindly) could be to try to *think* the truth of our time, accepting from the start to be-in-error and thus to "err." The thinking that accepts "erring" as the constitutive element of its truth does not insist; rather, it per-sists in being open to the experience of truth.

FOURTH COROLLARY

On the strength of what has been said so far and although it may at first appear strange, we have to conclude that every philosophy is absolutely (ab-solutely) true. The remark becomes less strange if we remember that Hegel, as we have seen already, upheld a similar thesis, although, in his case, he regarded every philosophy to be a stage and a form of the final and absolute truth. This is precisely what we do *not* want to claim, so that the strangeness of this dissimilar similarity remains (but it is also a useful comparison for those who may wish to ponder it). In what sense, then, can we say that every philosophy is absolutely true?

Let us suppose that a philosophy says of the previous one that it is an ideological superstructure, the conceptual disguise of the reality of economic relations of production. This judgment lowers the previous philosophy to the level of the succeeding one, that is, reduces one interpretation to another. In other words, this is equivalent to positing every philosophy in relation "to us." It is in this relation and only for this relation that the previous philosophy appears untrue—untrue with respect to us and to our interpretation of reality. All the same, let us suppose that this judgment on the superstructural character of previous philosophies is, in turn, a philosophy, *i.e.*, Marx's philosophy. Then, even this philosophy cannot be judged as untrue unless in relation, once again, to "us" who have a third philosophy that is neither superstructural nor structural but, let us say, hermeneutical. In other words, even Marx's philosophy is a philosophy, just as are those that judge this philosophy as superstructural; and since it is a philosophy, it is ab-solutely true. It can eventually appear false only to us and with respect to us, as previous philosophies appeared false to Marx. Insofar as a philosophy occurs, it is ab-solutely true. It has all the truth of its occurrence, *i.e.*, of its interpretation of the world.

Naturally, it too runs up against its own untruth and this is precisely what happens in subsequent interpretations, *i.e.*, in other philosophies that do not say the truth of its event but the truth of its meaning. All that happens is ab-solutely true. The fact is, however, that what happens is never ab-solute; it requires the chain of interpretations and, finally, the failure of this chain. Thus, Marx is an Interpretant destined to his catastrophe as any other. And the theory of the Interpretants destined to their catastrophe is destined to catastrophe and, at the same time, it is ab-solutely true.

All this can be summed up as follows. The event of meaning is ab-solute, but meaning is not ab-solute. Thus, from the point of view of meaning, philosophy is a continuous erring, a linking together of interpretations of interpretations. It is an erring founded on the fact that any interpretation is a "being-in-error." But the event of every interpretation is also "true" in an ab-solute sense since it expresses a mode of positing of the interpretation of the world that in fact occurs. We must not look at things only from the "objective" point of view of the public eye and its interpretations, *i.e.*, from the point of view of the "history of philosophy." This mode of seeing is narrow and ultimately nonsensical since it takes away the sense of experience.

Every interpretation is an error, but error, too, has its force of truth. Giordano Bruno thought that the Hermetic Books were authentic.[86] This belief of his and of his own time was an error, from the point of view of the objective and public historical-philological meaning that we embody today, and yet this error was Bruno's fortune. He was able to turn, what for us is an error, into the passion of his life and into the truth of his thinking (which is not to say that we can do equally well with our own philological "truth"). Thus, Bruno's thesis of the authenticity of the Hermetic Books is absolutely true and so remains, even if the meaning of this statement is now for us false and unacceptable.

Any passion and any judgment pays for its ek-static error, but this is how *sense* "is given." By erring, Columbus discovered America. Naturally, every *insisting* has a price. Bruno was burned at the stake and Columbus did not fare much better. And when the Indians believed that the Spaniards were sent by their gods to bring peace and prosperity to their people, this belief was ab-solutely true, but it exacted the price of a catastrophe that brought their civilization to ruin. In the same way Othello carried his passion to the tragic fulfillment of his destiny because he believed Iago's proof of Desdemona's guilt.

It is only natural that we want to protect ourselves from tragic catastrophes, but even this insistence in wanting to be assured has its price. Man, today more than ever, does not trust anyone and thus does not place his trust in anything. He protects himself with infinite laws and with the bureaucratic organization of life because he does not want to put himself, as the expression goes, "in the hands" of another man. Thus, to be sure, he avoids many evils, oppressions, injustices, and much violence, but he encounters many other problems; but, above all, he renounces many possible benefits, such as the gift of generosity and sincere and disinterested friendship. And, overall, his experience becomes devoid of sense since everything is made "public," "objective," *i.e.*, nonsensical. The experience of error is the sense of truth.

26

◆

Beyond the Crucial Truth

After examining the four corollaries, let us turn to the last step, which must still be taken in our journey. The experience of truth is the experience of *its* being-in-error. But, in the end, what "is true"? The "public" world and its common experience present an unlimited, infinite quantity of "truths" on which our intersubjective and social lives are based. The "public" truths, we have said already, are "publicly" true. But the interpretive framework within which they are instituted (their "Interpretants") are in their turn events that are subject to "erring." This is how, for instance, the "public" truth, unshakably and undisputably certain, which used to assert that "the earth is flat," fell through and was replaced by "the earth is round," which works for us today. Public truths, just as everything, change with time and, furthermore, they have no "sense," do not say the *what*, but only the *how*.

In the last instance to the question, what is true? we must answer: it is true that *one* runs up against the untruth of one's own truth. The falling, the catastrophe is true. Every truth entails assuming a perspective. For the astronomer and the astronaut who experience it concretely, the earth is round, but for the man in the street the earth remains flat, inevitably. If our point of view happens to be "walking" (the "interest" that moves us) the fact that the earth is "flat" remains inexorably "true." But, every point of view is also a way of taking one's own distance. Now, every distance, since it occurs, is ab-solutely true (for "walking" it is ab-solutely true that the earth is flat). But since what occurs is never ab-solute but an interpretation (interpretation of the earth on the basis of walking on one's own two feet), every distance is also in-error. Thus, the way is opened to "erring," *i.e.*, to running after the untruth.

What has been said sums up the experience of the crucial truth insofar as it ties together Event and Meaning. This knot illustrates the concrete "taking place" of experience. And yet, can we say that in so doing we have exhausted the *sense* of experience? Can we say that we have defined the concrete "whole" just as it comes toward us in every instant of our life? Is this all, and only this, that the walking man of our example experiences on his windy day and in the ubiquity of his "emotional" and "public" relations? The answer can only be negative, and this for a reason that is as fundamental as it is simple. So far we have considered experience and its knot still and always through the public eyes of the *ratio*, even though this vision has reached by now the extreme confines of its nihilistic destination. Let us understand this last point well.

Both Hegel and Heidegger (but also Nietzsche) by assimilating error to truth have fulfilled the destiny of the public Western *ratio*. This destiny was born with Parmenides on the strength of the division between error and truth and the rigorous exclusion of the former from the latter. Then, as we already know, the "true" *logos* was instituted for the first time, to which "being" corresponds, and against it, mere *doxa*, false and deceitful opinion. *Episteme-doxa*, being-beings, public-private, light-darkness, day-night, thinking-feeling,and so on, emerged, then, as essential oppositions on which Western "knowledge" has since been founded. But it was Hegel who put all these oppositions in motion, in a circle of circles, in which they lost their traditional appearance. As will be remembered, Hegel views error as an essential and necessary moment of the becoming of reality. Heidegger, for his part (and we shall return to it in more detail shortly), viewed error (or "erring") as the *mysterious* pre-supposition of truth. Thus, both of them brought to its dissolution the original and perennial Eleaticism of our civilization.

It is from their radical thinking, in every way inevitable, that our journey has taken its first steps to arrive, fatally, at an even more radical and, in a certain sense, "definitive" stage. In fact, in the conclusions we have reached, truth and error appeared to us even more entangled, or better, they appeared to us in every sense and without residue as the "Same." This in the twofold cor-responding formula of (*a*) being-in-error as event of truth; (*b*) erring as the meaning of truth. The be-falling (*ac-cadere*) of truth is the same falling (*cadere*) of interpretations. This is how nihilism, as destiny of the *ratio*, arrives at unveiling the ground of its sense (or its non-sense).

All the same, as we have observed, this mode of reasoning on truth, on its erring and its "being," pursued to the end of its enigmatic relation with error and nothing (*nulla*), is still fundamentally *ambiguous*. In fact, it continues to wander around and within the "public places" (truth, error, being, nothing) instituted by the public *logos* of metaphysics. Thinking *insists* on the places of public meaning. In so doing, and in spite of everything, this thinking remains blind to the event of these places and meanings, to their *sense*. Even though the *ratio* has for a long time now started the "deconstruction" of its own foundation and the display of the non-sense of its sense, all the same these procedures that claim to "see" the metaphysical roots of our culture remain nonetheless blinded by the great light of tradition. Thus, they do not have eyes for the *non*-metaphysical "sense" of experience or for what concretely happens in experiencing which, meanwhile and always already, moves and moves *us*.

A typical example, as well as one of the finest, of what we are saying is provided by Heidegger himself, through whose example much of contemporary thinking stumbles in the "dark" and is trapped. To be sure, Heidegger has posed in his own terms what we have defined here as the question of the event of truth in its difference with respect to meaning. In so doing, Heidegger brought to its nihilistic conclusions Aristotle's distinction, from which we started, between truth as measure of Being and truth as judgment. We also know that faced with the problem of the event of truth, Heidegger's journey came to a halt; the event of truth is a "mystery." With this term Heidegger emphasizes the radical difference of this event with respect to "knowledge." On the strength of this insurmountable difference, Heidegger concludes in "silence," that is, with an equally radical refusal of interpretation, the word and the sign. This conclusion, which to Heideggereans seems so "coherent" and "inevitable," in actual fact is the *sign* that reveals how Heidegger continues to think metaphysics with metaphysics and within metaphysics, that is, on the basis of Parmenidean, Platonic, Aristotelian, and, finally, Hegelian categories. His difference, in fact, that difference that takes the name of "Being" and then of "*Ereignis*," is always thought with relation to knowledge and against knowledge. From the point of view of knowledge, the event of truth appears to be negatively qualified as enigmatic and mysterious.[87]

The event of truth "differs" from any other "logical" meaning, from any *logos* (even though it refers "mysteriously" to the "historicizing" of meanings and *logos*). As it differs from "knowledge," the event of truth is considered solely from the point of view of knowledge that continues to provide the foundation and the norm. We can speak of "mystery" only by reference to this norm: the event of truth is something *we would like* to know, is a having-to-know. But this having-to-know remains unsatisfied, and its nature is such that it can never be satisfied—a correspondence *not* corresponded to, and as such, for us who would like to see it correspond, "mysterious." Heidegger thinks the event of truth still on the basis of "metaphysical wonder." As Nietzsche would say, he still takes his firebrand from Plato's great fire. Thus, Heidegger *says* he wants to leave metaphysics to itself, but this saying is still a metaphysical saying *of* metaphysics.[88] Thus, very little or nothing at all is done about metaphysics, about techno-scientific culture and its interpretation of the world. It is the nothing (*niente*) of a silence that has no more room to interpret.

Undoubtedly, Heidegger thinks of the withdrawing of truth (of the truth of Being, of *Ereignis*) as the unconcealedness of the impossibility of the Parmenidean *tauton* of Being and thinking. On the one hand, Being and thinking are identical because Being is always the same revelation of beings, and thinking is always ontic (metaphysical) thinking. This means that Being (the Being of beings) and thinking are radically "historical." The "history of Being" is an "epoch" of the world and nothing more than this.[89] Being and thinking of being are not the truth of the world. Thus, Being declines and fades away, *is weakened* and disappears. This conclusion, which today appears after all "acceptable" to some as the sign of a "softer," less dogmatic and more "humane" culture, is nothing more than a nihilistic judgment, totally contradictory (as we have shown many times) and finally powerless in the face of the most banal historicist and sociological relativism. What is more, this conclusion reiterates, involuntarily, that the Parmenidean truth is the only one that can be thought except to add that this thinking should not be taken too "seriously" (too tragically). Its value is not *absolute*. But just what this means is not thought through at all, unless by some appeal to the "private" (as if this were not a form of the "public" and of Parmenidean truth) and its contingent truths.[90]

On the other hand, Being and thinking are not identical for Heidegger. Thinking, as ontic (metaphysical) thinking comes from Being's difference, from its "mittance" (*inviare*) and "withdrawing," "unconcealing" and "concealing." Thus, with respect to *this* Being that withdraws we cannot "say" in any way that Being and thinking are *tauton*. One cannot "say" Being. In this fashion, the implicit difference at the basis of the Parmenidean identity that made it possible to say "Being" is sublated. To sublate this difference, as we remarked, is the same as decreeing the end of metaphysics, which is what Hegel and then Heidegger accomplish after all, with differing degrees of awareness. For the implicit difference, Heidegger substitutes an explicit difference, posited radically beyond the correspondence of Being and thinking. But this more radical difference is always thought in terms of the Parmenidean difference-sameness of thinking and Being. In fact, it is in relation to this difference-sameness that this more irreducible difference is declared a "mystery," *i.e.*, the non-correspondence of thinking to Being.

The proposed alternative can be summed up as follows: to speak is equivalent to saying Being, but Being, because of its radical difference from knowledge, cannot be said; therefore, nothing can be said, and one can only be silent, or one can speak without any pretense to "saying," which is the same. But the conclusion of this argument, of *its* interpretation, derives from the premise that speaking is the same as Being, that is, from the Parmenidean premise of the public *logos*. Thus, we could call all this the metaphysical fulfillment of metaphysics. In our own terms, we could say, as we have already done many times before, that Heidegger thinks of the event of truth, of Being, as the always withdrawing Object of the sign and interpretation. On this assumption, Heidegger "throws out" the sign and interpretation since they are incapable of arriving at the Object (infinite semiosis, hermeneutic circle) and hence, in the end, at the eventuating (*evenire*) of being.

Still, even our "crucial truth," although it looks beyond metaphysics (since it thematizes the presence of the symbol in the sign), does not abandon its reference to metaphysical terminology, implicitly assumed to be exhaustive in relation to experience. Within the circle being-thinking-truth, the crucial truth is still a "public" interpretation of experience that remains as such even in its effort to take its distance from "public truth." This "crucial" interpretation leaves in the "dark," in fact, the non-public sense, or level, of experience. The last step we must take, then, is the questioning of this "darkness."

27

◆

The Enchantment
of the World

Since it occurs as crucial truth, experience is an infinite interpreting that addresses the enigma of the Object and, in this sense, the mystery. This aspect of experience must be kept firm. But to hold it firm is not to deem it exhaustive. To reduce experience to the event of interpretation is equivalent, in fact, to looking at experience only from the point of view of interpretation, *i.e.*, of Meaning and of sign which, of course, it also *is*. From the point of view of interpretation, of the Signified and the sign (and its co-essential infinite semiosis), the event of interpretation is, and remains, a mystery. But the *event* itself, this simple occurrence, the occurrence of its simple distance which resides (*di stanza*), all this is not experienced (*esperito*) at all as mystery. In its original provenance, the symbolic distance does not at all have the sense of mystery. Then, how is it experienced (*esperita*)? What is its sense? *It is experienced (esperita) as en-chantment.* Its sense is enchantment.

The en-chantment *knows* nothing of truth and error. For the enchantment, there is neither "wonder" nor will to knowledge (and nothing to know), no *aletheia* (revelation of the concealed), no *lethe* (concealment of the revealed). The en-chantment "does not know." For this reason it is the place of experience left "in the dark" by the public knowledge of the *ratio*, since it is incongruous with respect to any public knowledge and, more generally, to any knowledge and will to knowledge. In en-chantment, in fact, the distance and its difference are not experienced (*esperite*) primarily and essentially as "standing against," as Object. The en-chantment, instead, is precisely the experience of the Sameness of the Other. Its presence en-chants in every sense of the term, and among these, also and above all, in the sense of "chants-in," *i.e.*, it becomes sign and word. *In what* does that "in" occur? Obviously "in" the Response, "in" that response that we "are." Enchantment of moon for the look *of* moon. Enchantment in which the moon has its perspective, its internal difference, its primordial sign, which takes place in the nothing (*nulla*) of looking (of Response) which annuls itself: "enchantment of the present moon."

The experience of enchantment is the sense of this proceeding Sameness. Since it is "proceeding," the Sameness is eccentric and vanishing. By de-centering itself in the nothing (*nulla*) *of* moon (in that *where* that places the Response as moon's looking), the experience of enchantment (the properly symbolic experience) experiences (*esperisce*) *its* difference and *its* distance and experiences (*esperisce*) them in *its* ways. This experience, in fact, is characterized by the equilibrium (by the tension or in-tension) between presence and distance of presence, sameness and difference. This *equilibrium*, this staying in equilibrium, is the characterizing element of the experience of enchantment. By be-falling, it always already *falls* in the experience of Otherness (*Alterità*) of the Same, *i.e.*, in the mystery of its absence. In other words, the equilibrium, as moon that already has become look and edge of moon, is on the ridge of the abyss in which the vision is trans-lated into countenance and sign of moon, that is, into Object interpreted and lost. This is how the looking *of* moon becomes, or is always on the verge of becoming, as we said earlier, "moonlight."[91] In its balancing tension, the en-chantment is the experience of parti-cipation. It is a participating experience. If we are allowed to use the term "truth" here, just once for the purpose of clarity, we could say that the truth of the experience of enchantment is a "participating truth." For en-chantment, to participate means to be a part, to take part, to assume *the* part, in every sense and above all in the sense of being a part, finite and perfect, as *symbolon*. In our example, it means: to be part *of* moon, to take part *in it*, to take on its countenance. For this reason, as we said, the child's looking is *made of moon*.

Even more generally, it is also for this reason that the moon's presence *enchants*. To parti-cipate in looking, in the moonlight, to see *oneself* from the point of view of moon, to have (to be) a looking of moon, all these expressions are difficult to think and, at the same time, are very simple, perhaps too much so. They are difficult because they easily fall prey to the public distortion of the words that express them, words that have lost their original echo and sense of experiencing (*esperire*) the moon's looking. They are very simple, if not too much so, because they refer to a level so habitual and recurrent of experiencing (*esperire*), which, since being always with us and speaking continuously in us, is easily neglected.

This level is so obvious that the suspicion does not even arise that one is speaking *of it*; it seems impossible that one is really alluding and referring *to it*. This obviousness is hidden and, for the most part, misunderstood in the "private." Centuries of "public" dominion have made it obsolete as something that is not even worthwhile speaking about, in fact, as something that *one should almost be ashamed of.* On the other hand, it is also something that seems *useless* to speak about, since everyone has always "known about it," or more properly, since everyone "is" it, without there being anything else to add or "do." Insofar as enchantment is parti-cipating, "being a part of," it is not a having-to-be and not even a "looking for." Nor can there be in en-chantment any *wonder*, even though there are in it the roots and conditions of every wonder, as of every mystery.

The en-chantment is being in equilibrium, on the edge of the Same. That is why it is also always already a being ecstatic, ek-static, on the edge of the abyss, of the sign and its infinite semiosis: edge of world that is *at the point* of becoming sign and word. The relation between two nothings (*nulla*), of which we spoke earlier with reference to the symbol and the sign and their cor-responding relation, finds now its actual correspondence in equilibrium and at the point: point of nothing (*nulla*) that unites in itself the two nothings (*nulla*) of provenance and destiny, of enchantment and mystery.

Only in en-chantment does the *finiteness* of experience, already vindicated in the course of our journey, present itself finally complete and "perfect," because the enchantment, what en-chants, are *beings themselves* (in our example the moon, the world in countenance of moon). To use the language of metaphysics, then, *beings are the transcendens pure and simple*, but not so the Being (of beings), which only now, finally, can legitimately be released to metaphysics and to its public discourse. And to remain on the edge of transgression, which once again we have allowed ourselves with this refer-ence to metaphysics, we would like to add that here our distance and difference from Heidegger is most profound and decisive.

This applies, however, to the level of Meaning, not to the event, which for en-chantment is completely indifferent. What we have been stating, in fact, is *our* interpretation of Heidegger, who has become Object of those public signs that for us represent his philosophy. In the enchantment all this is indifferent because in it one ought to say, rather, that the event of Heideg-ger's philosophy and *its* enchantment are ab-solutely what they are or, as public language would express it, they are ab-solutely "true." In fact, it should not be forgotten that now we have finally entered the dimension of enchantment. In en-chantment, beings (moon) are the *transcendens* pure and simple. They are met and experienced (*esperito*) in the tension of equilib-rium, that is, *as the nearest presence of eventuating (eveniente) distance.* We could call it *the enchantment of equilibrium.*

This enchantment is the moment, or the point, at which the dancer, dancing, is drawn to the margins of the Chorus, to its extreme edge. From here, he can "see" his companions dancing and the dance which, while still dancing, he "is." That is, he can see the very provenance of his dancing and of his seeing *himself* as dance and dancer. The "dance" is a thing of the gods.

The dancer is he who "takes part" in the dance and who is a thing of men. His part-icipating is without doubt "dance" but also distance. He cannot take part without seeing himself from an extreme edge, in equilibrium between him who is all taken up by the god, which *is* "dance" and therefore does *not* dance, and him who is already falling off the outside of the dancing and, as a spectator (*i.e.*, "public" eye of the *public*), looks critically at his Object, analyzes it, and interprets it and can even write a "theory of dance."

Generally speaking, the entire human praxis is this equilibrium between participation and (interpretive) technique. One thing is to be a part and to take part in the game; another is to formalize and to know its rules. Perhaps this is why art, even with its techniques, is so attuned to enchantment that it seemed to Plato, logically, to be dangerous for "truth." Every technique requires first and foremost a *familiarity*, or, as we say, a *natural bent*. The player of billiards has to first of all "feel" the game, become cue and ball, just as the pianist must become at one with the keyboard. No rule can teach him this participation; in fact, every rule presupposes it—the hand's familiarity with the pen (with the "dance" of the pen, as Nietzsche says), or Odysseus' familiarity with his bow, or Penelope's with her man.

It will be remembered, to digress briefly, that the wise and prudent Penelope, although she is already intimately at-tracted to the Stranger in whom she recognizes her own sameness, does not let herself go to the enchantment before having questioned Odysseus at length and having *made him the sign* of careful interpretations, with the purpose of making sure of his *identity*. She *knows* that enchantment can also be dangerous and, therefore, she exacts interpretation. However, in so doing, Penelope also demonstrates the folly of her wisdom, besides the wisdom of her folly. Her stubborn wait for Odysseus, her *insistence* on getting him back, shows an extreme trust in the identity of the individual, with catastrophic consequences that no prudence can prevent. Both because the Odysseus who returns can no longer be the Odysseus she was waiting for, and because the "metaphysical" Odysseus, in love with the enigma of the Object, the wanderer who loves to "err," will move on, leaving Penelope alone once again.

Thus Penelope experiences (*esperisce*) the being-in-error of her passion, that is, the crucial truth. And yet this folly also contains, in its own way, a profound wisdom since only through the irremediable frailty of the individual and his evanescent identity is it possible, after all, to experience the truth of passion, with its constitutive catastrophe. What Penelope experiences (*esperisce*), what she does not withdraw from, is the fact whereby the symbolic event of passion, its enchantment, is not separable from the befalling and falling of the sign (but is the Same). In the age of nihilism we are too afraid, perhaps, of this truth. While we ideologically extol individuals (hallucinating that "people" are a reality and an end in themselves), we are wary, as we have said already, of trusting them and entrusting ourselves to them, *i.e.*, of letting them part-take in our passions. What we usually do, instead, is to demote individuals and the experiences that can be had *with them*, either to pragmatic utilitarianism or to indifferent and ephemeral chance encounters, that is, to the simulacrum of participation. For the "insisting," obsolete and dangerous (good only for poor Penelope, so little "civilized" as not to understand that, after all, any of the suitors would have done "just as well" as that arrogant Odysseus), we substitute "de-sisting"; for passion, we substitute pleasure as an end in itself, the fruition of the pure sign. No wonder, then, that we are surprised at the "poverty" of experience and at the emptiness of passions. Our age is so rich in signs but so poor in enchantment that it has not yet been able to find the way between insisting and desisting, that is, the way, if it exists, of a careful "persisting."

This brief digression can help us understand, perhaps, what is more important now, namely, "how" enchantment (and its being-in-error from the point of view of the sign) is the root of sense and of every sense. En-chantment, by itself, is the senseless, the "without-reasons," but it is the senseless that *gives* sense, since it allows the occurrence of the part-icipation of man in the world and "says" it. The senselessness of its distance is never in fact "extraneity." The peculiar balance of its nothing (*nulla*) (Response/object) at-tracts (in the world) and dis-tracts (from the world).

Events and their sense take place, precisely, in the place of en-chantment, in the enchantment of the balance, "beyond good and evil." In this balance, primordially, love and hate, creation and destruction, devotion and anger, calm and violence, serenity and terror, beauty and horror, are revealed as what they are. It is here that stars and mountains, trees and animals, storms and oceans and, finally, men, who walk along the edge of en-chantment, occur. All these "symbols" and countenances of world chant the *distance* of the joy and the pain that dwell in the "cosmic" order and disorder of every event. This does not mean at all, however, that the en-chantment is outside the sign, that the participating truth is outside the crucial truth. It is precisely the enchantment that pro-duces the ek-stasy of the Response: the des-cant (*dis-canto*) and echo of the world. This "double" chant (*des*-cant) gives way and activates the sign, in fact *is* already sign for the Object. Thus, the sign is caught (be-falls) between ecstasy and mystery. If en-chantment is the experience of the Sameness of the Other, and ek-stasy is the experience of the Otherness of the Same, then the *knot* of experience, taken in its globality, is the *ecstatic enchantment of the mystery*. Here is inscribed and *historized* (*istoriata*) the interpretation of truth, the erring of its infinite semiosis. Thus, en-chantment does not sublate at all the mystery, the experience that in its turn is constitutive of the mystery.

These last reflections allow us to discern, finally, where the place of philosophy is rooted—a philosophy and, therefore, a thinking that has metaphysics within itself and tries to *do* something with it rather than abandon it to the vultures. Furthermore, this allows us to show, as is necessary, whence our own discourse began and what made it possible. What, then, is *for us* its sense, its justification, and its reason for being. Now we can see, finally, without illusions but also without delusions, without pretenses but also without regrets, the place from which we speak, from where we make "public" speeches with "public" words (even the word "enchantment," since it is a sign, is a public word).

The sign, by being placed between ecstasy and mystery, experiences also the *en-chantment of the mystery*; the mystery also be-falls, it too is an event, just like anger, fear, or dawn's red. The occurrence of *this* en-chantment is the place of philosophy and of the philosophical word, and the place of "science" and of the sometimes terrible en-chantment of "research," which probes and upsets beings and introduces forces in the world as yet unknown.

If philosophy does not insist on the metaphysical will to dominate experience totally and to "resolve it" completely in "public" truths that are functionally effective and symbolically senseless; if philosophy, instead, persists in its task of trans-lating into "public" words the enchantment of mystery, the enchantment of its original wonder; if philosophy, discouraged, does not desist from the specific enchantment of its word and its precious gift, and leaves entirely to science the task of interpreting the public truth, and to short-lived chatter the task of talking nonsense on private truths; then, philosophy, once again, will be able to find in experience and in its structural knot of sign and symbol its own origin, its own justification, and its own destiny.

Many times, in the past, the greatest thinkers have been able to *say* the ecstatic enchantment of the mystery; they have been able to translate into words the enchantment of their passion, of their desire for knowledge, at-tracted by the mystery of the world that made them, in fact, philosophers. But, perhaps, in so doing they did not think they were saying it or could say it, since no one better than they could measure the shortcomings of the word and the sign in the face of the enchantment and the mystery in which thinking in its constitutive distance had taken "residence" (*stanza*). We would like at the end of our journey to let one of these great thinkers speak so that for once, at least, at the conclusion of these remarks, our discourse could measure up to the loftiness of the subject matter (the question of "truth") with which we have presumed to grapple.

In the words of this great thinker resound the experience of the cosmological enchantment of the world and its participating truth. But it resounds in a marvellous equilibrium with the sense of mystery that nourishes, as *its enchantment*, the cognitive and interpretive will to truth of the philosopher, who is aware of his insignificance but has not forgotten his dignity. A miraculous balance between a having-to-know, which lucidly is not resigned, and the participating feeling toward the event of that Same that one already is, precisely, by not knowing. In a note of 1763, Kant writes:

> When I examine, among others, microscopic observations, and I see in a single drop of water numerous races of animals, predatory species armed with instruments of destruction that while intent to persecute others are themselves destroyed by even more powerful species of this aqueous world; when I look at the intrigues, the power and the scenes of rebellion in a single drop of matter; and when I lift up my eyes to see the immense space teeming with worlds, atoms; no human word can express the feeling which this idea stirs up. And no subtle metaphysical analysis can even come close to expressing the sublimity and dignity of this intuition.[92]

Notes

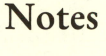

Except where indicated, all notes below are the translator's.

1. None of these works have yet to be translated into English. Their original titles and editions are: *Semiotica e filosofia*. Bologna: Il Mulino, 1978; *Passare il segno*. Milan: Il Saggiatore, 1981; *Kinesis. Saggio di interpretazione*. Milan: Spirale, 1982.
2. At times, for the sake of clarity or to provide the reader with more specific references, I have gone against Sini's wishes and added some academic "support." However, I have tried to keep the notes at a minimum, and the reader will find most of them at the end of the book.
3. Euthyphro is a character from a Platonic dialogue by the same name.
4. The analyses to which Sini is referring can be found in *Il silenzio e la parola. Luoghi e confini del sapere per un uomo planetario* (Silence and Word. Places and boundaries of knowledge for planetary man). Genova: Marietti, 1989; and in *I segni dell'anima. Saggio sull'immagine* (Signs of Soul. Essays on the Image). Bari: Laterza, 1989. Neither work has yet been translated into English.
5. I have used the W. D. Ross translation of the *Metaphysics* from the *Complete Works of Aristotle. The Revised Oxford Translation*, edited by Jonathan Barnes. Princeton, NJ: Princeton University Press, 1984. I have slightly modified the translation to adjust it to Sini's text.
6. W. D. Ross translates *exin* as "power of thinking." I have changed it here and elsewhere (p. 28) to "habit of thinking," since this is closer to the Italian version of "abito di pensiero" used by Sini for whom the meaning of a thing is in the "habit" of pragmatic response connatural to it.
7. On the importance of the Aristotelian distinction between homonyms and synonyms and on their ontological meaning see A. Cazzullo, *Metafora: Aristotele e l'ermeneutica contemporanea* (Metaphor: Aristotle and contemporary hermeneutics). Milan: Unicopli, 1983. (Sini's note)
8. These examples are taken from Plato's *Sophist*.
9. The reference is to W. D. Ross, *Aristotle's Metaphysics*. Oxford: Clarendon Press, 1966.
10. The translation here and elsewhere is from G. S. Kirk and J. E. Raven, *The Presocratic Philosophers. A Critical History with a Selection of Texts*. Cambridge: Cambridge University Press, 1957.
11. The translation of the *Sophist* is that of F. M. Cornford, *The Collected Dialogues of Plato Including the Letters*, edited by E. Hamilton and H. Cairns. Princeton, NJ: Princeton University Press, 1961.

12. See Chapter 11.
13. *Beyond the Sign* III. 46. See also the Preface.
14. I have used M. J. Inwood's revised version of William Wallace's translation of the third edition (1830) of the *Encyclopaedia of the Philosophical Sciences in Outline* from *Hegel. Selections*, edited with Introduction, Notes, and Bibliography by M. J. Inwood. New York: Macmillan, 1989. Since Inwood does not include the Additions I have used Wallace's translation from the second edition, *The Logic of Hegel*. Oxford: The Clarendon Press, 1892. These will appear in the text as "Additions" plus the paragraph number. Other quotations from the 1892 Wallace edition will appear as "Wallace" in the text. The quotations from Inwood appear with the paragraph number only.
15. I have slightly altered the translation to bring it in line with Sini's text.
16. Here and elsewhere I have changed Wallace's "notion" to "concept" to be consistent with Inwood's revisions.
17. I have slightly changed the wording of the first part of the quotation.
18. Here and elsewhere I have slightly altered the translation.
19. On this question see *The Philosophical Writings of Peirce*, selected and edited with an Introduction by Justus Buchler. New York: Dover Publications, 1955. Especially Ch. 7, "Logic as Semiotic: The Theory of Signs." Also *The Collected Papers of C. S. Peirce*, Vols. 1–8, edited by Charles Hartshorne and Paul Weiss. Cambridge, MA: Harvard University Press, 1931.
20. I have used the English translation of A. V. Miller, *Hegel's Science of Logic*. London: George Allen and Unwin, Ltd.; and Atlantic Highlands, NJ: Humanities Press, 1969.
21. See Miller, §701ff.
22. Here and elsewhere I have changed Miller's "notion" to "concept."
23. See Chapter 2.
24. I have slightly altered the translation of the last sentence to bring it in line with Sini's text.
25. See the first quotation from Aristotle's *Metaphysics* in Chapter 1.
26. The translation of the *Phenomenology of Spirit* is by A. V. Miller. Oxford: Clarendon Press, 1977. Here and elsewhere I have eliminated the capitals from the translation of German nouns.
27. See Karl Popper's *Open Society and Its Enemies*. London: Routledge, 1945.
28. See Chapter 13.
29. The reference is to Xenophanes of Colophon. See Kirk and Raven, *The Presocratic Philosophers*.
30. See Chapter 1.
31. Sini alludes here and further on (p. 43) to an important distinction between two conceptions of "nothing" (*niente* and *nulla* in Italian), which he discusses in greater detail in Chapter 18.
32. The question of the nothing (*nulla*) to which Sini refers is examined later in greater detail in Chapter 18. See also previous note.
33. See Luigi Pareyson, "The Wonder of Reason in Schelling," mentioned in the Bibliography.
34. See Max Weber, *On the Methodology of the Social Sciences*, translated and edited by E. A. Shils and H. A. Finch. Glencoe, II, 1949.
35. See Massimo Cacciari's *Icon of the Law*.
36. I have used the John Sallis translation from Martin Heidegger, *Basic Writings*,

edited by David Farrell Krell. New York: Harper and Row, 1977. All page references are to this edition.

37. I have substituted "thing" for "matter" to bring the translation in line with the rest of the text.

38. For reasons given in the previous note, I have replaced here "material truth" with "the truth of a thing."

39. However, as we have seen, this is precisely what Hegel does *not* do. For him untruth is neither the simple opposite of truth nor is it foreign to the essence of truth, but Heidegger seems to forget this. (Sini's note)

40. As in the previous two notes, I have replaced all the occurrences of "matter" with "thing" and I have slightly altered the final phrase.

41. Here and elsewhere, I have changed "statement" to "judgment" to bring the translation in line with the rest of the text.

42. See Chapter 26.

43. I have slightly altered the translation.

44. Sini alludes here and below to Parmenides' poem, *The Way of Truth*, which he quoted in Chapter 3.

45. Quoted in Heidegger's *An Introduction to Metaphysics*. New Haven, CT: Yale University Press, 1959. It is the first sentence of the first chapter, "The Fundamental Question Of Metaphysics," where Leibniz' phrase is translated as "Why are there essents rather than nothing."

46. The reference is to the question of "nothing" (*nulla*) to which Sini alluded in Chapter 9. The issue is taken up in Chapter 18.

47. A "house of tolerance" (*casa di tolleranza*) in Italian is a brothel and is synonymous with confusion. With this play on words, Sini wants to allude to the chaos that reigns now that thinking has become private, mundane, and indifferent.

48. See the *Critique of Practical Reason*, Bk. II, ch. 2, sec. ix.

49. I have used the D. F. Pears and B. F. McGuinness translation of L. Wittgenstein, *Tractatus Logico-philosophicus*. London: Routledge and Kegan Paul; and Atlantic Highlands, NJ: Humanities Press, 1961.

50. Max Weber, *On the Methodology of the Social Sciences*. See Chapter 9.

51. I have used the G. S. Kirk and J. E. Raven translation in *The Presocratic Philosophers. A Critical History with a Selection of Texts*. Cambridge: Cambridge University Press, 1963. The quotations are identified by paragraph number. For fragments §89 and §113 I have relied on Kathleen Freeman's *Ancilla to the Presocratic Philosophers*. Cambridge, MA: Harvard University Press, 1971. They appear in the text as "Freeman" with the paragraph number.

52. See, for instance, Hegel's *Lectures on the History of Philosophy*, Pt. I, ch. 1, sec. D.

53. Sini quotes from the Italian translation by Gabriele Giannantoni of Hermann Diels' *Fragmente der Vorsokratiker. I Presocratici. Testimonianze e frammenti*, 2 vols. Bari: Laterza, 1981. The English translation here and below is mine.

54. I have slightly modified the translation to suit Sini's text. The whole of fragment §199, partly quoted by Sini, is as follows: "Listening not to me but to the *Logos* it is wise to agree that all things are one."

55. This is Sini's version of Heraclitus' saying quoted earlier as part of fragment 1B, §197. The translation of Kirk and Raven is slightly different and is as follows: "all things happen according to this *Logos* (*kata ton logon*)." Later, Sini quotes this version.

56. On Xenophanes see also Chapter 8.
57. See Sini's *Beyond the Sign*, II. 80. (Sini's note)
58. See Sini's *Beyond the Sign*, III. 46ff. (Sini's note)
59. See Husserl's *The Crisis of European Sciences and Transcendental Phenomenology*. Evanston, IL: Northwestern University Press, 1970.
60. See Enzo Paci, *Science's Role and the Meaning of Man (Funzione delle scienze e significato dell'uomo)*. Milan: Il Saggiatore, 1963.
61. Sini is alluding to proposition §6.41 of Wittgenstein's *Tractatus Logico-Philosophicus*. "The sense of the world must lie outside the world. In the world everything is as it is."
62. See Pico della Mirandola's *De Ente et Uno* in the English translation by J. W. Miller, *On Being and the One*. New York: Bobbs-Merrill, 1965.
63. See Sartre's *Critique of Dialectical Reason*. London: NLB, 1976.
64. See *Beyond the Sign*, Part II. 38.
65. In Part II of *Beyond the Sign* this is said to be the "fundamental cosmological experience." (Sini's note)
66. See *Being and Time*, Pt. I, v. sec. 29.
67. Here and elsewhere, I have translated *esperire* and similar forms with "experiencing" to suggest the experiencing of something before its objectification as object. Thus, "experience" is not to be understood as sensation but, as Sini says later, as the unity of the sign and the symbol relations.
68. See Jean Piaget, *The Child's Conception of the World*. New York: Harcourt, Brace and Company, 1929. The reference is from ch. 4, "Realism and the Origin of the Idea of Participation," pp. 146ff. The sentence chosen by Sini is a composite of different answers by three children.
69. For a more detailed analysis of this issue, see the first part of *Beyond the Sign*. (Sini's note)
70. This is Peirce's triadic model of the sign. See the *Collected Papers of C. S. Peirce*, Vol. 2, ch. 2, "Division of Signs," pp. 134ff.
71. The expression used by Sini is "avere la luna," which in English translates "to be in a bad mood" (literally, "to be possessed by the moon"). Since the English equivalent does not show the use of "moon" in an idiomatic expression, which is what Sini wants to show, I have replaced it with one that approximates it.
72. To express the notion of a distancing that is also here, Sini plays on the word *distanza*, meaning "distance," and *di stanza*, meaning "to reside, to be stationed, to have room here." Since the play on words does not work equally well in English, I have rendered *di stanza* as "reside."
73. For Heidegger, see "The Principle of Identity," in his *Identity and Difference*, translated and with introduction by Joan Stambaugh. New York: Harper and Row, 1969. For Hegel see the *Science of Logic*.
74. As I indicated in notes 33 and 34, the question of the "nothing" is central to Sini's argument. He distinguishes between two conceptions of "nothing" (*niente* and *nulla*) to differentiate between a negation (*niente*), in the traditional metaphysical sense, and a negation (*nulla*), which is "not nothing" but that which determines something as what is. (See more detailed explanations in this chapter and further on.) Since in English both terms can be translated as "nothing," rather than selecting a special translation for *nulla*, I have opted simply to indicate all occurrences of *nulla* in parenthesis.
75. See Chapter 12, "Truth as Mystery."

76. See Husserl's *Logical Investigations*, translated by J. H. Findlay, Parts I and IV. London: Routledge and Kegan Paul, 1970.
77. As Sini explains, by "moon's look" is meant the look constituted, made by moon.
78. The expression *mirare-a* means both "to gaze at" and "to aim at." Both meanings are meant by Sini and I have translated the phrase with either according to context.
79. The notion of "catastrophe" is taken up again later in Chapter 11.
80. See Chapter 18.
81. See "Pragmatism's Conception of Truth," in *Pragmatism*. Cambridge, MA: Harvard University Press, 1975.
82. See section 7 of Heidegger's *On the Essence of Truth* and Sini's own discussion in Chapter 12.
83. The terms *istoriale*, *istoriata*, and later *istoriarsi* are meant in the literal sense of the dictionary definition of *istoriare*: "to illustrate with images or figures pertaining to historical events or facts." The crucial event of truth, therefore, is the event of a historical image or figure.
84. See Heidegger's "On the Essence of Truth."
85. The reference is to that "removed" dimension of experience that is displaced in the "private" by the institution of the *logos* and its public truth. See Chapter 17.
86. This is a reference to Giordano Bruno's *Cabala del cavallo Pegaseo* (1585).
87. See Heidegger's *Identity and Difference* and *Time and Being*.
88. See Heidegger's *Time and Being*, translated by Joan Stambaugh. New York: Harper and Row, 1972.
89. See Heidegger's *Nietzsche*, vol. 2.
90. Sini's obvious target here is the so-called philosophy of *pensiero debole* (weak thought), whose major representative is a Heideggerean, Gianni Vattimo. See Sini's Bibliography.
91. See Chapter 7.
92. From a footnote to the essay, "Beweisgrund zu einer Demonstration des Daseins Gottes," in *Kant's gesammelte Schriften*, 23 vols., Bd. II, p. 117. Berlin: Prussian Academy, 1902–55. To my knowledge, there is no English translation of this text. The translation is mine.

Bibliography

◆

In the bibliographical note at the beginning of *Images of Truth*, and in accordance with his intentions to reduce his notes to a minimum, Sini gives a list of authors he has quoted in the work. He also lists a number of Italian philosophers who have either influenced him or whose work is akin to his own. Rather than reproduce this list I have subdivided it into principal and reference works, with the addition of a section on articles in English on Sini and by other Italian philosophers.

PRINCIPAL WORKS

Aristotle. *Metaphysics*. Translated and edited by W. D. Ross. In *The Complete Works of Aristotle*, Revised Oxford Translation, Vol. 2, edited by J. Barnes. Princeton, NJ: Princeton University Press, 1984.

Hegel, G. W. F. *The Phenomenology of Spirit*. Translated by A. V. Miller. Oxford: Clarendon Press, 1977.

―――. *Encyclopaedia: Introduction and Logic. The Encyclopaedia of the Philosophical Sciences in Outline*, 3rd edition (1830). Translated by W. Wallace with revisions by M. J. Inwood. In *Hegel. Selections*, edited by M. J. Inwood. New York: Macmillan Publishing Company, 1989.

―――. *The Encyclopaedia of the Philosophical Sciences in Outline*, 2nd edition. Translated by William Wallace. Oxford: Clarendon Press, 1892.

Heidegger, Martin. *On The Essence of Truth*. Translated by John Sallis. In *The Basic Writings of Heidegger*, edited by D. F. Krell. New York: Harper & Row, 1977.

Heraclitus, Parmenides, Xenophanes. *The Presocratic Philosophers. A Critical History with a Selection of Texts*. Translated and edited by G. S. Kirk and J. E. Raven. Cambridge: Cambridge University Press, 1963.

Peirce, C. S. *Collected Papers of Charles Sanders Peirce*, 2 vols. Cambridge, MA: The Belknap Press of Harvard University Press, 1960.

Plato. *Sophist*. Translated by F. M. Cornford with an addition from the translation of B. Jowett. In *The Collected Dialogues of Plato*, edited by E. Hamilton and H. Cairns. Princeton, NJ: Princeton University Press, 1973.

Wittgenstein, Ludwig. *Tractatus Logico-Philosophicus*. Translated by D. F. Pears and B. F. McGuinness. London: Routledge and Kegan Paul; Atlantic Highlands, NJ: Humanities Press, 1961.

REFERENCE WORKS

Sini has this to say on the authors who at some time "have inspired, nourished and made possible" his research:

I believe it is useful to mention some writings recently published in Italy that deal with some of the same issues and problems and with which a critical comparison would be very useful. This list, although sketchy and limited only to the last four or five years, reveals the parameters of a theoretical debate that seems to me to be particularly lively, especially in our own philosophical culture. It would be of considerable importance if those who in one way or another participate in this debate were to become aware, over and above disagreements and oppositions, of the importance of the overall theoretical work being done in Italy today. The list that follows, of course, is not exhaustive and does not pretend in any way to establish a hierarchy of any kind. I am quoting from memory, so to speak, the writings of those scholars (including some young ones) whose works have come to my attention, whether by reason of affinity or contrast, especially in the concluding stages of my work. This subjective way of proceeding neglects, to be sure, many important works and writings, and betrays limitations and idiosyncrasies, not to mention momentary memory lapses for which I apologize from the start. Nevertheless, even within these contingent limitations, it is possible for the reader to discern in this list, as I have, the richness of Italian philosophical thought. This sketch, although casual and largely imperfect, is in my view a sign of how "vital" for us the present "death of philosophy" is.

In addition to these authors, Sini also mentions the Italian writer Italo Calvino with these remarks:

I would like to mention a "non-philosophical" work, Italo Calvino's *Palomar* (Turin: Einaudi, 1983). A young scholar in presenting me with this book suggested that I would find in it a familiar aura. Indeed, I have found it, with much joy and pleasure, and wish to express here my thanks to her as well as my admiration for Calvino.

With the exception of Vattimo none of the following authors have been translated into English. I have given the English title to give an idea of their subject matter.

Agamben, Giorgio. *Il linguaggio e la morte* (Language and death). Torino: Einaudi, 1982.

Cacciari, Massimo. *Dallo Steinhof. Prospettive viennesi del primo Novecento* (From the Steinhof. Viennese perspectives of the early 1900s). Milan: Adelphi, 1980.

———. *Icone della legge* (Icon of the law). Milan: Adelphi, 1985.

Caracciolo, Alberto. *Nichilismo ed etica* (Nihilism and ethics). Genoa: Il menangolo, 1983.

Cazzullo, Anna. *Metafora: Aristotele e l'ermeneutica contemporanea* (Aristotle and contemporary hermeneutics). Milan: Unicopli, 1983.

Curi, Umberto. *La linea divisa. Modelli di razionalità e pratiche scientifiche nel pensiero occidentale* (The divided line. Models of rationality and scientific practices in western thought). Bari: De Donato, 1983.

D'Alessandro, Paolo. *Darstellung e soggettività. Saggio su Althusser* (Darstellung and subjectivity. An essay on Althusser). Florence: La Nuova Italia, 1980.

———. *Linguaggio e comprensione* (Language and understanding). Napoli: Guida, 1982.

Dalmasso, Gianfranco. *Il ritorno della tragedia. Essere e inconscio in Nietzsche e in Freud* (The return of tragedy. Being and unconscious in Nietzsche and Freud). Milan: Angeli, 1983.

de Giovanni, Biagio. *Politica dopo Cartesio* (*Politics* after Descartes). *Il Centauro* 1 (1981).

Ferrarotti, Franco. *Il paradosso del sacro* (The paradox of the sacred). Bari: Laterza, 1983.

Galimberti, Umberto. *La terra senza il male* (The land without evil). Milan: Feltrinelli, 1984.

Givone, Sergio. *Dostoevskij e la filosofia* (Dostoevsky and philosophy). Bari: Laterza, 1984.

Leo, Rossella Fabbrichesi. *La polemica sull'iconismo (1964–1975)* (The controversy over iconism. 1964–1975). Naples: ESI, 1983.

Lisciani-Petrini, Enrica. *Memoria e poesia. Bergson, Jankélévitch, Heidegger* (Memory and poetry. Bergson, Jankélévitch, Heidegger). Naples: ESI, 1983.

Magris, Claudio. *L'anello di Clarisse* (Clarissa's ring). Turin: Einaudi, 1984.

Masini, Ferruccio. *Il travaglio del disumano. Per una fenomenologia del nichilismo* (The anguish of the inhuman. Toward a phenomenology of nihilism). Naples: Bibliopolis, 1982.

Moravia, Sergio. *Filosofia e scienze umane nell'età dei lumi* (Philosophy and human sciences in the age of enlightenment). Florence: Sansoni, 1982.

Papi, Fulvio. Canetti e la metafisica involontaria (Elias Canetti and unintentional metaphysics). *Materiali Filosofici* 11 (1984).

Pareyson, Luigi. Lo stupore della ragione in Schelling (The wonder of reason in Schelling). *Romanticism, Existentialism, Ontology of Freedom*. Milan: Mursia, 1979.

Perniola, Mario. *Dopo Heidegger. Filosofia e organizzazione della cultura* (After Heidegger. Philosophy and the organization of culture). Milan: Feltrinelli, 1982.

Rella, Franco. *Metamorfosi. Immagini del pensiero* (Metamorphoses. Images of thought). Milan: Feltrinelli, 1984.

Ruggenini, Mario. *Volontà e interpretazione. Le forme della fine della filosofia* (Will and interpretation. Forms of the end of philosophy). Milan: Angeli, 1985.

Severino, Emanuele. *Destino della necessità. Kata to chreon* (Destiny of necessity. Kata to chreon). Milan: Adelphi, 1980.

Vattimo, Gianni. *The End of Modernity: Nihilism and Hermeneutics in Post-Modern Culture* (La fine della modernità). Translated with an Introduction by Jon Snyder. Cambridge: Polity, 1988.

———. *Consequences of Hermeneutics* (Al di là del soggetto. Nietzsche, Heidegger e l'ermeneutica). Translated by Peter Carravetta. Forthcoming from Humanities Press.

Vattimo, G., and Rovatti, P. *Weak Thought* (Pensiero debole). Translated by Peter Carravetta. Forthcoming from the Johns Hopkins University Press.

Verra, Valerio. Immaginazione trascendentale e intelletto intuitivo (Transcendental imagination and intuitive reason). In *Hegel Interprete di Kant* (Hegel interpreter of Kant). Edited by V. Verra. Naples: Prismi: 1981.

Vitiello, Vincenzo. *Utopia del nichilismo. Tra Nietzsche e Heidegger* (Utopia of nihilism. Between Nietzsche and Heidegger). Naples: Guida, 1983.

———. *Ethos ed Eros in Hegel e in Kant.* (Ethos and Eros in Hegel and Kant). Naples: ESI, 1984.

RELATED WORKS ON SINI AND ITALIAN PHILOSOPHY

Borradori, Giovanna, ed. *Recoding Metaphysics. The New Italian Philosophy*. Evanston, IL: Northwestern University Press, 1988. Includes essays by Vattimo, Gargani, Perniola, Rovatti, Rella, Cacciari, and Severino.

Carrera, Alessandro. What Happened to Being? On Hermeneutics and Unlimited Semiosis in Carlo Sini and Gianni Vattimo. In *Romance Languages Annual*, edited by Ben Lawton and Anthony J. Tamburri, pp. 94–97. Purdue Research Foundation. West Lafayette, IN: Purdue University Press, 1990.

————. Consequences of unlimited semiosis. Metaphysics of sign and semiotical hermeneutics in Carlo Sini's thought. *Continental Philosophy* 8 (1992).

Carravetta, Peter, ed. *Differentia* 1 (Fall 1986). The issue contains articles by Vattimo, Gargani, Perniola, and Dal Lago among others. See also other issues.

Critique XLI, 452–453 (January–February 1985) is dedicated to contemporary Italian philosophers and includes articles by Rovatti, Gargani, Dal Lago, Vattimo, Cacciari, and Bodei.

Index

◆